ABOUT THE AUTHOR

Jackie Uí Chionna teaches histor in the west of Ireland. Primarily a she is also a skilled oral historian of businessman and politician M. *Was Galway*, was published in 20 *History of University College Galway, 1930–1980*, was published in 2019. A committed public historian, she is a frequent contributor to TV and radio documentaries in her native Ireland.

PRAISE FOR *QUEEN OF CODES*

'Completely compelling, endlessly illuminating and richly intriguing – Jackie Uí Chionna's wonderfully written and deeply researched work has at last pulled back the curtain of secrecy from one of Bletchley Park's most extraordinary unsung figures. This is a story not just of a pioneering codebreaking genius, working through two world wars, but also – movingly – about a dazzlingly brilliant woman creating a space for herself and her passions in a rigid world and at a rigid time'

– Sinclair McKay, author of Bletchley Park Brainsteasers
and The Secret Life of Bletchley Park

'Some women are missing from history books for the simple reason that – under the Official Secrets Act – they could not speak the truth about their lives. Among these was Emily Anderson, one of the greatest codebreakers of the twentieth century – an unsung heroine of both World Wars. In Jackie Uí Chionna she at last finds her biographer. In unravelling Anderson's story, Uí Chionna shines a light on an extraordinary woman who literally changed the course of history'

– Suzannah Lipscomb

'This book is a compelling biography, by any standard, and among the best studies of any intelligence officer. That this book could even be written is a wonder of research. Emily Anderson shunned publicity, and worked with British codebreakers who embodied skill and secrecy. That this book is so well written is a delight to match the grace of Emily Anderson's scholarship on Beethoven and Mozart'

– John Ferris, author of Behind the Enigma:
The Authorised History of GCHQ

QUEEN

OF

CODES

The Secret Life of
Emily Anderson, Britain's
Greatest Female Codebreaker

JACKIE UÍ CHIONNA

HEADLINE

First published in 2023 by
HEADLINE PUBLISHING GROUP

First published in paperback in 2024 by
HEADLINE PUBLISHING GROUP

3

Cataloguing in Publication Data is available from the British Library

ISBN: 978 1 4722 9550 7

Offset in 11.41/13.88pt Baskerville MT Pro by Jouve (UK), Milton Keynes

Printed and bound in Great Britain by Clays Ltd, Elcograf S.p.A.

HEADLINE PUBLISHING GROUP
An Hachette UK Company
Carmelite House
50 Victoria Embankment
London
EC4Y 0DZ

www.headline.co.uk
www.hachette.co.uk

For Mícheál,
for everything.

Contents

Introduction

On 1 November 1962 at St John's parish church, in London's Hampstead, the funeral took place of a seventy-two-year-old woman: the retired civil servant Miss Emily Anderson. As she had never married, there was no bereaved husband, nor long-term partner, nor were there any children to grieve her passing. Aside from one cousin, there were no family members – no siblings and no nieces or nephews – in attendance. To the outside observer, it must have appeared to be a typical funeral for an elderly woman who had perhaps led a solitary existence. Yet, had they but known it, the clues that she had, in fact, led a quite remarkable double life were there, hiding in plain sight. St John's was packed to capacity, and as the mourners filed into the church to pay their respects that day, there were those among the congregation who were well aware that this was the funeral of no ordinary woman, who had lived no ordinary life.

Emily Anderson had been a regular presence on the streets of Hampstead for nearly forty years. She had lived at a variety of addresses in the borough since 1923, but aside from her close friends, none of her neighbours really knew her. To those who encountered her, Miss Anderson appeared to be a pleasant, if unremarkable, figure. Her next-door neighbour in Ellerdale Road recalled a woman who was:

rather a solitary figure, and was rather shy, I reckon. She gave the impression of being very frail, with a very gentle manner. She was very self-contained, and very discreet, very pleasant to meet, and not interested in useless chatter. Her life's work was cataloguing, I believe. She probably looked older than she was. She had a very pleasant face, that I do know.[1]

While her neighbours may have considered Miss Anderson a quiet and solitary single woman, among the congregation that day there were those who knew only too well the varied – and, to a large degree, secretive – life this former academic, and later Foreign Office official, had lived since she moved to London from her home in Galway, in the west of Ireland, in 1918. The friends and former colleagues who attended the funeral were an eclectic bunch, reflecting the various strands of Anderson's life: strands that had occasionally intertwined but had remained largely separate over the more than four decades she had spent living and working in England. One aspect of the funeral that would have forcefully struck those who attended, however, was the quality of the music performed, which was exceptional. This was hardly surprising, given that music had been the grand passion of Anderson's life. Seated in St John's that November morning were the cream of London's musical community, including some of the best-known classical musicians and opera singers of the day, a number of whom performed during the service. Also seated in the congregation were a number of Anderson's Jewish friends – internationally renowned bookdealers and academics in the main, who had fled Nazi Germany in the years preceding the Second World War – as well as a high-ranking official representing the German Embassy. Finally, there among the mourners, and known to no one but each other, were some of the most senior figures in the world of British intelligence, going back decades.

The full details of Emily Anderson's life and career would have been known to very few of those who came to bid a respectful farewell to the tall, slim, quietly spoken lady who had lived at 24 Ellerdale Road. To all intents and purposes, Emily Anderson had worked as a civil servant with the Foreign Office, but she had put her free time to remarkable use. She had single-handedly collected and translated the correspondence of Mozart and his family, and then later performed the same monumental task for Beethoven. Both translations (*The Letters of Mozart and his Family* was published in 1938, *The Letters of Beethoven* in 1961) were immediately acclaimed as works of great scholarship, unlikely to ever be equalled (as they have remained). In a review of Anderson's *Letters of Beethoven* that appeared in her native Ireland, the writer observed:

> Miss Emily Anderson, whose brilliant editing of the letters of Beethoven has won her widespread praise, is an Irishwoman who, I am told, loathes publicity. She has had a varied and practical career.[2]

Miss Anderson's loathing of publicity was arguably directly related to just how 'varied and practical' that career had been. For had those who thought they knew her been told that this highly respectable woman, usually attired in a well-tailored skirt, silk blouse and pearls, who lived alone, travelled extensively, played the piano rather well, and had an international reputation as an exceptional music scholar, was also the foremost female codebreaker of her generation, her friends and neighbours would never have believed it.

But the proof was there for all to see, for laid side by side on her coffin, in velvet-lined boxes, were the two significant awards she had received during her lifetime. One box contained the OBE conferred on her by King George V in 1943, and the other the Order of Merit, First Class, the highest honour the Federal Republic of Germany could bestow, conferred on her only a year previously, in 1961. The first she had been awarded 'For services to the forces and in connexion with Military operations [. . .] GHQ, Middle East'. The second was for her significant contribution to Beethoven scholarship, as a result of her groundbreaking translation of the great German composer's letters.

Emily Anderson was a woman who had lived two distinct yet parallel lives – one, her public life, as an internationally respected music scholar; and the second, her scrupulously guarded professional life, as a codebreaker at the most senior level of British intelligence for nearly forty years. But her story began in a small city in the west of Ireland, when a shy, precocious little girl, with a keen intellect and independent spirit, first developed a love of languages and music. Those grand passions, carefully nurtured by her parents, would sustain her throughout her life. Her neighbour, who believed that Miss Anderson's 'life's work was cataloguing', could never have imagined the secret life that this shy, discreet, solitary figure with a 'pleasant face' had lived, quietly, for decades. After all, aside from her colleagues in the highest echelons of British intelligence, no one else knew about it either.

Until now.

1

Family, Early Life and Education

Emily Anderson was born on 17 March 1891[1] to Alexander Anderson and his wife, Emily Gertrude (*née* Binns). She was the second of the couple's four children, three girls and a boy. Raised in the city of Galway, in the west of Ireland, she was part of a respected and relatively well-off middle-class family. Her father, Alexander, was an academic, and at the time of her birth was Professor of Physics at Queen's College, Galway, the university where he himself had studied. Professor Anderson had been born in 1858[2] in Coleraine, County Londonderry, into a staunch Ulster Presbyterian family. At Queen's College, Alexander Anderson had been an exceptional student, having been awarded gold medals on the results of his BA examination in 1880, and also his MA examination in 1881. He went on to win first place in an open examination for a scholarship to Sidney Sussex College, Cambridge, and arrived there as a Foundation Scholar in 1881.[3]

At Cambridge, one of his fellow students was a fellow Ulsterman and physicist, Joseph Larmor, later Sir Joseph Larmor, Lucasian Professor of Mathematics at Cambridge. Both men had much in common, above and beyond being Ulstermen.[4] It was said of Larmor that he was:

[. . .] an unassuming, diffident man who did not readily form close friendships and whose numerous acts of generosity were performed without publicity. Larmor made few friends, perhaps; but while he lived, and they lived, he lost none.[5]

Much the same thing would later be said of Alexander Anderson, and he and Larmor remained firm friends for the rest of their lives.[6] In 1885, Alexander Anderson had returned to Queen's College, Galway, where he was appointed Professor of Natural Philosophy (in succession to Larmor, who had held the chair for two years), a post he held until 1934.[7] He subsequently became a Senator of – and the Vice Chancellor of – the National University of Ireland in 1915.

Emily's mother, the former Emily Binns, came from a well-respected Galway family. Her father, William J. Binns, was manager of the National Bank Galway, and her brother, William N. Binns, an engineer, was the Galway Borough Surveyor.[8] Emily Gertrude Binns was born in Rathkeale, Co. Limerick, in 1869. Her father was then manager of the Rathkeale branch of the National Bank, before being promoted to manager of the more prestigious Galway branch in the city's Eyre Square in 1881. The Binns family were also Presbyterian, and the couple are likely to have met when, as a student in Galway, Alexander Anderson attended services in the Presbyterian church at Nun's Island. Emily Binns was twelve years old when Alexander Anderson took his MA from QCG in 1881, and sixteen when he returned to Galway as Professor of Natural Philosophy in 1885. The young academic cannot but have been struck by the rather beautiful Miss Binns, and within three years of his return to Galway, the couple were married.

The wedding took place in Dublin on 18 July 1888, when Alexander Anderson was thirty and his bride just three months past her nineteenth birthday. That the wedding did not take place in the bride's home town is odd, and it appears likely that the couple had eloped in order to marry. Significantly, there had been no announcement in the local press of the engagement or impending nuptials of one of the university's professors to the daughter of a prominent local banker, as might have been expected. This, then, appears to have been a genuine love match, and the independent spirit, courage and determination shown by Alexander Anderson and his young bride in marrying in the face of parental opposition would be characteristics inherited by their middle daughter, Emily. The bride's youth is likely to have been the only reason for parental disapproval of the marriage, however, as in every other regard their new son-in-law was an eminently respectable match. Anderson's best man was Joseph Larmor, who had by then been appointed to the position of lecturer in mathematics at Cambridge.[9] Emily's bridesmaid was her cousin, Ann Binns.[10]

Following their honeymoon, the couple returned to Galway, where they rented a house in Mill Street. Their first child, Elsie, was born there in 1890, and she was followed a year later by Emily. Four and a half years after Emily's birth, in 1895,[11] a son, also named Alexander, was born, and in 1902, the couple welcomed their final child, a daughter named Helen.

When Emily was eight years old, her father was appointed President of Queen's College, Galway. The position required that the incumbent live within the college grounds, and a substantial nine-room residence in the Quadrangle of the college came with the presidency. The Anderson family, then comprising three children, moved to the president's quarters in 1899. They were in residence there when, two years later, the 1901 census recorded the city's population as 13,426; ten years later, it had declined to 13,255.[12] The Galway of Anderson's youth had ambitions to be a city of commerce and industry, but in reality was 'a relatively small market town and an administrative centre',[13] whose population was overwhelmingly Catholic. The opening of Queen's College, Galway, in 1849 had, however, attracted many Ulster Presbyterian students – including Alexander Anderson – to the city, and a vibrant and assertively Protestant subculture steadily emerged, whose principle characteristics were 'a siege mentality, a middle-class outlook and a disapproval of frivolity'.[14] Nowhere was this siege mentality more pronounced that in the university, where, by the 1880s, Ulster Presbyterians represented the largest student cohort in the college's population of $c.$ 200 students. For most Galwegians, however, the college remained a place apart.

Emily Anderson enjoyed something of a privileged existence as the daughter of the university president, living in a comfortable house, with an extensive library on her doorstep. By the time the 1901 census was taken, the Anderson household included a staff of four – a butler, cook, housemaid and governess. The governess, Elisa Curtet, was Swiss, and the children's early proficiency in French and German stemmed from being tutored by a governess fluent in both languages. The Anderson children also had as a pet a Pomeranian dog.[15]

Two images of Emily as a child survive. In the first, she is pictured on the steps of the doorway to the president's residence in the Quadrangle. Standing behind her is Elisa the children's governess. Emily is a rather plain, serious-looking girl with auburn hair and freckles. Also pictured are her elder sister Elsie, who has infinitely more cherubic features, and their mother, the older Emily, a beautiful if sombre-looking woman with dark, striking eyes, whose arm is wrapped protectively around her second daughter. The second image, taken around the same time, shows Anderson seated alone, on the banks of the River Corrib (which ran through the college campus), with her bicycle beside her and a book on her lap. Anderson could not have been more than nine or ten at the time the photograph was taken, yet she appears a serious, studious child. As the children of one of Galway's most prominent citizens, the Anderson siblings lived in something of a fishbowl, their conduct and behaviour on public view to the entire academic and student body of the university. Their father's status as college president, and the fact that they were Presbyterian, meant that the Andersons were limited in their choice of friends, who, in addition to sharing their religion, would need to match their social standing. There were few other children, other than the children of other college staff, for them to play with, and as they were educated privately, they had little if any opportunity for contact with children of their own age in the general population outside the university. A tendency towards reserve and solitude was to become, for Emily, a lifelong trait, which, ironically, in view of her future career in intelligence, would become a significant advantage.

In the absence of a wide social circle, it is hardly surprising that music became a source of solace and expression for at least two of the Anderson siblings. Both Elsie and Emily learned to play the piano from an early age, and Elsie also appears to have had a fine singing voice, winning various prizes at competitions. Living at the heart of a university ensured that the Anderson children grew up in a household where education and critical thinking were much prized. Their father's work ethos was firmly established in his children, all of whom were bright, conscientious students. Professor and Mrs Anderson had, by all accounts, a very happy marriage, and were loving and attentive parents. The children also grew up in a household where issues of gender were not perceived to preclude intellectual or personal advancement. Their mother was a committed suffragist, and encouraged her two oldest daughters to accompany her to meetings advocating that women be granted the vote.[16] Mrs Anderson was active in a number of civic spheres in Galway, and was not afraid to speak her mind. She was vice-president of the Women's National Health Association Galway branch, and honorary secretary of the Galway Total Abstinence Association.[17] A straight talker, in 1911 Mrs Anderson was the spokesperson of a delegation from the Women's National Health Association when they presented their case for the compulsory reporting of TB cases by doctors to the City Council. There was reluctance on the part of doctors regarding compulsory reporting of cases, but Mrs Anderson was clear in her view: 'We know that there are difficulties, but the best thing is to look the matter fair in the face.'[18] Mrs Anderson's view prevailed, reporting of TB cases became the norm, and she became a member of the visiting committee at the local sanatorium. She was also a founding member of the Connaught Women's Franchise League in

January 1913. The passion with which her daughter Emily later advocated for equal pay for women in the civil service undoubtedly shows she had inherited her mother's values.

Mrs Anderson could not have maintained such a high public profile, especially on contentious issues such as women's suffrage, without the support of her husband, and it is clear that Professor Anderson was very much of the view that ability transcended the issue of gender. The education of women had been much prized in Professor Anderson's own family, and his sister Elizabeth (known as Bessie) had been the first female student to attend Queen's College, Galway. Bessie Anderson subsequently graduated with a BA in Mathematics from the Royal University of Ireland, becoming a noted mathematician. Professor Anderson was also distinguished among other college presidents by being one of the first to appoint women to professorial positions.

When she was fourteen, Emily made the first of what would be numerous visits to Germany. Significantly, those trips appear to have been instigated by her father. Unfortunately, as no personal correspondence related to Emily Anderson or any of her family from this time survives, Professor Anderson's relationship with his middle daughter cannot be gleaned from any of the scant documentary evidence that does exist. However, in an interview Anderson gave to the BBC in 1961, she noted that although her father was a physicist, he was also a keen linguist, who had learned German during his time at Cambridge. Anderson also stated that she and her elder sister 'had German governesses', indicating that, as well as Elisa Curtet, there were a number of other governesses employed by the Andersons, which would explain the high level of fluency in German of all the Anderson siblings. Emily's brother

Alexander, who unlike his sisters was sent away to boarding school in Dublin,[19] was also a fluent German speaker, something that proved of significant benefit to him during the First World War.

It seems Professor Anderson was determined that, in addition to having German-speaking governesses, his daughters needed the experience of speaking German in Germany with German families to achieve full fluency. The fact that her busy father took the time to accompany his daughters on the journey to and from Germany, and as a consequence spent considerable time in their company, would appear to have fostered a warm, loving relationship between them. Having initially 'detested' her time living with German families, Anderson quickly overcame her dislike, and throughout her life she made and maintained numerous warm friendships with various Germans, and cherished a lasting love of German music and culture, which greatly enriched her life.

*

Professor Anderson's first decade as college president was a difficult one, in that it fell to him to defend the college from the threat of closure in the years preceding the establishment of the National University in 1908. But he was more than up to the task, and, as a Galway graduate himself, at a public meeting held in 1907 he concluded his staunch defence of his alma mater with an uncharacteristically poetic flourish:

> Woodman, spare that tree!
> Touch not a single bough!
> In youth it sheltered me,
> And I'll protect it now.[20]

Protect it he did, for the next twenty-seven years, until his retirement in 1934. He was an able university administrator, who successfully guided the college through a period of major change, including the transition from Queen's College, Galway, to University College, Galway, and the revolutionary period of 1916–22, which saw the university finally come under the jurisdiction of the new Irish Free State in 1922.

On a personal level, Professor Anderson was considered by many to be a somewhat aloof man, brilliant but remote. He was also a groundbreaking physicist. In February 1920, he published an article entitled 'On the Advancement of the Perihelion of a Planet (Mercury) and the Path of a Ray of Light in the Gravitational Field of the Sun'. In the article, he observed:

> We may remark, though perhaps the assumption is very violent, that if the mass of the sun were concentrated in a sphere of diameter of 1.47 kilometres, the index of refraction near it would become infinitely great, and we should have a very powerful condensing lens, too powerful indeed, for the light emitted by the sun itself would have no velocity at its surface. Thus if, in accordance with the suggestion of Helmholtz, the body of the sun should go on contracting, there will come a time when it will be shrouded in darkness, not because it has no light to emit, but because its gravitational field will become impermeable to light.[21]

What Professor Anderson was describing was the first published suggestion of the possibility of 'black holes', and he was also the first to speculate about what would happen if a star collapsed under its own gravity.[22] It was said of Professor Anderson that:

> he moved little beyond the walls of the university, mixed little with the men who battle in the world amidst worldly things. Perhaps, indeed, in this lay his fault, if fault it was, for one does not always perceive life whole through cloistered windows.[23]

A different picture of Professor Anderson emerges in a description by one of his colleagues. Affectionately known to his students as 'Alec', Anderson was described by Professor Mary Donovan O'Sullivan thus:

> in his leisure hours, like Churchill, rarely seen without a cigar. I used to travel home with him from meetings in Dublin when he proved a grand companion on the journey, bringing his wit and lively sense of humour to bear on men and events.[24]

He and his wife were generous and popular hosts, and Donovan O'Sullivan recalls that, following conferring ceremonies, the president would host an afternoon tea party – a *thé dansant* – in the Aula Maxima for graduates and staff. Professor Anderson, she noted, was:

> a physicist of European repute, he was also a fine classical scholar. He was [also] thoroughly at home in French and German, and even possessed a sound acquaintance with such languages as Czech, while he had all the feeling of the classical scholar for polished English prose.[25]

Alexander Anderson, then, was something of an enigma: a brilliant scientist who was also an excellent and passionate linguist and classical scholar; an aloof and somewhat austere workaholic who was also, in the company of close friends and colleagues, a charming, erudite man and a gregarious host. To a quite extraordinary degree, all of these characteristics, and apparent contradictions, came to be shared by his daughter Emily. In view of his daughter's future career as a codebreaker, it is interesting to note that 'right to the end of his life he used to love to do the classical crosswords in the *Athenaeum*'.[26]

*

In the absence of any family correspondence, we are fortunate in having a window into Emily Anderson's own student days at Queen's College, Galway, from one of her contemporaries at that time, Mary Donovan O'Sullivan – the same Donovan O'Sullivan who went on to become a colleague of Emily's father as the first Professor of History at University College, Galway.[27] In 1908, the first year of her BA, Emily Anderson took first place, and first-class honours, in English, French, German and Latin. At the time she came to know Emily, Donovan O'Sullivan recalls that the entire student body numbered about 120 students, '60% of whom were Catholics from the South and West, and about 40% Northern students, mainly Presbyterian.'[28] Of these, only eleven students were women. Donovan O'Sullivan noted that there was:

> a world of difference between the Northerners and Southerners, though both belonged to the same middle classes. The Northerners were quiet, plodding, and persevering, possessing all the qualities that command respect rather than admiration, and though by

no means brilliant, were nearly always successful. The Southerners, on the other hand, were more successful in brilliant dash than steady persistence, more prodigal than parsimonious, more addicted to sport and less to study, more capable of winning friendship than respect.[29]

As the daughter of a Northern Irish father and a Southern Irish mother, Emily Anderson was fortunate in exhibiting the best of both sets of characteristics throughout her life, and her stellar undergraduate career is a testament to how conscientious was her dedication to her studies. During her student days, aside from her interest in music, there was little to distract her from her pursuit of academic excellence. There were a few sports societies (rugby, cricket, tennis and hockey), and only one other college society, the Literary and Debating Society. There were 'no cinemas, no radio, and only once a year had we anything approaching a serious distraction when the Elster Grime Opera Co. gave a fortnight's opera at the only theatre[30] then existing in Galway'.[31] It was a university where students came to work, not to socialise, and, in the case of the Anderson siblings, they did so under the watchful eye of their father. With the entire academic and student bodies privy to their every action, there was little scope for spirited behaviour.

Anderson's elder sister, Elsie, had already completed the first year of a BA in Modern Languages at what was by then University College, Galway, when Emily formally began her studies in 1907. Just as her younger sister was to do, Elsie (who is listed on the college calendars by her given name, Elizabeth) had quickly established herself as a very bright student. She won scholarships in the first, second and third years of her degree, and won prizes each year in French and German.[32]

By the time the 1911 census was taken,[33] Emily was twenty, still living with her parents, and was within a few months of graduating with a BA in Modern Languages. Her brother Alexander was away at boarding school in Dublin at that time, and her only other sibling living at home was her younger sister, Helen, then aged nine. The Andersons no longer employed a governess, but still employed a cook and parlourmaid. It is likely that her elder sister Elsie had moved abroad to continue her language studies in Germany or France, as Emily intended to do, as she doesn't appear in the census.[34]

Emily Anderson held the Browne scholarship[35] in both 1909 and 1910, and graduated with a first-class honours degree in 1911. Significantly in her case, the examiners recommended that the words 'with special distinction' be added to the first-class honours in French and German in the BA Degree Examination, on the grounds that 'her answering was considered to be of quite exceptional merit'.[36] Professor and Mrs Anderson had every reason to be proud of their tall, auburn-haired daughter, and every reason to expect that she would continue to distinguish herself in her postgraduate studies, and in whatever career she chose to pursue thereafter. They were not to be disappointed.

2

Berlin and Marburg

With an excellent degree and impeccable academic record, Emily Anderson, with the approval of her parents, determined to further her education and undertake postgraduate studies abroad. The decision was likely not taken on purely academic grounds. Small and friendly as University College Galway may have been, it must also have been somewhat stifling for a twenty-year-old woman like Anderson. As Anderson spoke perfect German, she began her studies at the University of Berlin in the late summer of 1911. The Friedrich Wilhelm University[1] had, since its foundation in 1809, acquired an excellent reputation based on its academic standards, but also its ethos. The founding concept of the university, as envisaged by Wilhelm von Humboldt, resulted in its being given the title 'Mother of all modern universities'. Von Humboldt had envisaged a '*Universitas litterarum*', which would achieve a unity of teaching and research, and provide students with an all-round humanist education. Given her love of languages, music and literature, Anderson thrived there, and her time in Berlin engendered a lifelong love of the city, to which she returned frequently in later years in the course of her Beethoven research.

The sheer scale of Berlin, with its population of some

two million, was in stark contrast to the provincial city she had left behind. The expressionist painter Ernst Ludwig Kircher can be said to have captured something of the vibrancy, glamour and splendour of pre-war Berlin, depicting ladies in grand hats parading arm in arm on the elegant boulevards. The largest hotel in Europe, Berlin's Hotel Excelsior, had 600 rooms and hosted international stars such as Charlie Chaplin, as well as the Kaiser himself, who held 'gentlemen's evenings' there. It was a city of electricity and light – 'Elektropolis', Berliners called it – with tramways, underground railways, concert halls and cafés.[2] Anderson spent two years in Berlin, returning to her home in Galway in the summer of 1912, before travelling back to Germany, via England, in early September 1912.[3]

In 1913, after spending another year in Berlin, she moved 470 kilometres south-west to take up yet further studies at the university of Marburg. In contrast to the bohemian metropolis of Berlin, Marburg at the time had a population of 26,000, of whom 2,500 studied at the university. Built on the slopes of a hill and overlooking the River Lahn, many of the town's inhabitants still wore the colourful regional costume, the *tracht*.[4] Marburg was:

> picturesque in precisely the ways that a German university town should be picturesque: shadowed and dominated by a castle on the hilltop above it, the skyline broken by the twin towers of a Gothic church, its streets narrow, twisting, broken by sudden vistas, numerous tiny gardens, and gabled wooden houses.[5]

There were also numerous lively cafés, where students went to drink, laugh and argue. The Russian writer Boris Pasternak studied at Marburg in 1912, and described how the university was lit up 'operatically, on the top of the hill'.[6] As a languages scholar and Presbyterian, Marburg was an obvious choice for Anderson. Established in 1527 during the Reformation, it is the oldest university in the world that was founded as a Protestant institution, and had an international reputation in humanities subjects. There was a significant cohort of international students attending the university in the years preceding the First World War – during Anderson's time there, a fellow student was the poet T. S. Eliot.[7] Within a few weeks of Eliot's arrival in July 1914, however, studies were interrupted when Germany declared war on Russia on 1 August. Three days later, England declared war on Germany. Eliot's course was cancelled and he found himself stranded in Germany; 'after two weeks in seclusion at the university [he] left Marburg for the relative safety of London'.[8] He was not alone. Once war broke out, most international students fled Germany, including Emily Anderson. An interesting Galway perspective on events in Marburg in the weeks and days preceding and following the outbreak of war comes from a thirty-one-year-old teacher, P. J. Webb. Webb was principal of the Galway Technical School,[9] and had been in Germany from early July to the end of August 1914. In Berlin, he noted the city was 'unperturbed by the gathering clouds; he then proceeded to Dresden, where 'the excitement had increased and the war fever was in its first flush'. Webb continued his tour by train and, after 'travelling all night with men going to join their regiments', he arrived at Marburg, a place where, as recounted in a later interview for his local newspaper, 'he had friends'. One of those friends was very likely Emily Anderson; Webb would have known her father well, given their respective positions at Galway's two major educational institutions. Webb's time in Marburg was anything but pleasant. He spent ten days there, under police surveillance at all times, his American Express traveller's cheques no longer recognised and only ten shillings to his name. Intriguingly, he recounted when interviewed by a journalist from his local newspaper that 'a friendly American lent him ten pounds' and that with this, he 'made his dash from Marburg to Hanover'.[10]

Webb's dramatic account was published in a local newspaper, the *Connacht Tribune*, and must have terrified Anderson's family. As a woman, and a fluent German speaker, Anderson is likely to have had an easier time dealing with German officials and the military than Webb, but her forced departure from Germany, via the port of Hamburg, must nonetheless have been stressful. Anderson arrived in Southampton in late August 1914. She made her way to London and arranged passage back to Ireland.

The joy of Anderson's parents following her safe return to Galway in mid-September 1914 was tempered by the fact that their only son, Alexander, then aged twenty, had enlisted and was preparing to join his regiment in England. Alexander had been an undergraduate at University College, Galway, and was a bright, conscientious student, winning both Literary and Mathematics entrance scholarships in his first year, 1912–13, and a Faculty of Arts scholarship in his second year. He transferred to the Science faculty for the academic term 1914–15, but enlisted before completing his degree.[11] Like many of his contemporaries, he was gripped with war enthusiasm and determined to play his part in the 'great adventure', a war that everyone was confident 'would be over by Christmas'.

Unsurprisingly, as a town loyal to the Crown, with a large army barracks – home to the famous Connaught Rangers – located on the outskirts of the city, 'the town of Galway went recruiting mad'.[12] Recruitment rallies took place throughout the city and county, and Professor Anderson, a committed supporter of the war, encouraged students to enlist. Emily Anderson's one-time fellow student, Professor Mary Donovan O'Sullivan, headed up the city's Women's Recruitment League.

Emily's brother enlisted on 11 September 1914 and was assigned to the Royal Regiment of Hussars (19th Hussars). He did not seek a commission, and enlisted as a private.[13] He immediately made his way to England, where he joined his regiment in Bristol. Shortly thereafter, Private Anderson was 'discharged for the purpose of being appointed to a commission' on 31 October 1914, when he joined the 4th Battalion Connaught Rangers. He was sent to France with his regiment, quickly promoted to lieutenant, and sec-onded for service with the Trench Mortar Batteries. On Christmas Day 1915, Galway newspapers reported that Lieutenant Anderson had been 'sent to the firing line on the west front'.[14] Within a few months, however, on 1 April 1916, he was granted a temporary commission in the Royal Flying Corps, becoming 'Flying Officer A. Anderson of the 22nd squadron Royal Flying Corps', an air reconnais-sance unit then based at Bertangles (Amiens).

With her brother having enlisted, her father occupied with running the university and her mother also engaged in war-related works, for Emily Anderson the question of what she would do for the duration of the war must have been at the forefront of her mind. In the short term, she was employed as an assistant to Professor Steinberger in the department of

Romance Languages at University College, Galway, but there was very little assisting for her to do. With so many of the male students having enlisted, and many young women committing to the war effort by training as nurses or pursuing involvement with other war work, student numbers at the university plummeted. With insufficient work to keep her gainfully occupied, Anderson became bored and frustrated. Having lived abroad for three years, it is also unlikely that returning to live with her parents in the president's residence was an enticing prospect. Now aged twenty-three, and with no likelihood of a significant academic position opening up at University College, Galway in the foreseeable future, she sought employment elsewhere.

*

It is unclear how Anderson came to hear about the post of Modern Languages Mistress at Queen's College, Barbados, although it may have been advertised in the British or Irish press or professional publications. The school had been established in Bridgetown, Barbados, in 1883 as a result of an Education Commission report, which determined that Barbados required a first-class school for girls similar to the top educational institutions that existed in Britain. Over time, the school grew in size and reputation, and by the time Anderson applied for the position there, Queen's College was firmly established as the most prestigious girls' boarding school in Barbados. The quality of its teaching was recognised in the awarding of prizes for its students in competitions open to students from throughout the British Empire.[15] Anderson's application was successful, and having formally been offered the position, she arranged her passage to Barbados.

Committing to work in a far-flung part of the Empire, particularly in a time of war, was a brave decision, and Anderson's motivation in choosing to do so must be examined. A desire to live independently was certainly a significant part of what motivated her – apart from a brief period in the 1950s, Anderson chose to live alone for all of her adult life. If, as seems likely, her long-term intention at that point was to carve out a career in academia, teaching experience in a good school was absolutely essential. The Barbadian climate would also have been a great improvement on the cold, damp west of Ireland, and this may also have influenced her decision.

Regardless of what had motivated the move, Anderson made her way to England, and boarded the *Panama* in Liverpool on 22 April 1915. The ship set sail for the port of Valparaíso, Chile, that same day. On the passenger list, Anderson (who travelled first class) listed her occupation as 'Teacher'. After a journey of over 4,000 miles, she finally arrived at Bridgetown to begin her teaching career.

3

Barbados and the 1916 Rising

The school to which Emily Anderson committed herself was one with an excellent reputation. The principal of the school to which Emily Anderson had committed herself was a Miss Alicia James,[1] who was succeeded in 1916 by a Miss Billett.[2] The school syllabus consisted of Divinity, English, History, Geography, French and an undefined scientific subject. Anderson's position as 'Modern Languages Mistress' in reality meant that she was teaching only French, as there were no other languages on the syllabus.[3]

In spite of its reputation, the governing body minutes of Queen's College during the period 1901–14 reveal that the school had an ongoing difficulty in retaining teachers.[4] There were 120 girls enrolled at the school at the time Anderson took up her appointment, and, as Queen's College was a boarding school, mistresses were obliged to fulfil supervisory as well as teaching duties.[5] Teaching staff were required to live in at the school, with the main building housing both classrooms and bedrooms for teachers. The remoteness of the school's location at that time, and the lack of opportunities for the young female staff to socialise outside of school grounds, appears to have given rise to some unhappiness on the part of newer, and younger, expatriate staff. In the period 1915–17, college records indicate that these were four in number, including Anderson, and while some staff were unhappy with the posting, for the duration of the war, opportunities to find work elsewhere were extremely limited. Apart from Anderson, who returned to Galway to take up the Chair of German at the university in 1917, the other three members of staff remained at the school until the mid-1920s.[6] The number of pupils increased during the war years, as the Barbadian economy prospered due to the high demand for its key product: sugar. Traditionally, the sugar barons of Barbados had sent their daughters to be educated in boarding schools in England. The war, however, made this more difficult, and with sugar plantations working at full capacity, the white middle classes of Barbados could well afford to send their daughters to Queen's College.[7]

For Emily Anderson, however, it appeared she had exchanged the oversight and claustrophobia of one educational institution for another. Living in with her fellow teachers, she had little privacy and was called upon to supervise students night and day, with limited options for recreational activities during her free time.

Back in Ireland, the outbreak of war in August 1914 also heralded the beginning of a period of great turmoil on home ground, culminating in the Anglo-Irish Treaty of 1922, which saw Ireland finally sever its links with the British Empire and gain independence. But, at the outbreak of the war, most Irish people, regardless of their political affiliation, supported the war in much the same way as their British counterparts did. Nationalists (predominantly Catholics) who had long sought a degree of independence for Ireland in the form of Home Rule – the establishment of a separate Irish parliament in Dublin – enlisted in great numbers, confident that they would be rewarded with the enactment of Home Rule legislation as soon as the war ended. The Home Rule Act of 1912 had been due to come into effect in 1914, but its enactment had been postponed for the duration of the war. Unionists in the north of Ireland, on the other hand, were largely Protestant, and bitterly opposed to Home Rule as an undermining of the link to Crown and Empire. They enlisted in their thousands to show their commitment to the union and to ensure that Home Rule legislation would *not* be enacted and that Ireland would remain part of the British Empire. In spite of differing objectives and expectations, over 200,000 men from Ireland, nationalist and unionist, fought in the war, almost 50,000 of whom died in the course of the conflict. For a small minority of more radical Republicans, Home Rule was a poor compromise, and nothing less than a fully independent Irish Republic would suffice. Believing that 'England's danger was Ireland's opportunity', and that the time was ripe for Ireland to strike for full independence, an armed rebellion against British rule occurred in April 1916. What became known as the Easter Rising was originally planned as a nationwide rebellion, but a countermanding order sent by the leader of the Irish Volunteers, Eoin MacNeill, ordering Volunteers not to muster for 'exercises' on Easter Sunday, resulted in the rebellion being mostly confined to Dublin, Ashbourne in Co. Meath, and Galway city and county.

Galway had always been a city loyal to the Crown. King Edward VII had visited in 1903, and was enthusiastically greeted by cheering crowds.[8] By 1916, however, a number of strong companies of Volunteers had been established in the city and county, and approximately 500 men took up arms in Galway during the Easter Rising. The city of Galway was in lockdown, and a British naval destroyer, the HMS *Gloucester*, sailed into Galway Bay and began shelling rebel strongholds inland. The rebels finally admitted defeat, the leaders fled and went into hiding, and most of those who remained were arrested the following week and imprisoned in English and Scottish jails, before being transported to Frongoch in south Wales, where the rank-and-file men were detained until August. The more prominent rebels were finally released at Christmas 1916. Although the rebellion in Galway was militarily a failure, its putting down was largely brought about because of widespread resistance to it among the local population. Galway was a garrison town, and many Galwegians had husbands, sons and brothers serving in the British armed forces. Support for the war effort was very high, and condemnation of the actions of the rebels absolute – at least initially. The subsequent decision by the British authorities to execute the leaders in Dublin in the immediate aftermath of the Rising – a group of fifteen men,[9] who included teachers, poets, civil servants, shopkeepers and a prominent Labour leader – changed all that. Within days, the mood of the Irish people had swung dramatically, and animosity towards the rebels quickly turned to support for the idea of an independent Irish Republic.

One unexpected consequence of the Easter Rising in Galway was to have a significant impact on the course of Emily Anderson's life. This was the arrest of a German national, Valentine Steinberger, who had been Professor of Romance Languages at University College, Galway, since 1886. A native of Bavaria, Steinberger had taught for a time in Belfast,[10] before moving to take up the position at UCG. Steinberger had taught Emily as an undergraduate, and as we have seen, she subsequently taught as his assistant following her return from post-graduate studies in Germany. A kind, cultured man, who was extremely popular with his students, Anderson was not alone in holding him in very high regard. The outbreak of war, however, meant that as one of very few Germans living in Galway, his loyalty and allegiance to the Crown became the subject of public scrutiny and innuendo. Xenophobia, spy-mania and detention of enemy civilians as 'aliens' featured across combatant nations during the First World War, and Galway was no exception. Professor Steinberger, perceived to be in a position to influence young minds at University College, constituted something of an 'enemy within' for many in Galway, with the pro-unionist *Galway Express* newspaper thundering:

> A number of German born spies are hovering round Galway at the present time. May we suggest to the police and other authorities protecting the British interests that any persons found undermining the cause of England, France and Russia, be at once placed in a position that his (or her) venom will be permanently extracted. This is no time for sentiment. We are fighting to the death.[11]

Professor Steinberger's home in Salthill overlooked Galway Bay, and unsubstantiated rumours began to circulate of flashing lights being seen emanating from his windows at night, the inference being that he was signalling enemy submarines off the coast. Ironically, at the time such accusations were circulating, Professor Steinberger's son, Charles, was serving with distinction with the Royal Navy. Steinberger was not a member of the Volunteers, but a number of his students were, and in principle he supported their aims. Following the outbreak of the Easter Rebellion, those suspected of rebel sympathies were swiftly arrested, including Steinberger. Then aged sixty-three,[12] Steinberger was arrested at home in Salthill on 29 April 1916 (four days after the Rising had begun), and imprisoned 'like the vilest criminal', an article in the college magazine claimed.[13] Also arrested was the Professor of Pathology, Thomas Walsh, and two students, Thomas Derrig and Cornelius O'Leary, who were known Volunteers. One striking fact regarding Professor Steinberger's arrest was that while the college authorities loudly protested the arrest of Professor Walsh and the two students, their silence regarding the esteemed Professor of German was deafening. The Governing Authority were concerned that public opinion would be against them were they to appeal for the release of a German citizen whose loyalties were being openly questioned, in spite of there being no evidence to substantiate claims being made by a frenzied Galway public. Initially at least, the president and governing authority of the university opted instead to patently exclude Professor Steinberger from their pleas for clemency, and so the unfortunate man was left to his fate by his academic colleagues.

Already weakened by poor health, Steinberger developed pneumonia during his two-week confinement and deportation to England aboard a cattle ship. A student who had been imprisoned alongside him later recalled that 'he treated with calm contempt the gibes and jeers, the insults and indignities he had to undergo and was never in the least afraid of the worst that could be done to him'.[14]

Professor Steinberger was released and returned to Galway on 23 May 1916, taking up his duties in the college the following day.[15] His arrest and detention, and the privations he had endured, irreparably damaged his health, and he died of pneumonia on 3 November 1916. By then, however, public opinion had shifted considerably as a result of the executions, and those involved in the Rising, instead of being spurned and castigated, were treated as heroes. It was at this stage the university, in part to make posthumous amends for the manner in which its former employee had been treated, decided to make a bold statement. The vacant Chair of Romance Languages was to be divided in two, with the appointment of a Professor of German, and a Professor of Romance Languages (incorporating French, Spanish and Italian). Creating, for the first time in the college's history, a designated Professorship in German was a remarkable gesture in a time of war, but the events of Easter week had brought home to President Anderson and the rest of his academic staff that great changes were taking place in Ireland, and the university and its student body would inevitably be impacted by those changes. In the interregnum between Steinberger's death and the filling of the two new chairs, Professor Mary Donovan O'Sullivan, whose husband was serving with the Royal Engineers, taught German and French.

Emily Anderson applied for the position of Professor of German in December 1916, and she had more than one reason for doing so. It was a position for which she was well qualified, and which represented a significant career advance. It also meant a return to teaching German, as opposed to French, as she had been doing in Barbados, which was never her preferred language. Finally, it meant a return to Galway at a time when her family were in need of her. For, as difficult as things were for her father and the university during and in the aftermath of the Easter

Rising, worse was to come, of an infinitely more personal nature. In early November, a telegram arrived for Professor Anderson, informing him that on the same day that Professor Steinberger had died, his son Alexander's plane had been shot down over German lines during the Battle of the Somme. Emily's brother was now a prisoner of war.

For months, the Andersons would have read accounts in the press of the Somme Offensive, which had begun on 1 July 1916. Intended to hasten a victory for the Allies, the battle dragged on for nearly five months as both sides became entrenched,[16] involving more than three million men, one million of whom were wounded or killed, making it one of the bloodiest battles in history. Sir W. A. Raleigh, in his memoir *The War in the Air,* records the crucial role played by the Royal Flying Corps in the battle, in difficult weather conditions:

> [. . .] pilots and observers struggled through the rain, mist and sleet to give their help to the army in the teeth of the westerly gales, they flew perilously low, registering the guns, reconnoitring the trenches and villages and attacking infantry and transport with bombs and machine gun fire.[17]

Lieutenant Anderson later gave evidence[18] that, on 3 November 1916, at Barastre, near Bapaume:[19]

> While on Reconnaissance duty over enemy country my machine was attacked by 3 hostile aircraft. My pilot, Captain Lord Lucas, RFC, was killed almost immediately; and, slightly wounded, with my engine shot through and stopping, I was forced to descent in the German lines near Barastre.[20]

At the time he was captured, Anderson was serving with the 22nd squadron Royal Flying Corps. Though not the pilot of the F.E.2d plane, he was what was termed an 'observer', as in the crew member whose duties are predominantly reconnaissance, but was also required to operate forward- and rear-firing Lewis guns in engagements with the enemy. The difficult task faced by observers was recalled by an American pilot who served as an F.E.2b observer in 1916:

> When you stood up to shoot, all of you from the knees up was exposed to the elements. There was no belt to hold you. Only your grip on the gun and the sides of the nacelle stood between you and eternity. Toward the front of the nacelle was a hollow steel rod with a swivel mount to which the gun was anchored. This gun covered a huge field of fire forward. Between the observer and the pilot a second gun was mounted, for firing over the F.E.2b's upper wing to protect the aircraft from rear attack [. . .] Adjusting and shooting this gun required that you stand right up out of the nacelle with your feet on the nacelle coaming. You had nothing to worry about except being blown out of the aircraft by the blast of air or tossed out bodily if the pilot made a wrong move. There were no parachutes and no belts. No wonder they needed observers.[21]

Raleigh records the circumstances in which Anderson's plane crashed and its pilot was killed:

> Bright intervals on the 3rd of November brought out many German fighters. Five of our aeroplanes were

shot down during the day, three of them from a photographic reconnaissance formation of No. 22 squadron led by Captain Lord Lucas who, it was afterwards known, had been attacked by three enemy pilots and shot in the head and leg. His aeroplane was landed by the wounded observer, Lieutenant A. Anderson. Lord Lucas never regained consciousness after he was hit, and died the same day.[22]

Anderson's heroic actions in landing the plane when his pilot had received fatal injuries and he himself had been wounded were remarkable. But he was not the only hero in that F.E.2b plane. Auberon Herbert, Captain Lord Lucas, was the second – but eldest surviving – son of the Hon. Auberon Herbert, younger son of Henry Herbert, 3rd Earl of Carnarvon. Educated at Bedford School and Balliol College, Oxford, Lucas Herbert had worked as a war correspondent during the Boer War, where he was wounded and lost a leg.[23] In April 1908, he was appointed to his first ministerial post as Under-Secretary of State for War (with a seat on the Army Council) by Prime Minister Asquith. A succession of other senior appointments followed before he entered the cabinet as President of the Board of Agriculture and Fisheries in August 1914. However, in 1915, aged thirty-nine and unwilling to spend the remainder of the war behind a desk, he took the only course open to him with a disability that made field service impossible, and joined the Royal Flying Corps, training first as an observer, and then as a pilot. He was posted to France in October 1916, and 'was the oldest in years but youngest in heart, of all the pilots of his squadron'.[24]

Lucas's death was recorded in one of the best-known

poems of the First World War, *In Memoriam A. H.*, written by his friend Maurice Baring. The last lines of the poem, in which Baring reflects on those who mourn their lost friends and loved ones, have become synonymous with the bravery and sacrifice of those who served in the air force:

> [. . .] it is well with them because they know,
> With faithful eyes,
> Fixed forward and turned upwards to the skies,
> That it is well with you,
> Among the chosen few,
> Among the very brave, the very true.

Emily's brother was lucky to escape with his life.[25] Though injured, and with Lucas unconscious and close to death, Alexander managed to land the F.E.2b.[26] His achievement in doing so is made all the more remarkable by the fact that the engine had stopped and he had to glide the plane to the ground. He was removed from the plane by his German captors, but by then his pilot had died, and Lieutenant Anderson recorded that he had 'witnessed his burial'.[27] A Standing Committee of Enquiry into the circumstances of his capture concluded that Lieutenant Anderson had acted entirely properly, and that 'no blame attaches to him in the matter'.[28]

The injured Lieutenant Anderson was taken first to a military hospital for prisoners of war in Aachen, western Germany, where a number of hospitals had been established for the care of prisoners awaiting repatriation. When he was sufficiently recovered, he was transferred to Stralsund, a prisoner-of-war camp for officers. For Alexander Anderson, the war was effectively over; within a year of his capture, however, for his sister Emily, the war was only beginning.

4

Academic Career

Anderson's decision to leave Barbados in 1917, then, was motivated both by the prospect of applying to become Chair of German at University College, Galway, and also by a desire to be at home with her family in the aftermath of the Easter Rising and her brother's capture. Having made the decision to resign her post at Queen's College and apply for the new position back home, she must have been hopeful that there was a reasonable chance of her being appointed.

There were seven candidates for the position, two men and five women. The governing body's assessments of all the candidates make for interesting reading. Anderson was deemed joint second in respect of academic distinction, and joint first with regard to general scholarship. Her teaching experience was calculated as '1 year in University, and two in secondary school'.[1] No publications were recorded for any of the candidates, and overall the 'general view' was that a Miss Stack was deemed the top candidate, with Miss Anderson ranked joint second. Nonetheless, it was Anderson who was appointed to the position, having (perhaps unsurprisingly) received the majority of governing body votes.[2] Anderson's appointment was confirmed at a meeting of the National University held on 1 June 1917.[3]

What the governing body minutes do not reveal is that when another prospective candidate, Hanna Sheehy Skeffington,[4] whose husband Francis had been murdered during the Easter Rising, had written to enquire about the vacant chair of Romance Languages, she had been told by Fr Hynes, the College Registrar, that 'a Galway graduate would almost certainly be awarded any such post'.[5] As it transpired, Fr Hynes was incorrect; while it was a Galway graduate, his friend Emily Anderson, who was appointed to the Chair of German, it was a University College, Dublin, graduate, Liam Ó Briain, who was appointed to the Chair of Romance Languages.

Despite having had the inside track, Anderson was eminently qualified for this new position, and quickly made her mark as Professor of German with a radical reform of the curriculum. She supplemented texts from the eighteenth and nineteenth centuries with those from earlier periods in German literature, and expanded the language programme to include Middle and Old High German, as well as emphasising a theoretical knowledge of phonetics as related to German. She also expanded existing courses on German literature to include 'a detailed knowledge of the history of German literature from the twelfth to the sixteenth century, inclusive'.[6] It was a bold and ambitious syllabus, and 'was to be Emily Anderson's legacy to UCG when she eventually resigned from the professorship in 1920'.[7]

Anderson was twenty-six when she was appointed as the first Professor of German at University College, Galway; her colleague Liam Ó Briain was twenty-eight. Ó Briain had been chosen from ten candidates for the position, and was also well qualified. A first-class honours graduate in Irish, English and French from University College, Dublin, with an MA and several years of lecturing experience behind him, he too had studied at Berlin, and at Bonn, Freiburg and Paris as well. While Anderson and Ó Briain were on cordial terms with each other, the differences in the political ideologies of the two new appointees could not have been more stark. The Andersons were staunch supporters of Home Rule for Ireland. Ó Briain was a committed Republican, who had fought under Countess Markievicz at the College of Surgeons Garrison in Dublin's St Stephen's Green during the Easter Rising. A lecturer in French at University College, Dublin, following the Rising, Ó Briain spent two months in prison and six months at Frongoch internment camp in Wales, before being released to discover that he had been fired from his job at UCD. He applied for the position at University College, Galway, and his appointment was confirmed mere months after his release from Frongoch in 1917.[8]

The fact that Professor Steinberger had been replaced by two much younger professors, one of them a woman, was the injection of energy the university needed, and the appointments of Anderson and Ó Briain were welcomed, particularly among the student body. Anderson was one of only two women professors at UCG – the other, Mary Donovan O'Sullivan, Professor of History, welcomed her new colleague as 'not only a fine German scholar, but [someone] deeply interested in music'.[9] The announcement of Anderson's appointment observed that 'the Chair of German could not have been better filled'.[10] But it was Ó Briain who won the hearts of students, with the college calendar noting: 'we are glad to see that Professor O'Brien[11] is another of these professors who take an active interest in students' societies and social life – "Si sic omnes".* Ó Briain, however, did not have a great deal of time to enjoy either his relationship with his students or his new position, as his openly Republican sympathies led to his arrest and internment on a number of occasions during the War of Independence.

*

With Irish Republican turmoil attending the career of her colleague, the Professor of German was quietly waging a war of her own, the precise nature of which would, had he but known of it, have likely appalled Ó Briain, who was vehemently anti-British. Just as everything changed in Ireland in the aftermath of the Rising, 1916 had also been a landmark year in the course of the war, and, as it transpired, the course of intelligence history. By 1916, the Germans had started to move away from the telephone and ground-based wire systems that had underpinned their military and diplomatic intelligence systems, and to move towards wireless telegraphy. Telephone systems were vulnerable to damage from artillery and easily intercepted. Blockades instigated by the Allied powers compelled the Germans to use their copper resources wisely, and a wireless set was a much more efficient use of such resources. This seismic shift in communications systems resulted in the volume of encoded German traffic mushrooming, such that by late 1916, it was imperative that the British Expeditionary Force ramp up its collection capability and establish stations that could intercept and decipher the encrypted messages being sent by wireless telegraphy. As

* The Latin phrase translates as 'If only they were all like'.

encoded messages, using a combination of numbers and letters, were encoded in the language of the host nation, it was imperative that linguists fluent in German, French, Italian and Japanese be recruited and trained in decoding such messages. Anderson's fluency in German and French, and her knowledge of Italian, rendered her eminently suitable for the task.

On the surface, nothing much had changed in the life of the newly appointed head of the German Department. Professor Anderson was building up her department, mentoring her students, and overseeing the expansion of the new German syllabus. But unbeknownst to her colleagues, the need for intelligence officers with a particular skill set to help in the war effort had intensified, and Emily Anderson had been secretly approached to assess her willingness to serve for the duration of the war in Europe.

Staunchly pro-war in her sympathies, Anderson had a more compelling reason than most to respond to the overtures made to her in the summer of 1917, only months after her return to Ireland and her appointment to the Chair of German. Her willingness to become involved in the war effort was inevitably influenced by the fact that her only brother had been languishing in a German prisoner-of-war camp since his capture in November 1916. In agreeing to play her part in defeating the Germans and bringing the war to a speedy conclusion, which would hopefully see the return of her brother and millions of serving soldiers to their families, Anderson was embarking on a career that would determine the course of the rest of her life.

5

'Passed Under the Microscope'

The passing of the Official Secrets Acts of 1911 and 1920 resulted in an official secrecy policy discouraging disclosures even during peacetime. As a consequence, how, when, and by whom Anderson was recruited to the intelligence service remains something of a mystery. It is widely acknowledged that the recruitment of intelligence officers, male and female, tended to come about principally at that time as a result of connections and recommendations from those already serving within the armed forces, and trusted civilians with strong connections with the armed forces who knew the kind of people required. Of his own recruitment to Room 40 (the Navy's intelligence division, later known as ID25), Richard Hippisley observed: 'Room 40 was, as it should have been, a watertight compartment & very few of the people working in it knew or cared how the staff was got, and who got it.'[1]

Women recruited to the intelligence service appear to have been subject to a great deal more scrutiny than was the case with their male counterparts. Francis Toye, who worked in Room 40, observed that, when it came to recruitment, 'Ladies [were] passed under the microscope of every kind of social and political scrutiny', while the 'gentlemen [were] of established reputation.'[2] Intelligence records for the First World War are extremely limited when it comes to the issue of recruitment,[3] so in Anderson's case, the question of who elected to put her 'under the microscope' may never be definitively known, but there are some compelling possibilities.

One is a fellow Irish academic, Douglas Lloyd Savory, Professor of French at Queens University, Belfast, and later a Unionist MP. Savory had been recruited to Room 40, but immediately prior to taking up the professorship in Belfast in 1909, he had taught French and English at the University of Marburg, and may have had contacts there who would have known Anderson.[4] Another significant observation was made by Anderson's colleague, Professor Mary Donovan O'Sullivan:

> The thing that struck me most about College Staff in my time was their close contact with Cambridge. Four members of the staff in those days were Fellows of one or other of the Cambridge Colleges.[5]

This is telling, as Cambridge colleges proved a significant recruiting ground for cryptographic talent. James Bruce has observed that Room 40 recruited many of its personnel:

> [. . .] from existing and overlapping personal networks including Cambridge University (16 per cent), the naval educational system (24 per cent), and 'the City' i.e. London's financial institutions (7 per cent). This homogeneity meant that existing social contacts persisted after 1919, including reunions of what was effectively an 'old comrades' association; it also resulted in those who returned to academia acting as recruiters

for GC&CS, and in some former Room 40 staff being asked to join GC&CS in 1939.[6]

Anderson's recruitment may have been due to her father's good friend Sir Joseph Larmor, Lucasian Professor of Mathematics at Cambridge. Mathematicians and modern language graduates were the first choice for those recruited for cryptographic work. As the daughter of a physicist, with a sound grasp of mathematics, and a skilled linguist, Anderson was in many ways the perfect cryptographer – and Larmor would have known that.

The Cambridge connection is rendered even more compelling by an intriguing reference in Anderson's correspondence with the college during her time in London. In March 1919, she wrote to the college registrar, Fr Hynes, concerning one of her students, a Miss Dermody, who had left college due to ill health. Anderson wrote:

I was very sorry to hear from Miss Milner-Barry that Miss Dermody was in poor health and had to go home. I think it is very wise that she should not attempt an examination until she is quite strong again. I have just written to her.[7]

While Anderson's concern for her student is laudable, it is the reference to 'Miss Milner-Barry' that is significant. Alda Milner-Barry was a graduate of Newnham College, Cambridge, and later became a fellow and served as vice-principal of the college until her death in 1938, at the age of just forty-four. Milner-Barry was the daughter of Edward Leopold Milner-Barry, Professor of Modern Languages at the University of Bangor, and the granddaughter of Dr William Besant, a renowned mathematical fellow of St John's College, Cambridge. Milner-Barry graduated with first-class honours in English and German in 1916, and, immediately upon graduation, 'for a year she was a translator in the Intelligence Department of the War Office, for another year acting Professor of German at University College, Galway'.[8] Having herself worked in intelligence for a time, Milner-Barry became Anderson's deputy[9] when Anderson was appointed to MI1(b), the army's intelligence division.* Anderson would come to know Alda's younger brother, Stuart Milner-Barry, during the Second World War, when he worked as a codebreaker at Bletchley Park.[10]

Academic skills were not the only criteria relevant to the recruitment of women for intelligence work. Anderson was Irish, and in Ireland, religion and political loyalties were inextricably linked, with Catholics generally nationalist (and increasingly Republican) in their ideology, while Protestants traditionally identified as British and loyal to the Empire. The fact that Anderson was Presbyterian, and although a supporter of Home Rule was staunchly in favour of Ireland remaining within the United Kingdom, would undoubtedly have been a factor in her recruitment.

Initial soundings regarding a possible role in military intelligence were made to Anderson sometime in the autumn of 1917, just months after she had taken up her professorship at UCG. The need for codebreakers who could decrypt German SIGINT (signals intelligence) became a priority on the Western Front, and a code-breaking bureau, called I(e)C, was established at Saint Omer in northern France. With every available man

* MI stood for 'Military Intelligence'.

needed for active service, women with the requisite skills had already been recruited and were working in the two existing cryptographic organisations: the navy's Room 40, and the army's MI1(b), for which Emily Anderson was destined.

After an initial approach in the autumn of 1917, Anderson appears to have agreed to join MI1(b) once the 1917–18 academic year had ended, and she moved to London in July 1918. At the time she joined, MI1(b) had a total of thirty-eight staff. Most of the female staff were employed as clerks and typists, but there were three university-educated women – Florence Hayllar, and the Misses Carleton and Chichester – already engaged on cryptanalytic work. Anderson was set to join them.[11]

Her formal letter of resignation was dated 19 July 1918, and written from the Hotel Stuart,[12] Cromwell Road, London, and addressed to the governing body of UCG. In it, Anderson stated:

> I beg to tender my resignation of the Chair of German Language and Literature to which I was appointed by the Senate of the National University of Ireland in June, 1917, and which I have filled during the Session 1917–1918. I have accepted an appointment in the Military Intelligence Department in France for the duration of the war. I much regret to have to give up my academical work in Galway, but as the work in the Intelligence Department is extremely important at the present crisis, I feel it is my duty to undertake it.

Anderson formally joined MI1(b) three days later, on 22 July 1918. However, a second, and private, letter accompanied the above formal resignation, and was addressed to

Anderson's friend and confidante, Fr John Hynes, the college registrar.[13] This letter was not meant for the eyes of her father or the governing body, but it throws significant light on the reasons behind Anderson's life-changing decision to give up her academic post, move to London and commit herself to working as a secret cryptanalyst. Anderson wrote:

> You will perhaps remember that I spoke to you last autumn of what I felt was my duty at that time. This summer I came to London with every intention of returning to my work in Galway in September. I have been told, however, that people with a thorough knowledge of Modern Languages are very badly wanted for Military Intelligence work in France and I was asked to apply. Up to the present only four girls have been taken for this work; they are university lecturers in England. I feel that I cannot do otherwise than go and help, since I am qualified to do so. So I have agreed to go for the duration of the war. After four or five weeks work in London I am to be sent to France.
>
> I need not assure you that I am extremely sorry to resign my work in Galway and I do regret leaving my students, some of whom I took a special interest in. I sincerely hope that they will prove to be as thorough as they were promising to become last session. I should also like to thank you very much for your kindness to me during last session and for making things easy for a newcomer.[14]

The reference to Anderson having spoken to Fr Hynes 'last autumn' is highly significant. It reveals that, shortly after taking up her position as Professor of German in June

1917, Anderson had been approached regarding intelligence work, and had been keen to do her 'duty', as she saw it. What is also clear is that she never envisaged this as a permanent career change: in both letters, the phrase 'for the duration of the war' imply that she was prepared to undertake intelligence work only as long as the war lasted, and thereafter it was her intention to return to academic life. The implication for the university governors was that they would be honour bound to keep her post open for her – which, as her father was college president, was pretty much a given.

Of even greater significance in the letter to Fr Hynes is the reference by Anderson to her being 'sent to France'. This was undoubtedly a reference to the codebreaking bureau established at St Omer, which was contributing vital intelligence for the British and French military. With the war on the Western Front intensifying considerably by mid-1917, the need for SIGINT in France was so great that an unprecedented decision was made to deploy suitably trained women directly with the British Expeditionary Force (BEF) in France. The first contingent of six women, all members of the Women's Army Auxiliary Corps, known as WAACs, arrived in St Omer on 29 September 1917. Once deployed, these women codebreakers were affiliated to the army's Intelligence Corps. It was to this elite group of women codebreakers, known as 'Hush WAACs',[15] deployed to France to intercept German signals in the field, that Anderson was set to be deployed by MI1(b).[16] The female 'university lecturers' Anderson refers to are almost certainly Florence Hannam,[17] Gwendoline (Gwen) Watkins,[18] Mabel Peel[19] and Olivia Chevalier.[20]

We are fortunate that Gwen Watkins wrote wonderful account of her recruitment and time as a Hush WAAC in France, written by Gwen Watkins, survives. Anxious to play her part, Watkins had applied to several government offices for a job, but was eventually called for an interview at the War Office, where:

> [...] to my extreme astonishment one of the first questions was 'would you go to France?' I was told that a party of women was being sent there almost immediately for special work.[21]

She was subsequently asked to read 'various specimens of German handwriting'. Such was the demand for this as-yet-undefined 'special work' that:

> [...] in an incredibly short space of time I found myself consulting surprised but proud relatives, being interviewed at Devonshire House,[22] medically examined, vaccinated, inoculated, dressed up in uniform, received at Connaught Club (where for the first time I experienced the odd sensation of being called 'Ma'am' and saw rows of 'other ranks' jumping to their feet when I passed) and finally hustled across the Channel with the other five.[23]

By the spring of 1918, the complement of women codebreakers deployed in France had reached its peak of twelve. By then, the work of the Hush WAACs had become essential, as in March 1918 the Germans had changed their codes and I(e)C were under intense pressure to break them. An intensification of German attacks in April saw the British being driven back, and with St Omer no longer a safe area, the unit was moved to Paris Plage on the coast to enable codebreaking operations to continue. It is likely at this juncture that Anderson's recruitment as a Hush WAAC, and her planned deployment to France to join the other twelve women already there was initiated.

Having committed to the required training in London, and ready and willing to go to France, wider events were to significantly alter Anderson's plans. By the time she wrote her resignation letter, the tide had already turned in the Allies' favour. America's entry into the war had proved decisive, and only a day earlier, on 18 July 1918, a combined French and American attack along the Marne River marked the first in a series of coordinated Allied counter-offensives on the Western Front. Three French armies and five American divisions had crossed the Marne, and as a result the German 7th and 9th Armies had begun a withdrawal. At this critical juncture, the need for speedy and consistent British signals intelligence was still acute, and in spite of her obvious willingness to go, it is clear that Anderson's services were no longer needed in the field in France. Back in London, however, her quite exceptional skills as a codebreaker had been noticed by her superiors in MI1(b), and they were anxious to retain her services, not just for the duration of the war, but for the fledgling intelligence service already being planned by senior officers in military and naval intelligence for the post-war period. Anderson had already been earmarked for the new organisation, but there were still four months to go before the war ended, and for Anderson, those months in London were to change her life for ever.

6

'A Shadowy Entity'[1]

The First World War would bring about a remarkable revolution in how war was waged, with nineteenth-century military science giving way to twentieth-century technology. Yet, at its outbreak, no plans had been made for the interception of enemy wireless traffic and its subsequent analysis to produce intelligence – as a result, British SIGINT 'was started from scratch in 1914'.[2] The fledgling intelligence service had a champion in Winston Churchill, First Lord of the Admiralty in 1914, who was deeply concerned about naval intelligence, and was among the first 'to appreciate the great intelligence potential of the ability to read secret messages intercepted by the new method of wireless signals'.[3]

In evaluating the origins of SIGINT, the Second World War codebreaker Mavis Batey noted:

On the day WW1 broke out instructions were given to cut the German transatlantic cables in the Channel which meant that in future their communications overseas would have to be mainly through wireless telegraphy. France suggested they should be jammed but Britain, having realized the potential of signals intelligence, with great foresight insisted that all messages should be intercepted [. . .] the race was then on to set

50

up a cryptographic bureau to break the enciphered messages. SIGINT, as signals intelligence would be known, would work side by side with HUMINT, intelligence gained from agents.[4]

The first intercept stations (known as 'Y'* stations) were set up by the Royal Navy along the east coast, and these stations began to intercept the wireless traffic of the Germany navy. Intercepting was one thing; making sense of the traffic was entirely another, and Sir Alfred Ewing, Director of Naval Education, was allocated this task. Ewing began to gather together a group of German speakers from among the officers at the naval academies at Dartmouth and Osborne. Those recruited were given a relatively small room, Room 40, in the Old Admiralty Building[5] in which to begin their operations. Among the first of those recruited was Alastair Denniston, whose career, from 1918 onwards, would run in tandem with Emily Anderson's. Born in Scotland in 1881, Denniston was educated at Bowdon College in Altrincham, and later studied at the University of Bonn and the University of Paris. A talented sportsman, he won a bronze medal playing hockey for Scotland in the 1908 London Olympic Games. In 1909, he secured a job at the Royal Naval College, Osborne, teaching French and German.

Ewing identified Denniston as someone who, as well as being a German linguist, had an inquisitive mind, and Ewing's instincts proved to be correct: Denniston was a natural cryptanalyst. In addition to working in Room 40 throughout the war, he also served as an interpreter at

---

* The term originated as 'Wireless Interception', or WI, pronounced 'Y'.

Scapa Flow when the German fleet surrendered, and led a SIGINT team at the Paris Peace Conference in 1919. He later became the first Head of the Government Code & Cypher School (GC&CS) when it was established in 1919.

Churchill, then the First Lord of the Admiralty, had assumed a proactive role in establishing the naval cryptanalytic bureau, and:

> [. . .] installed the bureau in Room 40 of the Admiralty Old buildings, close to his own rooms. He liked nothing better than slipping in to watch 'the quiet men' silently scribbling on coded intercepts with growing tension. He gave Room 40 personally its charter in 1914[6] and called for a study of 'all intercepts, not only current but past, and to compare them continually with what actually took place in order to penetrate the German mind and movements'.[7]

The War Office had established its own cryptanalytic unit, MI1(b), the division of military intelligence responsible for interception and cryptanalysis.[8] Anderson was one of a number of women cryptographers specifically recruited to MI1(b). Regrettably, MI1(b) was to become 'the worst documented of British intelligence agencies between 1900 and 1945'[9] for a number of reasons, including the naval dominance of British COMINT* history, thanks to which Room 40 was deemed to have 'conducted all British signals intelligence during the Great War'.[10] This was emphatically not the case, and MI1(b) did decisive work against diplomatic communications, work at which Anderson became particularly adept. The lack of records (for which

* Military communications intelligence.

the head of the section in Anderson's time, Major Hay, was partially responsible)* saw to it that the roles played by Anderson and her colleagues received relatively little attention until recent times.[11] However, it was at MI1(b) that Anderson's boss recognised her exceptional skills and became her first mentor.

MI1(b)'s development as a military cryptanalytic bureau was down to the remarkable group of people, from a variety of backgrounds, who worked there. Finding people with the right skill set was not easy. William 'Nobby' Clarke, in his history of MI1(b), observed:

> Really expert cryptographers can never be found ready made; only experience can make 'expert' the individual who possesses the necessary mental qualifications and aptitude for the work.[12]

During the First World War, cryptanalysis was viewed as work for linguists rather than mathematicians, and as a result those candidates with 'high linguistic qualifications' were deemed the most suitable.[13] Fortunately for Anderson, her linguistic skills were matched by a natural mathematical ability, honed by her physicist father in her youth, something that contributed to her exceptional ability as a cryptanalyst, and the longevity of her career.

In addition to Watkins and Hannam who had served as Hush WAACs in France, among Anderson's other female contemporaries in Room MI1b were Florence Hayllar and Claribel Spurling. Born in Brighton in 1868, Hayllar was 'a natural scholar'[14] and, at the time Anderson met her, was aged fifty.[15] The 1911 census lists her as a 'writer/authoress',

* See p. 61.

living 'on her own means'. Many of the women who worked in MI1(b) were supporters of greater rights for women, and had been involved in the women's suffrage movement – Claribel Spurling, for example, had been Secretary of Bristol and West of England Society for Women's Suffrage.[16] Spurling was forty-two when she joined M.I.1(b),[17] and prior to the war had been Headmistress of Birkenhead High School, where she taught German. In December 1917, her brother, Captain Francis Spurling, was killed in action in Flanders,[18] and Spurling immediately joined the Wrens.* Her fluency in German brought her to the attention of Major Hay, who recruited her as a translator. Spurling distinguished herself as the only person to score 100 per cent in a supposedly 'unsolvable' test set by Hay for potential recruits. Like Anderson, neither Hayllar nor Spurling ever married.

Anderson's male co-workers at MI1(b) were an eclectic bunch, comprising military men invalided out of active service and private individuals from every walk of life. A large cohort were academics from a variety of disciplines. One such was John Fraser, a lecturer in Celtic and Comparative Philology at the University of Aberdeen, who was fluent in twenty-one languages.[19] John Maxwell Edmonds, a graduate of Jesus College, Cambridge, was a classicist, poet and dramatist. Edmonds would later be credited with authorship of perhaps the most famous wartime epitaph:

> When you go home, tell them of us and say
> For their tomorrow, we gave our today.[20]

MI1(b) was housed in offices at 5 Cork Street, Mayfair. Staff worked in shifts, around the clock, and as a

* Women's Royal Naval Service.

consequence some of those who worked there developed insomnia.[21] But aside from insomnia, stress and the repetitive nature of the work itself, one of the main physical discomforts that those who worked in MI1(b) had to contend with was the cold of the building. War restrictions meant coal rations were limited, and a building constructed in the late eighteenth century required large quantities of fuel to make the space bearable. Hays' habit of opening windows to let in fresh air served to make the problem even worse for his staff.[22] Their counterparts in Room 40 struggled equally with the cold, with one of their number 'accused of bringing a bag in which to take coal home'.[23]

*

When it came to the work of codebreaking, Hay believed 'anyone of average intelligence can learn to read cryptograms. Success in solving difficult problems depends of course on individual talent':[24] talent which, as a result of a rigorous selection and training process, he had to hand in abundance. The task of 'attacking'* enemy codes was nonetheless daunting, as Hay explained:

> Every message, every sentence in a message, has its own distinctive pattern, and contains repetitions of letters, or combinations of letters, and sometimes of complete words. These repetitions can be disguised, they cannot be destroyed. All possible methods of disguise can be classified under the two systems 1) substitution, 2) transposition. By the system known as

* This is the term used by Hay, and others, in relation to the systematic process of breaking enemy codes.

substitution the letters of the text are replaced by various symbols; or letters, or figures, are generally used. By the method known as transposition, the letters of the text change their position according to some predetermined arrangement, or key. Both methods can be used simultaneously.[25]

While it was generally agreed that attacking military codes was difficult, the complexity of diplomatic traffic was infinitely more so. By early 1917, Hay noted:

[...] we had already begun to attack a number of other foreign codes. Thousands of telegrams filled up cupboards at Cork Street. Although my staff at the end of the year had enormously increased, it was impossible to read everything. Even if we had been provided with the code books, the task of decoding all the diplomatic cables which reached and left London every day would have kept busy at least a hundred people [...] All these difficulties were overcome. Cork Street was never defeated.[26]

Diplomatic traffic focused on what governments were saying to their embassies abroad, affording a window into their political intentions. The nuances of diplomatic correspondence demanded a particular skill set from cryptologists, who needed to be fluent in a range of languages and able to draw from a breadth of knowledge, just as those who worked in the diplomatic service were able to.[27] It was in this aspect of attacking codes that Anderson showed exceptional skill: a skill quickly identified by Major Hay.

By the time Anderson was recruited, the codebreaking process had evolved from the improvisation of the early days of the war, to limited effectiveness during 1915–16, to 'increasing effectiveness and cryptologic sophistication in the last two years of the war.'[28] The process of breaking codes was done without the use of machinery, and involved 'almost unimaginable mental gymnastics',[29] which ultimately yielded information that proved invaluable to the war effort. MI1(b), along with its sister organisation the Navy's Room 40, had proven definitively by war's end that SIGINT was now an intrinsic component in military and diplomatic intelligence.

*

What has become known as 'The Cork Street Book', an album compiled at the war's end by his staff as a memento for Major Hay, now held at the University of Aberdeen, provides a fascinating insight into MI1(b). The work was of a high-pressure, often repetitive nature, but with a diverse mix of clever and talented individuals working together, there was also considerable intellectual stimulation. It is hardly surprising that the Cork Street Book includes challenging and amusing puzzles and poems (often variations on classical works of literature) in Gaelic, French, Spanish, Latin, Greek and even Egyptian hieroglyphics. It also provides one of only three photographs of the adult Anderson known to exist. Taken in August 1919, on the roof of the Cork Street building, it shows Anderson in the company of her female colleagues and Major Hay. Anderson is seated in the second row on the extreme left, affecting an almost jaunty pose, with her legs crossed, her head held high and a broad smile on her face. She is one of the few women pictured to have her hair styled in the short 'shingle' hairstyle, which was just coming into vogue.[30]

The album closes with an image of Hay's chair in an empty room at Cork Street. The ghost-like image of a vacant chair, with no trace of its former occupant, was a subtle nod to the fact that as the vast majority of its staff went back to their pre-war lives and careers, their remarkable contribution to the war effort would remain completely unknown, because it could not be talked about. The Official Secrets Act, and its implications for those who had worked in MI1(b), is obliquely referred to in a quote from Shakespeare's *Hamlet*:

> And now, good friends –
> As you are friends, scholars and soldiers –
> Give me one more request,
> Never to speak of this that you have heard.[31]

For Emily Anderson, however, such secrecy was never a burden; rather, it became a way of life. Her exceptional skills as a codebreaker had been recognised, and as a consequence her career in academia was about to end, just as her full-time career in intelligence was about to begin.

7

War's End

It is a measure of just how vital the codebreakers of MI1(b) and Room 40 had been to the war effort that 'they were the first to know that the war was over'.[1] They were also among the first to celebrate the victory, and from the windows of their offices in Cork Street, the staff of MI1(b) witnessed the jubilant scenes that followed the realisation that the war had finally ended. But the scenes of unbridled joy were initially slow in coming. Lionel Fraser, who worked in Room 40, recalled:

> Everybody rushed out into Whitehall, which before very long was a packed mass of happy and excited people, not knowing how to give vent to their feelings, and, being truly British, they were too shy to shout or dance, or do anything, so they stood and swayed about like sheep.[2]

Fraser was moved to act, and the manner in which he did so was later recorded by Rear Admiral Sir Douglas Bowrigg:

> The situation was saved by a young subaltern [Fraser], who [. . .] happened to find himself on a bus bound down through Whitehall to Westminster.[3] As the

speed of the bus was reduced to rather less than foot pace, he solemnly stood up at the back of the roof, and beating time with his cane, he started three cheers which lifted the safety valve of the crowd, and they began to give voice to the ferment of joy that was inside them [. . .] He travelled to and fro many times on buses, keeping the crowd yelling and cheering in a perfectly orderly manner, his face remaining sphinx-like with not a trace of a smile on it. He did good work that morning.[4]

Few in Britain's military or naval command were in any doubt that a great deal more 'good work' had been done by the codebreakers of MI1(b) and Room 40 during the conflict. By war's end, MI1(b) had a staff of eighty-five, of whom fifteen were working on military targets.[5] Anderson was, in many ways, fortunate that although the need for military intelligence was now at an end, MI1(b) 'actually grew in size during the early months of peace to meet the requirement for diplomatic intelligence, using personnel awaiting demobilisation'.[6] Many of those employed in MI1(b) and Room 40 began to drift back to their previous lives in business, academia and the arts. Anderson left London and returned to her home in Galway on 9 December. The visit was prompted by the impending arrival home of her brother, Alexander, a prisoner of war since November 1916, who had survived the war and was repatriated to Ireland, arriving in Galway on 13 December 1918.

Anderson then returned to London and MI1(b) to resume her codebreaking work in the new year, when it was clear that negotiations were taking place to form a new, dedicated codebreaking organisation, combining military, naval, air and diplomatic intelligence. Soundings were already being made to staff whose services would be needed in any new organisation. In considering their decision, prospective employees from both organisations, would have been influenced by who was set to lead this combined operation. Hays, one of the candidates, was a complicated man, and when he was passed over for the position of head of the new combined cryptologic section that succeeded MI1(b) and Room 40 – to be known as the Government Code & Cypher School (GC&CS) – his unilateral decision to destroy most of the records of MI1(b) was at best vindictive and at worst an act of archival vandalism of the most reprehensible kind. Most historians agree, however, that although his superiors found him 'difficult',

> Hay engendered loyalty and affection in his staff, as reflected in the 'Cork Street Book'. This took time to compile and bind and it was not until 31 October 1919, the day before GC&CS came into being, that it was ready to be sent to Hay, Brooke-Hunt noting in a laconic PPS to his best wishes that 'MI1(b) died today.'[7]

The actions of Hay in destroying records (and removing some to his own care, without official authorisation), coupled with the paucity of primary sources related to the inside story of how places such as Room 40 or MI1(b) operated, renders the Cork Street Book of even greater importance than it might otherwise have been. The album does much more than serve as a farewell gift to a former boss. The tone of the Cork Street Book reflects the collaborative effort and team spirit that prevailed. It also provides an insight into the nature of the work Anderson and her colleagues undertook in MI1(b), which is vividly recalled and reflected in the imaginative and often witty individual entries in the album. What is clear from many of the entries is that the work was repetitive and gruelling, and required persistence, a broad outlook, and often a great deal of luck. In this regard, one of the entries, by J. Maxwell Edmonds, cites Coleridge's *Rime of the Ancient Mariner* in describing the process of finding a way into a complicated code or cipher:

> At first it seem'd a little speck
> And then it seem'd a mist
> It moved, and moved, and took at last,
> A certain shape, I wist.*[8]

By the time the book was sent to Hay, Anderson had already returned to Galway to take up her academic duties, and a page was left blank for her contribution to be inserted at a later date. Anderson's contribution is therefore dated 'January 15th 1920', and is a poem that she begins 'With apologies to Ronsard', a reference to the French poet Pierre de Ronsard.[9]

The poem reads as follows:

> *Mais quelle recompense aurois-je de tant suivre*
> *Vos travaux nuit et jour, allant venant?*
> *De tirer doulce saigesse des livres*
> *Pour fournir conseil à nos grans?*

* The word 'wist' is an old English way to say someone has knowledge of something.

Nous aurons tous de vous fresche memoire,
Toujours chez nous votre nom fleurira.

Translated, the poem reads:

But what reward should I receive for following so closely
Your labours night and day, going and coming?
For drawing sweet wisdom from books
To offer advice to our great men?
We shall all keep you fresh in our memory
Your name will bloom for evermore.[10]

Anderson's lines reveal an accomplished linguist, who succeeds in recreating a Ronsard-sounding verse by embroidering on the well-trodden theme of immortality found throughout his poetry, and the idea that great men live on through memory and reputation. What is abundantly clear from its content is the high regard and admiration Anderson had for her former boss.

It is also inferred in the Cork Street Book that even before the issue of pay for the women codebreakers became a burning question when it came to the establishment of GC&CS, rumblings were already being heard from the female codebreakers of MI1(b), who were paid less than their male colleagues. Anderson was at the forefront of these rumblings, and remained so when, in 1920, she made the momentous decision to leave her academic career behind and commit herself to working fulltime with GC&CS. The signs were there even before the establishment of GC&CS that women codebreakers felt there was an uneven playing field when it came to their pay and conditions in comparison to those of their male counterparts. The Cork Street Book makes reference to the dissatisfaction that was already being felt among the women, and in a section titled 'Equal pay – for equal work?', Cowley quotes from Aristotle's *Politics*, stating:

> [. . .] and the unsatisfactory condition of the women seems [. . .] not only to create a certain indecorum in the polity itself, but to contribute something to the avarice of the citizens.

The issue of equal pay for equal work was one that undoubtedly concerned women codebreakers like Anderson, but it was not the only one. Much as his staff – male and female – may have respected Hay, there is confirmation from one of Anderson's contemporaries, Claribel Spurling, that women staff were subject to a great deal more scrutiny than their male colleagues. Spurling addresses Hay in a poem entitled 'The D.M.I.'* and observes:

> Our names, weights, ages, heights & sex,
> The way we do our hair,
> Which tongues we talk, what ways we walk,
> Were objects of his care.
> From Aberdeen to far Japan
> Without a pause his queries ran.
> Our lurid pasts he found invest-
> -ed with peculiar interest,
> We dared not baffle nor perplex
> His 'How?', 'What', 'When?' and 'Where?'
> Return! Return, O, D.M.I.!
> Prithee return and tell us 'Why?'

* Director of Military Intelligence.

Spurling's plaintive 'Why?' reveals a frustration that women codebreakers were treated differently to their male colleagues on a variety of levels. Disparities in pay and career prospects eventually led to a full-blown stand-off, led by Anderson.

But before that battle could be fought, Anderson, like many others whose lives and careers had been upended for the duration of a gruelling four-year war, had decisions to make. With the future role of SIGINT still being worked out, for the vast majority of those non-naval or non-military personnel who had worked in MI1(b) and ID25 (as Room 40 became), a return to their former lives and careers was inevitable. But while the precise nature of the organisation that would continue the work of wartime intelligence gathering had yet to be fully defined, it was certainly the case that:

> Consideration of post-war intelligence arrangements began before the Armistice was a week old. Thwaites wrote to the Admiralty and Foreign office on 14 November 1918 proposing a joint structure for 'Secret Service, Contre-espionage and Censorship [. . .] in time of peace'.[11]

The structure that eventually emerged was the Government Code & Cypher School, and with a wealth of experience gained in high-pressure wartime conditions, and a cohort of highly skilled cryptanalysts having risen to the top of both Room 40/ID25 and MI1(b), that organisation was to become what is widely acknowledged as probably the most effective cryptanalytic bureau the world has ever seen. Recruiting the right staff to the new intelligence organisation would be crucial to its success, and it was by no means certain that those earmarked for retention would be willing to stay. Writing of the decision to stay or leave facing the staff of Room 40, Patrick Beesley observed:

> [. . .] most of them wished to return as speedily as possible to their old careers – to the Stock Exchange or the City, to the universities, to literature or antique furniture, to haute couture or to the stage. But for a few Room 40 had become a way of life, something they could not give up. Denniston, Clarke, Dilly Knox and one or two more were 'hooked'. They would all have earned much more by returning to civil life than the five or six hundred pounds a year which they were paid in Intelligence, but not one of them had ever, or could contemplate ever having in the future, a career which would give the fulfilment and satisfaction they had experienced in Room 40. They decided to stay on with the Old Firm. Thank God they did.[12]

The staff of MI1(b) faced a similar dilemma, but their responses were identical – the vast majority, including Emily Anderson, gave an indication that, subject to pay and conditions, they were prepared to stay on. Whether she knew it or not as she packed her bags and prepared for a return to her academic life in Galway, Emily Anderson was already destined for a role at the heart of that new organisation.

8

'Double Jobbing'

In spite of their contribution to the war effort, after the war women were dismissed from, or politely asked to leave, their posts to make way for the men returning from the front. A Ministry of Labour pamphlet went so far as to call on women to 'help renew the homes of England' by cooking, cleaning and rearing babies.[1] For Anderson, it was not a life of domesticity that beckoned but a resumption of her academic career in Ireland. In December 1918, she returned to take up her duties as Professor of German at University College, Galway, and the issue of her resignation letter of July 1918 was quietly allowed to drop. The armistice in November 1918, however, was to prove as much a beginning as an end to Anderson's career.

Anderson was fortunate that it was MI1(b) and not Room 40 to which she had been recruited. Room 40's female employees had largely worked in clerical roles, with cryptanalysis exclusively a male domain. By 1919, however, a third of the civilian cryptanalysts and linguists of MI1(b) were female,[2] whereas in ID25, the successor to Room 40, the number of staff working on diplomatic decryption had remained as low as it had been at its height in late 1917, and was an exclusively male preserve.[3] Anderson was doubly fortunate that her exceptional skills had not only been recognised by her first boss, Major Hay, but were to be equally valued, and for far longer, by her second, Commander Alastair Denniston, the man tasked with the job of heading up GC&CS.[4] Denniston became Anderson's boss, and friend, for the next thirty years. The Cabinet Secret Service Committee made the ultimate decision to establish GC&CS, with Winston Churchill in particular convinced of the value of retaining those who had:

> [. . .] developed a particular kind of aptitude for the work, which depended for its success more on the psychology of the persons sending out the messages and an instinctive flair for what they are saying than of careful study and analysis.[5]

The Admiralty had made a strong case for the establishment of GC&CS, with Denniston arguing that 'the majority of the experts employed by the Admiralty during the war have gone to their own spheres of work, but there still remains a certain number whose capabilities and experience in cryptography entitles them to a place in any joint scheme'. Hay, from the military side, agreed, and brought a number of his female staff to the attention of his naval colleagues in a document that identified individuals who had the required expertise, and were also willing to stay on and continue their cryptologic work in a permanent capacity during peacetime. Hay singled out Anderson, Florence Hayllar, Barbara Freire-Marreco and Claribel Spurling, noting: 'The services of these ladies are invaluable. They are experienced in the working out of all kinds of codes.'[6] Hay's regard for the talents of Anderson and her other female colleagues is significant in that he could be extremely dismissive of female staff whose work and talents he felt were below par. In his memoirs, Hay recalled an incident that occurred in late 1918:

> A few weeks before the New Year, someone in the War Office asked me to provide temporary work for 'a lady who had done excellent service in France.' The lady arrived; I turned her over to one of my officers who reported later that she was very good at pouring out tea. When Major G— paid his next visit to my room he brought the conversation round to the subject of the New Year's Honours list, and then to the talents of the lady. I pretended not to understand.[7] At last he asked me to outright to put her name down on the Cork Street list. I replied with equal frankness: I told him I would prefer to recommend the office cat.[8]

With a 'wish list' of personnel now identified, the staff selected by Hay and Denniston in their respective organisations were approached. Hay's report indicates that Anderson expressed a willingness to remain, as a tick appears against her name.[9] Expressing a willingness to stay was something of a leap of faith among those identified as being 'most desirable to retain', the category into which Anderson, Hayllar and Spurling[10] fell. Hay's report stated that 'all the persons named, with the exception noted[11] have intimated their willingness to stay so far as they can do so without knowing the actual conditions'. This was a significant point, as initially it was unclear what status the staff of this new organisation would have within the civil service structure, and what their salaries and pension rights would be. It is a measure of Denniston's leadership abilities, and his powers of persuasion, that the vast majority of those asked to stay on and serve in the new organisation elected to do so.

Much work had yet to be done on putting together the bones of the fledgling intelligence organisation, with its deceptively academic-sounding title of the Government Code & Cypher School, before it was formally established on 1 November 1919, and became the foundation for the modern British intelligence service we now know as GCHQ. Anderson was to serve in GC&CS, and all of its subsequent iterations, from the outset until her retirement in 1950.

In the interim, with no indication of the terms and conditions she could expect if she committed to a career as a cryptanalyst, Anderson elected to do what she had done since her recruitment in 1917 – she kept a foot in both camps. Anderson's contract would eventually confirm that her employment with GC&CS formally began in January 1920, but until then for the remainder of 1918, throughout 1919, and until June 1920, Anderson was effectively 'double jobbing'. Having taken up her professorship in German at University College, Galway, again, she continued to spend almost all her time, and all of her academic holidays (Christmas, Easter and the long summer vacation), working in MI1(b) in London. Having spent Christmas 1918 with her family, and reunited with her now safely repatriated brother Alexander, she returned to London in January 1919, and took up residence in the Hotel Madrid.[12]

Necessitating a gruelling travel schedule and affording precious little leisure time, retaining a foothold in academia while engaging in intelligence work was something that had been facilitated by those charged with recruiting academics with codebreaking skills at both MI1(b) and Room 40 during the war. In striving to retain the best cryptanalysts, Denniston and his superiors were prepared to smooth the way for Anderson and others as necessary while GC&CS

was being constituted. Anderson returned intermittently to her home in Galway, and a life of relative normality was reestablished for the Anderson family in the Quadrangle. Whether Anderson confided in her parents or siblings the true nature of her wartime work for the 'Foreign Office' in London is unclear, but it appears highly unlikely that she did, as no hint of her codebreaking activities was ever spoken of in Galway or within the small, intimate academic community of UCG, where her colleagues were also in many cases her neighbours, living in staff quarters within the walls of the university. It appears, then, that Anderson's cover story of her linguistic skills being of wartime use in the Foreign Office was completely accepted by everyone, including her own family.

*

Lieutenant Flying Officer Anderson arrived at his parent's residence at University College, Galway, on 19 December. Having not seen his family for almost three years, it is striking that one of his first actions was to complete his repatriation documentation, and provide an account of his shooting down and capture. The account, dated the day of his return, recorded that: 'while on reconnaissance patrol on the Somme 3 E.A.'s* attacked, killing my pilot. Engine being shot through and stopping. Slightly wounded.'[13]

There is evidence to suggest that the circumstances of the crash, his capture, and his time as a prisoner of war had a traumatising effect on Alexander. Memories of his flying career certainly remained with him sufficiently long that his grandson, Stephen Andrews, recalls how, when he was a child, his grandfather would pick him up in his

* Enemy aircraft.

arms and imitate the sound and motion of a plane flying, including a sharp descent.[14] Initially, however, Flying Officer Anderson did not have much time to physically or mentally recover from his trauma, or to reconnect with his family, as he was 'retained on his temporary commission while serving with the Inter-Allied Aeronautical Commission of Control, Germany'.[15] Established under the terms of the Treaty of Versailles, the role of the IACC was to represent the governments of the principal allied and associated powers in dealing with the German government 'in all matters concerning the execution of the air clauses'. This required the officers of the Commission to:

> [. . .] make an inventory of the aeronautical material existing in German territory, to inspect aeroplane, balloon and motor manufactories, and factories producing arms, munitions and explosives capable of being used by aircraft, to visit all aerodromes, sheds, landing grounds, parks and depots, to authorise, where necessary, a removal of material and to take delivery of such material.[16]

It was a complex brief, rendered all the more difficult by the fact that the Commission's officers were ex-Air Corps personnel, many of whom had lost comrades, or themselves been injured during the war, or, as was the case with Alexander Anderson, had been shot down and spent time in a prisoner-of-war camp. Alexander's appointment was likely influenced by the fact that, like his sisters, he was a fluent German speaker, and well placed to interact with German authorities and manufacturing personnel.[17]

*

While in Britain the end of the war had brought a much-welcome degree of stability, in Ireland the first post-war general election, in December 1918, had seen a seismic shift in the political landscape. The moderate Irish Parliamentary Party, who had dominated the political landscape and campaigned for Home Rule, were defeated in a landslide victory by the more radical Sinn Féin. Sinn Féin had vowed to establish an independent Irish Republic. The party's elected members refused to attend the parliament in Westminster, and formed an independent Irish parliament in Dublin. On the same day that the first gathering of that parliament, Dáil Éireann ('Assembly of Ireland'), took place, the first shots in what was to become known as the Irish War of Independence were fired. For almost three years, until a Treaty was signed in December 1921, Ireland was the scene of a bloody war, with Republicans engaging in guerrilla warfare with Crown forces, including the notorious Black and Tans.[18]

During this time of major upheaval in her native country, Anderson was experiencing an internal conflict of her own: deciding where her future lay. It was by no means the case that she was considering relinquishing her position as Professor of German for a career in the intelligence service – quite the contrary. In February 1919, she wrote to the college registrar, Fr Hynes, from the Hotel Madrid, stating: 'I hope to be released from my work here in June, and resume work in Galway in October.'[19] In December 1919, using her UCG address,[20] she made her recommendation in respect of the Browne Scholarship, an academic prize for language students, whom she had personally examined.[21] On the same day she wrote to the college president, her father, advising that: 'I shall be pleased to act as a member of the College Restaurant Committee in the event of its being established'.[22]

Every indication was being given by Anderson that she planned on remaining in academia. This is hardly surprising, as her future career with GC&CS was still the subject of high-level negotiation regarding the grade to which she would be appointed and her salary. She continued to hedge her bets, and in her letter to the registrar, she requested proofs of the 'Regulations for Degrees etc, 1920–21', as she wished to 'correct any misprints in the German section.'[23] Following the Christmas vacation, Anderson once more returned to her work in London, but by then GC&CS had been formally established on 1 November 1919, and an offer of employment with the organisation awaited her signature. Significant pressure was brought to bear on Anderson to commit to a full-time career in intelligence, and finally she was forced to choose. This she did, formally agreeing to join GC&CS in January 1920, but, significantly, delaying the submission of her resignation letter to UCG until 24 June 1920. Writing to her father from her new lodgings in London,[24] Anderson stated:

> I beg to tender my resignation of the chair of German Language and Literature at University College, Galway, which I have held since October 1917, as I have been appointed to undertake research work at the Foreign Office, London. I should like my resignation to date from September 30th 1920.[25]

Given the implicit secrecy surrounding the real nature of the work she had been engaged to do, Anderson's cover story, that she had been appointed to undertake 'research work' at the Foreign Office, is entirely understandable. But the request that her resignation date from the end of September 1920 – three months after her formal letter of resignation was written – is odd. Odder still is that, at the time of writing, she had already been appointed as a Junior Assistant with the Foreign Office almost six months previously, on 10 January 1920, shortly after her return from Ireland. The reasons for such subterfuge likely relate to two distinct issues: her unwillingness to accept anything less than a Junior Assistant position, and her determination to hold out for a salary commensurate with that of her male colleagues in the Foreign Office, something unheard of for a woman. As a result of her sheer bloody-mindedness, and both Hay and Denniston's desire to keep a top-class cryptanalyst, Anderson had succeeded in her efforts by January 1920, but her appointment proved problematic, and formal confirmation of her new position was deferred in view of 'certain technicalities'. When finally confirmed on 20 November 1920 – ten months later – Anderson's appointment was deemed to be 'on a temporary basis' only.[26] Confident in the backing of Denniston, Anderson once more opted to play for time as she waited to see whether there was any pushback from senior civil service figures regarding the details of her contract and salary as the first ever female Junior Assistant. Anderson had judged the situation regarding her resignation from UCG correctly, to the extent that interviews for her vacant chair took place on 24 November 1920 – four days after her appointment as Junior Assistant to the Foreign Office had been confirmed, albeit temporarily.

Anderson had given ample notice of her intention to resign her chair, but one aspect of her departure from the university is striking. Given that she was leaving to take up a 'research position' in the Foreign Office, it is odd that her departure was not in any way marked by the university. The college annual for 1920–21 did not acknowledge her resignation, and her departure is only recognised in that her successor, Miss Margaret Cooke, was congratulated 'on her appointment to the Chair of German'.[27] It was as if Anderson had not existed. There are two possible reasons for this. Firstly, her father may have been bitterly disappointed by his high-achieving daughter giving up a professorship for a career in the civil service. However, it is also possible that he knew (even if the governing body did not) that his daughter would be working not in research but in intelligence, and there was therefore an imperative to keep that work secret. Maintaining strict secrecy regarding intelligence work came at a heavy price. Regardless of gender, one issue that impacted former staff of Room 40 and MI1b was the question of recognition for their wartime service. It raised a question mark about what they had been doing – if they were not serving in uniform, then what kind of war work had they been engaged in?

For women, especially those who had given up academic careers in order to work in intelligence, it meant glaring holes in their CV, which often predicated against their gaining advancement when and if they returned to academic life. Anderson's sudden and permanent departure for London in 1920 raised a few eyebrows among her colleagues and students, who were unaware of the work she had been doing during the war. As far as they knew, Professor Anderson had been working in a translation capacity, albeit one related to military intelligence. She would have been lauded for having 'done her bit for the war effort', but it would have been expected that she would resume her academic career once that service ended. For a twenty-nine-year-old woman with an impeccable academic record to surrender a professorship in order to become a civil servant must have appeared inexplicable to her colleagues and students, not to mention something of a slap in the face to her father. Had the university community known of her wartime activities, it is unlikely that what appeared to be her sudden and surprising departure would have been greeted with the degree of indifference it was when she decided to give up her academic career and move to London.

The simple fact was that they did not – could not – know of her wartime service, and the implications for Anderson were damaging to her reputation. Rumours of what had prompted her sudden resignation from what would have been seen as a plum job cast something of a cloud over her departure from Galway, as if she had been guilty of some transgression. Of course, nothing could have been further from the truth, but such was the price to be paid: not just by Anderson, but by many women involved in wartime intelligence work. In addition to the difficult work they undertook, they also had to forgo public recognition for it, and were left with the problem of explaining away a glaring gap on their CVs, or in Anderson's case, a surprising change in career trajectory.

Ultimately, Anderson's decision to join GC&CS was likely more complex than having become 'hooked' on cryptology, or the satisfaction the work undoubtedly gave her. Having enjoyed the independence of her college years in Germany, and having tasted freedom again in London, returning to take up a professorship in a small university in the west of Ireland, and facing the prospect of living with her parents once more, must have been a far from appetising prospect for a woman about to enter her thirties. In addition, student numbers were low (there had only been eight First Arts students in Anderson's first year when she began teaching in the academic year 1917–18), and enlistments during the war had seen the number of male students attending the university fall even further. The small number of students, and the prospect of even fewer electing to study German in the aftermath of the war, represented a far from challenging prospect for a scholar of Anderson's calibre.

For Anderson, the die was cast. She made the decision to walk away from academic life and commit herself to a life that, by its very nature, would always be couched in the greatest secrecy. While to her family and the wider public, Professor Anderson would now become 'Miss Anderson of the Foreign Office', she could never be 'Miss Anderson of the Government Code & Cypher School', or, even more impossibly, 'Miss Anderson, ace codebreaker and diplomatic intelligence officer'. But it is certain that, to Anderson, none of this really mattered. What did matter, more than anything, was that, for good or ill, she had committed to a life that would enable her to leave behind the claustrophobic atmosphere of a small, provincial university, and the oversight of her parents, and instead live an independent life in one of the most exciting cities in the world. She had chosen a life where she could be herself and not have to conform to the expectations of others. A life, in short, which she was guaranteed would never be boring. As was ever the case, Anderson's instincts in that regard proved entirely correct.

9

'Miss Anderson of the Foreign Office'

Anderson's career with GC&CS began on 10 January 1920, when she and Florence Hayllar were appointed as Junior Assistants with the Foreign Office,[1] and reported for duty at the new GC&CS headquarters at Watergate House, on the Thames Embankment near Charing Cross. On the same day, Miss C. Lunn, Miss J. F. Carleton and Miss Claribel Spurling were appointed as translators. The appointment of women to a government department was problematic, as civil service rules mandated that women resigned upon marriage, and there was a perception within the Foreign Office in particular that women were 'wasteful as recruits; for after they have been trained for some years, they marry and must go out of the Service'.[2] When the 'wish list' of staff to be appointed to GC&CS was made, such perceptions were set aside – as they had been during the war – and at the outset, women made up 25 per cent of GC&CS's managers. Of those managers, almost all were clerical supervisors, 'with only one codebreaker'.[3] That codebreaker was Emily Anderson.

Anderson was the only woman Junior Assistant at the formation of GC&CS in 1919, and was, regardless of gender, recognised as being by far the most capable of the JAs. She would eventually be appointed Head of the Italian

Diplomatic Section[4] in 1927, and was considered the leading bookbuilder in GC&CS during what was deemed 'the cryptanalytical golden age of the 1920s'.[5] The fact that she had worked primarily in diplomatic traffic was to prove significant, for once the war ended, the importance of such traffic was steadily growing. Diplomatic traffic was very different to the services traffic dealt with during the war, with Clarke observing:

> [. . .] it was a very different matter to deal with the formal language of diplomatic telegrams[6] after a training devoted to the telegraphese of service messages. The methods of recypherment were also very different and the staff had to learn a great deal about cryptography in its more complicated forms.[7]

Anderson was one of very few of the academics of MI1(b) asked to join the fledgling intelligence service prepared to give up their university careers to do so. Her former colleague in MI1(b) John Fraser was asked to join GC&CS, but missed Scotland and his academic work on obscure Gaelic inscriptions, so chose to return to the University of Aberdeen, before being appointed Professor of Celtic at Jesus College, Oxford in 1921.[8]

As we have seen, another reason why senior staff left the intelligence service and returned to their pre-war careers was the fact that the war work they had been engaged in – which had contributed significantly to the war effort – was done without a single medal to show for it. If the secret world of codebreaking and intelligence gathering was to be of any use in the future, it had to remain just that: secret. Those engaged in intelligence work had to forgo credit for what they had achieved if their methodology, and very existence, was to have any chance of operating successfully in any future conflicts. This was something that impacted particularly on the male codebreakers, who felt that they had done their duty, often with great personal sacrifice, but saw family, friends and colleagues receive the honours and awards they were due, while they remained silent. Major Hay recognised this, and he recalled 'the barely contained frustration' some of his men experienced.[9] Such frustrations resulted in a number of those involved in wartime intelligence operations breaking rank and divulging how much codebreaking had contributed to the identification of critical intelligence and the successful outcome of the war.[10] As a direct result of these indiscretions, the Germans took immediate action in the 1920s and acquired commercial Enigma code machines, which the manufacturers claimed were unbreakable. The German military modified these machines for use by their armed forces, and the scene was set for another grand showdown should hostilities resume.

*

From the outset, GC&CS's future was far from secure, and it was recognised that 'beyond a salary and accommodation vote, GC&CS had no financial status. It became in fact an adopted child of the Foreign Office with no family rights, and the poor relation of the [Secret Intelligence Service].'[11]

A problem also arose in defining grades and salaries for GC&CS personnel whose roles were unique and didn't 'fit' wider civil service rules. Anderson stood out among her colleagues as being exceptionally good at her job – too good, in fact, to be graded as anything lower than a

'Junior Assistant'. From the outset, she was determined that, regardless of gender, she and her female colleagues would be paid appropriately. On their appointment in 1920, they were on a salary of £120, and this increased to £125 in July 1920. In contrast, the salary of male JAs was £420 p.a. The salaries of the women were eventually raised to £220 p.a.[12] – still less than half that of their male colleagues. Anderson continued to lobby for a more equitable salary for her and her female colleagues. A Foreign Office report on the matter by the Chief Clerk noted:

> Commencing in April 1921 an agitation arose in the GC&CS based on the apparent impossibility of promotion [for women], and the fact that the older Junior Assistants were the same age as the [male] Senior Assistants. This resulted in the increase of the basic rate of pay for Seniors from £600–£25–£800 to £700–£25–£900. No alteration was made in the pay of Juniors.[13]

The message was clear: female staff could complain as much as they liked, but they would never have the same promotion prospects or be paid the same salaries as their male colleagues within the civil service.[14] While her former colleagues in MI1(b) fully recognised and were prepared to reward Anderson's worth, resistance to women becoming Junior Assistants within the civil service was intense, particularly when GC&CS passed under the control of the rigorously grade conscious Foreign Office on 1 April 1922.[15] As was so often the case, Anderson proved to be the exception to the rule. The Admiralty decided that 'Miss E. Anderson could not be admitted as a Junior Assistant in view of certain technicalities, but must be regarded as on a temporary basis only'.[16] The precise nature of these 'technicalities' was not specified, but clearly Anderson carried enough weight, and was sufficiently indispensable, that even the senior civil servants in the Foreign Office could not deprive her of the grade she had been awarded when she first committed to GC&CS. All they could do was to begrudgingly state that her appointment was on a 'temporary basis'. All Anderson had to do was wait, continue to impress, and continue to agitate, which is precisely what she did.

Within the civil service structure, issues related to pay for women employees were longstanding, and, even prior to the FO assuming overall control of GC&CS, in 1921 when plans were afoot to reduce Anderson's salary and those of the other women codebreakers in GC&CS, Hugh Hugh Sinclair, in overall charge of GC&CS, rallied to Anderson's defence. In a memo to the Treasury Office describing her work in building codebooks, Sinclair noted that the work required 'an exhaustive knowledge of one or more languages, an alert sort of mind with a lot of knowledge of current affairs in the sphere in which it specialises and a distinct flair for the job', and noted that finding someone of her skill and experience 'would be nigh on impossible'.[17] In a separate memo to Denniston, Sinclair observed that Anderson was:

> [. . .] in full charge of the Italian section & is doing about the best work done by Juniors in the school. The work is clearly not suitable to the administration class, nor in my opinion to any other general c.s.* grade. I doubt if competitive examination of any sort will produce the right people.[18]

* Civil service.

Denniston and Sinclair were cognisant of the value of Anderson's work and abilities, and were of the view that if she was not treated fairly, she would leave. Sinclair noted:

> As regards Miss Anderson, I think her case is very hard & that something more should be done for her. She obviously has a distinct gift for the job and is carrying rather more responsibility than most of the established Juniors.[19]

A letter to the Under Secretary of State at the Foreign Office in June 1922 noted that although rates of pay for graded clerks had been reduced, 'we refused to establish Miss Anderson but apparently allowed her the minimum of the scale laid down for male established officers'.[20] As the civil servants argued, Anderson's superiors in GC&CS had lobbied on her behalf, and in May 1922 it was agreed that Anderson would receive a salary increase of £40, effective the following month.[21] It was a measure of Anderson's tenacity that three women translators who had joined GC&CS with her, Lunn, Carleton and Spurling (Hayllar had left and returned to academia), had their salaries reduced from £215 to £200 at the same time as she saw her salary as a Junior Assistant increased 'to £240 with bonus from 25th June'.[22]

Being viewed as the 'poor relation' of the intelligence service was but one of the issues that GC&CS faced from the outset. Apart from frustration with civil service grading protocols, the pressure of the work itself,[23] and the relatively modest pay, was sufficient that within a year or two, a number of staff resigned. Others gave way under the strain, and in early 1924 one of Anderson's colleagues, Sydney Fryer, who had served with her in MI1(b), took his own life by jumping in front of a train at Sloane Square tube station.[24] Sinclair was sufficiently troubled by the suicide, and its implications around the conditions under which his employees were working (many of them having done so, without a break, since the beginning of the war in 1914), that he improved working hours and conditions for codebreakers. Staff were required to work from 10 a.m. to 5.30 p.m., with an hour and a half for lunch.[25]

By 1923, Hugh Sinclair was both the Chief of Secret Intelligence Services (SIS) and Director of GC&CS. In 1925, working conditions for SIS and GC&CS improved considerably when both organisations were relocated to better offices on the third and fourth floors of 54 Broadway Buildings, opposite St James's Park.[26] The offices were conveniently close to an underground station and the entrance was an unobtrusive doorway at No. 21 Queen Anne's Gate. In spite of security precautions, many London taxi drivers became aware of its role as an intelligence location. Kim Philby, later revealed as a Russian spy, worked with SIS at Broadway Buildings during the Second World War, and described it as 'a dingy building, a warren of wooden partitions and frosted glass windows [. . .] served by an ancient lift'.[27] It was, nonetheless, a considerable improvement on the cramped offices that Anderson and her colleagues had previously occupied, and GC&CS continued to be based at Broadway Buildings until the outbreak of war in 1939, when the organisation moved to Bletchley Park.

As a colleague (and later as a boss), Anderson was forthright and diligent, with a ferocious capacity for work. She tended to lead by example, and whenever possible sought out and encouraged co-workers who had both an aptitude for the job and who shared her work ethic. One of those was Wilfred Bodsworth, a Spanish expert, who would later play a significant role in the cracking of Enigma.[28] He recalled being headhunted by Anderson in 1927:

> As I was selected for the vacancy on the strength of my Spanish, I was expecting to use this language from the beginning. However, the Head of the Italian Diplo section, (Miss E Anderson), had contrived to pull strings, persuading Cdr. Denniston that as Italy was a first class Power, her need was greater than that of the Head of the Spanish Section.[29]

Such was Anderson's determination to acquire a new talent, and her influence with Denniston, that Bodsworth was assigned to the Italian Diplomatic Section. He provides a fascinating insight into the tight ship run by Anderson:

> The Italian Diplo section was flourishing. The main book was well out and key solution was easy [...] I spent the first three months on key breaking and decoding, and learning diplomatic Italian from decodes, documents, magazines and newspapers. I was then taught how to build books and after a year I was sharing this work with Miss Anderson and doing some translation.[30]

Bodsworth held Anderson in high regard, describing her style of book building as 'neat and ruthlessly methodical'.[31] Such training served him well in his later work on Enigma,[32] but he learned from the outset that working for Miss Anderson would be no picnic:

> My first chief, Miss Anderson, set herself and her subordinates a standard to which the output of her section

had to conform at all costs. She could be critical of the work of her subordinates to the point of undermining their confidence. Her fault, if it is a fault, lay in not knowing where to stop being critical and to begin to be encouraging for a change.[33]

Bodsworth's observation that Anderson was overly critical of subordinates is qualified by his comparison with the management style of William 'Nobby' Clarke, who worked in the Italian Naval Section. Bodsworth observed:

In my experience, Clarke did not seem to know when to start being critical. He allowed his subordinates to set their own pace and standards and he was too prone to accept them at their own valuation.[34]

Ultimately, it was Anderson's 'ruthlessly methodical' approach that won out, and her promotion to Senior Assistant in 1928 was recognition that she had by then become one of the best bookbuilders in the intelligence service, if not *the* best. Book building, the first phase in book breaking, is the process whereby codebreakers:

[. . .] guessed the value of unknown groups, by checking their context in every telegram where they featured. Then, by generalising lessons learned from analysing messages, bookbreakers defined punctuation (indicators of sentence structure), parts of speech, groups for letters and numbers, prepositions, address groups, and some words, particularly proper nouns. Bookbuilders hunted alone, or as a team, but always under a leader.[35]

In the Italian Diplomatic Section, Anderson was that leader. And although her colleagues in GC&CS would not have known it at the time, the skills honed by Anderson in finding 'cribs', i.e. anything that suggested the possible content of a message, or an individual word or phrase, would later be used to remarkable effect by her in decoding the ciphers often employed by the Mozart family in their letters, and in translating the almost illegible handwriting in the letters of Beethoven. Josh Cooper, who joined GC&CS as a Junior Assistant in October 1925,[36] intimated as much when he stated: 'I gained much valuable training working on Italian under Emily Anderson whose qualities as a scholar-linguist were afterwards shown in her translations of the letters of Mozart and Beethoven.'[37]

Finding 'cribs' and making sense of documents to which a crib gave access required a great deal of lateral thinking. In the Italian Diplomatic Section, Cooper also worked with the ex-Room 40 codebreaker Dilly Knox, a man who was 'a very powerful intellect but tended to be incomprehensible and intolerant of people who could not understand him'. Cooper recalls an occasion when Knox approached him with a problem:

He worked at one time on Hungarian, and did not trouble to learn the language, treating the whole thing as an abstract problem. I remember him coming to me with a piece of paper covered with cipher groups with marks in coloured chalks over them. It was, he said, an interview with an Italian diplomat. Had I anything on the same subject from the Italian angle (I was by then doing Italian diplomatic). 'This group, taken with that one means that either Mussolini or

Stalin did, or did not, say that the man named in this group (who may be Sir Samuel Hoare[38]) is going to speak to the League of Nations'. I could only reply that there was nothing in Italian diplomatic to fit. 'Well, the Hungarian is probably lying anyway', and Dilly shuffled out of the room.[39]

It was typical of Anderson that, unlike Dilly Knox, she *did* take the trouble to learn Hungarian, a notoriously difficult language to master. Working in conjunction with Knox, Anderson began to build Hungarian books in 1933.[40]

Once the question of the 'technical difficulties' associated with Anderson's status had been dealt with, notice of Anderson's appointment as a Junior Assistant with the Foreign Office was published in the *London Gazette* of 6 March 1923. It noted that the appointment had been made 'After competition under the Reconstruction Scheme.'[41] In her home town, Anderson's appointment made headlines in the local newspaper. An article headed 'Galway Lady's Distinction: First to Enter British Foreign Office As Official', recorded that 'this is the first time in the history of the Civil Service that women have been, as a result of a recent examination, offered posts in the administrative grade'.[42] Anderson, of course, had sat no such examination. The article proudly described Miss Anderson as 'a young lady of considerable charm, and a brilliant career is sure to await her in the Foreign Office, where she has the distinction of being the first lady official in what is really the hub of the diplomatic service'.[43] Any lingering regrets her parents had that their brilliant daughter had forgone a career in academia for the life of a civil servant were no doubt compensated for by their pride that she had accomplished what no other woman had in the diplomatic service, and in doing so had struck a blow for the rights of all women who came after her. No doubt her parents were also relieved that the rumours that had persisted about her sudden departure from Galway in 1920 appeared to have been finally put to rest. The college president's daughter was clearly well thought of in the British Foreign Office, and as a result of her prestigious appointment, her respectability was now assured.

It is, however, possible that Professor Anderson had not surrendered hope that his daughter had not fully given up her academic work. One remarkable aspect of Anderson's early career with GC&CS is the fact that she published a significant academic work – an English translation of the Italian author Benedetto Croce's *Goethe* – in the same year that her appointment was officially gazetted, 1923. As a linguistic exercise, Anderson's skill in taking on a work by an Italian author, written in Italian on a German subject, citing German sources and translated into English, was impressive. But it was her motivation for doing so which distinguishes Anderson as a woman who would go to extraordinary lengths to hone her skills as a codebreaker. Wilfred Bodsworth provides a revealing insight into Anderson's determination to put her linguistic skills to use in the most effective way possible.

> Though Italian was not her best language, she was a fine linguist. It is typical of her that she translated one of Croce's works in order to fit herself for the job of translating decodes and breaking books, at both of which she was an acknowledged expert. She expected of her subordinates the same high standard she set herself.[44]

In undertaking the translation of Croce's *Goethe*, therefore, Anderson's objective had not been to maintain a foothold in the realm of academia by publishing a scholarly work of translation. Instead she had, of her own volition, taken on a formidable task specifically to hone her Italian translation skills, and thereby improve her ability to build Italian codebreaking books. Anderson's dedication to her task was exceptional, particularly when compared to her fellow codebreakers. Bodsworth, who had left the Italian Diplomatic Section in November 1930 and moved to the Italian Naval Section, noted of his three colleagues in this section (Clarke, Titterton and a Miss White):

> [N]one of them had taken the trouble to learn Italian even moderately well – not even Titterton, who I believe was drawing interpreter's allowance for knowledge of the language. At that time, this officer was learning Russian, and with the same lack of success.[45]

In voluntarily undertaking such a task, and completing it in her own time, Anderson was certainly exceptional, but her choice of this work by Croce may not have been entirely random. As a music lover, Anderson would have known that the German poet Johann Wolfgang von Goethe had actually met Beethoven, along with Mozart, two of her favourite composers, whose letters she would later translate into English.[46] Beethoven, in particular, was such an admirer of Goethe that he later wrote the incidental music for his play *Egmont* as a commission for the Hoftheatre in Vienna in 1809, and did so without payment, 'merely for love of the poet'.[47]

Benedetto Croce's *Goethe*, translated by Emily Anderson, was published by Methuen & Co., and it is notable that

Anderson did not write the introduction to the book herself – instead, she chose to leave that task to Douglas Ainslie, who had written the first translation of Croce's work into English, which had been greeted with mixed reviews.[48] Why she made this decision is not known, but it may have been that Anderson was unwilling to reveal too much about herself, and preferred to allow someone else, an acknowledged (though not widely celebrated) Croce scholar, to perform that task. Remarkably, it is only in the last paragraph of his introduction that Ainslie acknowledges Anderson as the author of the translation, remarking that 'this very able and sympathetic translation is the work of Miss Emily Anderson, formerly Professor of German Literature in University College, Galway'. That is as much as the public were told about the author, perhaps as Anderson intended. Her reticence aside, the book was well received and favourably reviewed.

Anderson's desire to remain anonymous with respect to her professional life was not matched by others in the world of signals intelligence,[49] some of whom failed to stifle the desire for recognition alongside their more visible military colleagues. One such was Sir Alfred Ewing, a former Director of Naval Education who had been appointed as the first head of Room 40 in 1914. He delivered a lecture on Room 40 in Edinburgh in December 1927.[50] Arthur Balfour, the former Prime Minister and Foreign Secretary, and a good friend of Ewing, wrote a letter of introduction to the lecture, declaring that, as a result of it, 'the veil will be partially removed from the labours in which your distinguished lecturer took so important a part'.[51] Ewing's desire to set the record straight and gain recognition for the work of those under his command was not uncommon,

but there was also in it a sense of establishing his own reputation as a result of his envy of Admiral Reginald 'Blinker'
Hall, the hero of the Zimmermann telegram[52] affair.[53] But
the lifting of the veil was not something everyone welcomed, particularly those, like Anderson, who recoiled at
the prospect of their secret operations becoming public
knowledge.

Ewing delivered his lecture, 'Some Special War Work',
on 13 December 1927 to a rapt audience of 1,500 in
Edinburgh.[54] Reaction was swift. The following day,
Ewing received a visit from a Lieutenant Mackeson of the
Naval Intelligence Department, who informed him that,
due to security concerns, on no account was the text of his
lecture to be published. That same day, the Admiralty
warned Room 40 veterans now employed by GC&CS
that they viewed Ewing's lecture 'with grave concern', as it
was prejudicial to the interests of the State, and 'contrary
to the provisions of the Official Secrets Acts of 1911 and
1920'.[55] It ordered them to 'continue to maintain the same
degree of secrecy and discretion which you have observed
hitherto.'[56] But by that stage, the damage was done. The
arrogance and recklessness of the few (and certainly more
than Admiral Hall were at fault in this regard)[57] had seen to
it that much of the progress in cryptanalysis that Anderson
and her colleagues had made during the First World War
had, as a result of leaks, became common knowledge, and
spurred German innovation in cryptology – the development of Enigma being one such innovation.[58]

Anderson saw out the rest of the 1920s, and most of the
1930s, concentrating on her cryptologic work by day, and
her next major project by night. Stimulated by the success
of her Croce translation, she felt confident enough to

embark on an infinitely more ambitious task, one that enabled her to combine the three great passions of her life: music, German and travel. She committed to the task of compiling and translating the letters of one of her favourite composers, Mozart, and his family. It was yet another formidable undertaking, but Anderson proved more than up to the task.

10

Life in London and Family Matters

Outside of her working life at GC&CS, Anderson's leisure time in London was largely taken up with her love of music and musical pursuits, and occasional family dramas. The absence of any personal correspondence makes it impossible to know if she maintained contact with her family back home, or met with siblings or relatives in London. It is, however, clear from her active social life, and the warm friendships she developed with many of those involved in the London music scene, that Anderson loved London, living there from the age of twenty-eight until her death in 1962, aged seventy-two. There was certainly much to like for the cultured, artistically inclined Irishwoman from a quiet west-of-Ireland backwater. The 'wonderful immensity' of the city never ceased to lose its hold on her, for, as Samuel Johnson famously observed 'when a man is tired of London, he is tired of life, for there is in London all that life can afford'. For Anderson, that meant the city's grandeur and beautiful buildings, its theatres, museums, parks, art galleries and, most of all, its concert halls, where she could indulge her love of music.

In the early years, she fully immersed herself in the vibrant cultural life of her adopted city, and did so by basing herself right at the heart of it. The fact that her choice of accommodation placed her in the company of other independent-minded women was no accident. By June 1920, when she submitted her resignation letter to University College, Galway, Anderson was writing from her new address at the Forum Club, a club for women located at 6–7 Grosvenor Place, Hyde Park. Formerly the residence of Sir Henry Campbell-Bannerman, who served as Prime Minister from 1905 to 1908, the Forum Club was founded in October 1919[1] as 'The London Centre for Women's Institute Members'.[2] Renamed 'The Forum Club' to mirror the numerous Gentlemen's Clubs that proliferated in London at the time, it became one the most successful ladies-only clubs of its era, with over 1,600 members, and over time expanded into adjacent houses on Grosvenor Place.[3]

The Forum Club held a prime location in Belgravia, its upper street-facing rooms affording a view of Buckingham Palace. Its membership included a number of suffragettes and early feminists, including Elizabeth Robins, Mary Sophia Allen, Sybil Thomas and Viscountess Rhondda. After the quiet and isolation of Galway, the Forum Club must have been a heady change for Anderson, as she found herself living at the very heart of a meeting point for many well-known female authors, artists, speakers, public figures and political activists. As well as accommodation for members (and their maids), the club contained a lounge, a salon that could by hired for exhibitions, a bridge room, a billiard room, a library, a photographic darkroom and a hairdressing room. A buttery and a large dining room offered excellent cuisine, prepared and served by an entirely male staff.[4] The club had a policy of welcoming women from different classes of society (the only requirement being that they could pay the fees), and provided a uniquely support-ive environment for women, while at the same time affording networking opportunities on a par with its equivalent gentlemen's clubs. Anderson lived at the Forum Club until 1923 and commuted daily to her work at GC&CS at Watergate House, Adelphi, a thirty-minute walk, or twenty-minute tube ride away.

Emily was not the only member of the Anderson family living in London at that time. As we have seen, after the war, her brother Alexander had served with the Inter-Allied Aeronautical Commission of Control in Germany.[5] Flying Officer Anderson was on the Air Force List for April 1920, and in July of that year he was awarded the Distinguished Flying Cross. The award was presented by the Duke of York (the future King George VI) at Buckingham Palace.[6] It is not known whether Emily Anderson accompanied her brother to the confer-ring ceremony of the DFC, although as his only relative living in London, and living so close to the Palace, it is likely that she may have done so. Flying Officer Ander-son remained working with the IACC in Germany until 1922, when his commission ended and he returned to London and civilian life.

Alexander Anderson left the air force as a qualified pilot with significant mechanical skills. Like his sister, he decided to make a life for himself in London, and with money saved from his service with the IACC, he estab-lished his own business, a car dealership selling top-end cars, such as Rolls-Royces, to post-war Londoners who could afford them. Anderson's first-hand knowledge of mechanics was never in doubt – sadly, his knowledge of the world of commerce proved to be infinitely less strong. His lack of business acumen and poor financial management meant that, within two years of its establishment, Alexander Anderson's car dealership business was in difficulty, and eventually went bankrupt. News of their only son's failure and bankruptcy was greeted with dismay by his parents in Galway, who had always had high hopes for their clever, gifted, and now decorated-war-hero son. Yet the disapproval of his parents, and his own disappointment at the failure of his business, were the least of Alexander Anderson's problems, foremost of which was the residual effect of the psychological trauma he had experienced during the war. The dramatic shooting down of his plane, the death of his pilot and his own subsequent capture and imprisonment in a German prisoner-of-war camp had left their mark on him, and having tried, and failed, in his initial attempt to overcome his wartime experiences, he sought another way to deal with the trauma and reinvent himself. This he did, in dramatic fashion, by making the decision to leave London, on foot, and walk until he found a place where he felt he could put down roots.[7] It is unclear how long this odyssey lasted, but Alexander Anderson eventually arrived in Liverpool.

As a destination, Liverpool was to prove fortuitous for him, for shortly after his arrival there, he met the woman who was to change his life. Lilian Redman was twenty-four when she met Alexander Anderson (he was then thirty). How and where they met is not known, but they appear to have instantly bonded, and the relationship developed quickly. From a large family of solidly working-class Liverpudlian stock (there were nine children, and her father was a baker), Lilian was, according to her family, a kind, warm and vivacious woman who was always cheerful.[8] Lilian Redman may have recognised in the troubled Alexander Anderson a man in need of healing, stability and direction, and he in turn appears to have responded to the warmth and vivacity that he so desperately needed and she provided. Alexander Anderson made the decision to remain in Liverpool, and as a result of his mechanical knowledge, found a job as a control room engineer at Liverpool Power Station. With Alexander now having a steady job, the couple decided to marry, but the simmering tensions with his family in Ireland intensified when he informed them of his intention to marry. His parents either did not respond to the announcement of his impending nuptials, or responded in a less than enthusiastic, and possibly even negative, manner, but the precise details are not known. What *is* known, however, is that the breach was sufficiently serious that it was at this point that Alexander Anderson made a momentous decision that severed his connection with his family for ever. He changed his name by deed poll from Alexander Anderson to Arthur Andrews, and it was as Arthur Andrews that he married Lilian Redman[9] in Liverpool in July 1925.[10] Their son, and only child, Arthur Henry Andrews, was born two years later.[11] Thereafter, Alexander Anderson disappears from the historical record, and had no further contact with his sister Emily or the rest of his family.

*

The conflict within the Anderson family in the early 1920s was replicated in the events in their home country. As Emily Anderson was beginning her full-time career with GC&CS, back in Ireland, a bloody war of independence, which had begun in January 1919 and continued until July

1921, was raging. Tensions ramped up considerably in May 1921, when Ireland was partitioned under British law by the Government of Ireland Act, which created Northern Ireland. This came into effect on 3 May. It was an indication of the turbulent times that less than two weeks later, on 14 May 1921, Professor Anderson presided over a remarkable meeting, the object of which was to nominate academics to represent the National University in what was described as 'the Parliament of Southern Ireland'. Of those nominated, Professor John (Eoin) MacNeill was noted as being 'at present in Mountjoy Jail', Dr Ada English was 'at present in Galway Jail', Professor William Stockley was 'on the run', and Michael Hayes of University College, Dublin, was 'at present in Ballykinlar'.[12] All four candidates were duly elected,[13] and Professor Anderson was complimented on 'the courtesy and impartiality' with which he had conducted the election.[14]

The war of independence ended on 11 July 1921, with a ceasefire and negotiations towards a treaty to resolve the Irish question taking place in London. The signing of the Anglo–Irish Treaty on 6 December 1921 ended British rule in most of Ireland and the Irish Free State (Saorstát Éireann) was created as a self-governing Dominion on 6 December 1922. This was followed by a bitter and bloody civil war between those who supported the Treaty as the best deal Ireland could get in the circumstances, and those who opposed it as betraying the ideals of those who had fought and died for a fully independent Irish Republic. Anderson's own family were directly impacted by the conflict when Professor Anderson's sister (Emily's aunt) Bessie Anderson, a mathematician and Principal of Rutland High School in Dublin, had to vacate the premises at short notice in June 1922 when a group of Irregulars, members of the anti-treaty IRA, took over the building for use as a hospital for 'five or six days'.[15] But for Emily Anderson, such events were at a far remove from her work in GC&CS. By 1925, two of her three siblings were also living in the UK. None of the Anderson siblings, apart from the oldest, Elsie, would ever live in the new Irish Free State – for Emily, Alexander, and the youngest sibling, Helen, England was to be their home for the rest of their lives.

*

In December 1925, five months after her brother had married in Liverpool, Dr Helen Anderson married Dr Francis Lydon in a registry office in Wharfdale, West Riding, Yorkshire.[16] Helen Anderson shared her mother and sister's support for the cause of women's rights, and she continued to style herself Dr Helen Anderson after her marriage, never taking her husband's name, professionally or otherwise.[17] Dr Anderson had met her husband when both had studied medicine at University College, Galway, Francis Lydon being in the year above her. In common with all of her siblings, Dr Anderson was academically gifted, and after what was described as a 'brilliant' course of medical studies,[18] she had graduated, with first-class honours in 1925, and moved to England to continue her training at a hospital in Leeds.[19] She subsequently took up a position at Charing Cross Hospital in London.[20]

Emily Anderson's new brother-in-law, Francis Leo Lydon, was the second youngest in a family of nine children born to John Lydon, a professional angler employed by the Galway Salmon Fishery.[21] After graduating in Medicine from University College, Galway, in 1924 (with

first-class honours), Dr Lydon moved to continue his training at St James University Hospital ('Jimmy's') in Leeds,
and later Sheffield, before being awarded a consultant post
at King's College, London. There, he lectured in derma-
tology, and was attached to a number of London hospitals
as a consultant dermatologist.[22] Unlike his wife, who in
common with the rest of her family was a Presbyterian,
Francis Lydon was a Catholic, and for this reason the marriage took place in a registry office.

*

Having lived at the Forum Club for three years, in 1923
Emily Anderson moved to another, smaller, ladies' club,
the Landsdowne, at 13 Lyndhurst Gardens, Hampstead.
Guests were provided with breakfast and dinner on week-
days, and all meals on Sundays.[23] Including Anderson,
there were fourteen women living there in 1924–25. After
spending three years at Lyndhurst Gardens, in 1926
Anderson made the decision to rent her own private, self-
contained flat at 38 Arkwright Road, and she lived there
until 1938. Offering more space, and a greater degree of
privacy, her new home was a second-floor flat with two
reception rooms, two bedrooms, a small kitchenette and a
bathroom, for which the rent was £125 p.a.[24] For a single
woman, living on her own, a flat of this size was something
of an extravagance, but as she was in receipt of a good
salary,[25] she could well afford it. More importantly, at both
this flat, and her subsequent flat at Ellerdale Road, Anderson used the second bedroom as her office, a place in which
she could organise her research material, conduct her correspondence and focus on her writing.[26]

Now living in a spacious flat, Anderson finally had the

opportunity to re-engage with her love of music, and specifically her love of playing piano. Sometime after her move to Arkwright Road, she purchased a Bechstein boudoir grand piano. The piano was built in Berlin in 1906,[27] and despatched for sale to the Bechstein showroom in London in July of the same year.[28] Always an accomplished pianist, and now with a fine instrument of her own to practise on, in typical fashion, Anderson set herself a specific task, and by 1930 her playing had improved to such a standard that she successfully completed the London College of Music's Associate's examination (A.L.C.M.) in pianoforte.[29]

On 14 February 1930, Emily's older sister Elsie married, at the age of thirty-nine, John Joseph Rochford, also thirty-nine, a farmer's son and a native of Co. Wicklow. The marriage took place in St Kieran's church, Moate, Co. Westmeath, where Rochford was employed as manager of the local Ulster Bank branch. It is unclear how the couple met, or how their relationship had developed, but the marriage certificate gives Elsie's address as Galway city, and her occupation as 'daughter of university president'. As had been the case with Dr Helen Anderson, Elsie had married outside the Presbyterian faith – her husband was also a Catholic. The professional life of Elsie Anderson prior to her marriage raises a number of questions. The photograph of her as a child, with her mother, governess and sister Emily, reveals a pretty blonde girl, with arguably more striking features than her younger sibling. With Emily, she had been sent to Germany as a teenager to learn German. Although Emily would later say of their initial experience of living with a German family, 'we hated it',[30] the experience had a significant impact on the two sisters, and their subsequent love of languages. Elsie appears to have been an excellent linguist, and was 'a fluent speaker in German, French, Russian, Flemish, Irish, English and Greek. She read and could converse on the literature of all these countries with amazing skill.'[31] The references to Russian and Flemish are particularly intriguing, and it is unclear how, where and why she acquired her fluency in these languages.

However, the question remains: with such beauty and accomplishments, why was Elsie living at home with her parents at the age of thirty-nine, appearing to have had no career to speak of following her graduation, and at the time of her marriage able only to list her occupation as 'daughter of university president'? Very little has emerged in the archives to provide an answer to that question. She did not appear on the 1911 census of Ireland or the UK, suggesting that she was then living abroad, most likely in Germany, furthering her studies, much as Emily had done following her own graduation a year later. We know nothing of Elsie's life during the war, or in the after-war period. The little we do know reveals that Elsie applied for a position as a part-time teacher of German at the Limerick Technical Institute in 1926, but was unsuccessful on the grounds that she had no previous teaching experience.[32] If such was the case, when she was aged thirty-five, it begs the question: if she had not been teaching or lecturing, what exactly had she done with her BA in Modern Languages until then? At the time of her application, her address was given as 'Strand Barracks, Limerick'.[33] This is significant, as at the time the Strand Barracks was leased to the German company Siemens Bauunion, the firm employed to construct the Shannon hydroelectric scheme at Ardnacrusha, Co. Limerick, the largest infrastructure project undertaken by the Irish Free State. A number of the senior engineering and administrative staff had quarters in this building – a former army barracks – as accommodation in the area was very limited at the time due to the influx of workers employed on the scheme, who numbered some 3,000 at its height. This would indicate that Elsie Anderson was working – possibly as an interpreter or liaison officer for the Siemens staff– on the Shannon scheme.[34] Such an appointment would make sense, given that the engineer who first suggested, and later designed, the Shannon scheme was Dr Thomas McLaughlin, a former lecturer in engineering at University College, Galway,[35] and that the chief engineer of the scheme was Frank Rishworth, professor of engineering at UCG, who in 1925 was appointed Chief Engineer of the Shannon scheme.[36] Other than this position, likely acquired via her personal connections to two college staff, Elsie's professional career, up until her marriage, remains something of a mystery.

*

With both of her sisters and her brother now married, Anderson herself remained resolutely single, and lived alone. She was well established, professionally and financially – particularly so following her promotion to Head of Italian Diplomatic Section in 1927. In her spare time during the rest of the 1920s and all of the 1930s up until the outbreak of war, Anderson's work on her translation of the Mozart letters had begun in earnest. Her pursuit of these letters in archives and private collections would see her establish a wide network of friends and collaborators internationally, including some of the foremost collectors, dealers and academic scholars in the field. But it was also to be a time during which she was to suffer great personal tragedy within her family.

11

Mozart and the Interwar Years

During the interwar years, along with Agnes Driscoll
and Elizabeth Friedman in the United States, Anderson
was the leading female codebreaker and among the
best cryptanalysts in the world.[1]

The above assessment of the codebreaking skills of Emily
Anderson is rendered all the more remarkable for two reasons. Firstly, while the careers and achievements of Agnes
Driscoll[2] and Elizabeth Friedman[3] are the subject of significant publications, virtually nothing was known or published
about Emily Anderson. Secondly, while Driscoll and
Friedman focused during the interwar years on their codebreaking work, Anderson was, for practically all of the
1930s, living an increasingly demanding double life. In addition to her work as Head of the Italian Diplomatic Section at
GC&CS, Anderson undertook another project that incurred
a workload which few would have had the intellectual or
physical energy to match. While she set about tracking
down and translating the complete letters of Mozart and his
family, she was at the same time establishing a reputation as
one of the best codebreakers in the world.

*

One reason why Anderson's cryptanalytic efforts remained unacknowledged is the fact that keeping secret the real nature of her work in cryptanalysis was something that Anderson was not only willing to do, but that suited her preference for attracting as little attention to herself as possible. In this, she was not alone. Her former colleague in MI1(b), Oliver Strachey (brother of the writer Lytton), was, like Anderson, a talented pianist and music lover.[4] It was said of Strachey:

> When those who knew him less well asked him what he did, he would playfully refer them to the reference books, which described him as being 'employed in a department of the Foreign Office'. That suited Oliver Strachey quite well.[5]

It suited Emily Anderson equally well, especially when it came to the undoubted grand passion of her life, and what she was later to describe to her Bletchley Park boss Commander Denniston as her 'real work', i.e. the translation of the letters of her two favourite composers, Mozart and Beethoven. From the outset, Anderson accepted that, in order to live one aspect of her private life in the public domain, it was imperative that the other side of her life, her professional life, remain entirely secret.

*

One significant point regarding Anderson's career as a musicologist must be considered. In 1928, James Turner[6] of GC&CS wrote a series of notes on intelligence and cryptography, and the differences between the two. Turner, described by Wilfred Bodsworth as a 'classic bookbuilder' in the same mode as Anderson, observed that:

A cryptographer is not a person who by mysterious and secret processes arrives at results which he does not understand, and which only the intelligence officer can appreciate. The cryptographer needs in the first place a wide range of information concerning the country with which he is dealing and cannot be successful unless he does know 'what they are talking about'. In short, he must himself have at his disposal all the intelligence available regarding his particular country.[7]

In other words, codebreaking is not done in the abstract – only in living in and experiencing the wider world can the cryptographer have the depth of knowledge with which to find a 'crib' that will enable them to break into a code. As a classic 'bluestocking', Anderson was ideally qualified to perform that role. Her part-time career as a musicologist enabled her to travel widely, forge friendships and alliances, and explore archives to which few would have had the access she did. It was a happy – and, as it transpired, productive – bonus.

To her work colleagues, Anderson's translation of the Mozart letters would have been considered little more than an exercise in antiquarianism. The fact that the end result is so far removed from the more familiar output of the classic antiquarian is a testament to Anderson's remarkable intellectual vigour, sense of purpose and astonishing work ethic. There were, however, dangers inherent in a Foreign Office cryptologist travelling internationally and collaborating with archivists, collectors and scholars in countries such as Austria and Germany – something that Anderson did extensively during the interwar period. Another of those who worked in intelligence with the Foreign Office was Group Captain M. G. Christie, who was based in Berlin during the interwar period. In 1928, Christie's boss wrote to him, and acknowledged:

> [. . .] it is always difficult for an officer working in a foreign country to avoid looking through the spectacles of the people in whose country he is working, and, while going out of his way to be on extremely friendly terms, at the same time maintaining that segregation and unbiased point of view which is essential to enable him to see a true and clear picture. The more intimate a friendship the more difficult it is to judge one's friend impartially.[8]

For Anderson, as far as we know, no such conflicts ever arose. For the more than thirty years she lived a 'double life' as a codebreaker by day, musicologist by night (and during vacation time), she kept her two lives entirely separate. As a linguist and former academic, it was naturally assumed by most who knew her through her musicological work that her Foreign Office role was largely of a translation or diplomatic administration nature. There was never any indication that the refined, well-spoken and reserved lady who spent her annual vacations working in archives, sometimes for weeks on end, and spent her evenings writing innumerable letters to scholars, dealers and collectors around the world, was anything other than a genuine and committed scholar, and a single woman who had little else with which to fill the vacuum of a non-existent family life.

There was nothing strategic in the manner in which Anderson undertook her first major work on the Mozart letters.[9] She did it because she could. She had the skills, she had the time, and it gave her pleasure to use that remarkable brain of hers in pursuit of an objective that was the polar opposite of the work she did from nine to five – work that had to remain secret. It had the added advantage that it gave her a genuine reason to engage in her lifelong love of travel, and gained her a wide circle of friends throughout the world, with whom she collaborated and corresponded for decades, greatly enriching what was a challenging and often stressful career in intelligence. When Anderson left her office in Broadway Buildings for the evening, she entered another world. She was answerable to no one except herself. There would be no line of enquiry unpursued, no archive un-mined and no possible contact unexploited. The finished volumes were a testimony to the impeccably high standards Anderson set herself, and always delivered on.

It is unclear when Anderson first decided to embark on the Mozart letters project, or secured the commission from Macmillan Publishers Ltd to do so, but faith in her ability to deliver the project came from the most senior member of the publishing house, who became a good friend to Anderson. In the preface to the first edition, published in 1938, Anderson thanked Harold Macmillan 'for his unfailing help and interest in the production of my edition'.[10] A politician and future prime minister,[11] Macmillan had joined the family publishing firm in 1920. In 1936, he and his brother Daniel took control of the firm, with Harold focusing on the political and non-fiction side of the business. He resigned from the company on appointment to ministerial office in 1940, but not before he oversaw the publication of *The Letters of Mozart and his Family* in 1938.[12]

Anderson's choice of Mozart was in no way accidental, and exemplifies the manner in which her two lives – as cryptologist and musicologist – overlapped almost seamlessly. Anderson herself flagged it, albeit subtly, in an article she wrote for *Music and Letters*, a leading international journal of musical scholarship, published in April 1937. In her article, entitled 'An Unpublished Letter of Mozart', Anderson observed that the letter in question 'helps to solve a problem which so far has baffled all students of Mozart's operas'. Highlighting phrases in the letter, Anderson noted that, following the accession of Hieronymus Colloredo to the Archbishopric of Salzburg in 1772:

> [. . .] the Mozart family made occasional use of a simple substitution cipher (certain letters of the alphabet being replaced by others) in order to be able to express their opinions freely. They adopted this device because they had good reason for believing that before their letters were delivered the Salzburg post office sent them to the Archbishop's residence for inspection.[13]

Here, then, was a codebreaker working on the correspondence of a composer and his family who wrote in codes. The article is rich in content concerning unknown aspects of Mozart's life, the footnotes revealing a thorough and exhaustive research process – a perfect taster for the publication of *The Letters of Mozart*, which she announced in the first footnote would be published by Macmillan 'in the course of the year'.[14]

The task that Anderson undertook was monumental and daunting. She had elected to compile and translate the extensive correspondence, numbering over 900 items,[15] of a composer who was something of an enigma. Dr Charles T. Harrison, in his review of Anderson's *The Letters of Mozart and his Family*, declared: 'Mozart is like his music. He seems immediately the most intelligible of geniuses, but he is ultimately elusive [. . .] the most inaccessible of the great masters.'[16]

Accessing the inaccessible and pinning down the elusive was something of a specialism of Anderson's, so it is hardly surprising that the task attracted her. In her introduction to the collected *Letters*, Anderson reveals what underpinned that attraction. She viewed the correspondence not merely as shining a light on the music of the great composer, but also as an exercise in breaking into – in effect, decoding – his distinctive way of thinking and composing. Anderson writes:

[. . .] in many of his letters Mozart, while expressing himself in words, seems in reality to be thinking in terms of music. Thus when we come upon passages which are curiously involved, words written backwards, phrases reversed, and other similar oddities of expression, we remember his description of how on a certain occasion he extemporised fugues on a given theme in a minor key, playing all kinds of tricks with it, reversing it, turning it into the major and so forth. Again, when we take up one of Mozart's autograph* letters, many of which are untidily written, larded with erasures and splashed with ink-blots,[17] and suddenly find him weaving delicate scrolls and fantastic flourishes round a capital, we remember certain themes, upon which he has embroidered a wealth of variations, deliciously interlaced and flawless in texture.[18]

* The term 'autograph' in this context refers to a letter handwritten and signed by the author.

Anderson's delight in the 'wealth of variations' and 'deliciously interlaced and flawless' texture employed by Mozart in his writings is indicative of the pleasure she herself took in deciphering the complex codes that made up her daily work with GC&CS. Yet instead of revealing the inner workings of the Italian diplomatic service, here was a great mind, a great composer, at work, and, for Anderson, cracking that code served to add even greater pleasure to her enjoyment of the music she so dearly loved listening to and playing. Her work as a codebreaker was contingent on her remaining permanently silent on what she had discovered – her work on Mozart, however, meant that she could share her discoveries with the world.

As a woman with a demanding career, she had precious little leisure time to devote to the task. Yet she devoted what time she did have to becoming the first person to publish Mozart's scatological letters in unabridged form in any language. Though much of the correspondence was known to exist, it was either printed privately or had been heavily censored or bowdlerised. In addition to translating and annotating over 900 letters, the work necessitated travel to, and correspondence with, archives, manuscript dealers and private collectors around the globe. In chasing down Mozart autographs, Anderson collaborated with the leading Mozart scholars and collectors in the world at that time. These included Professor Otto Eric Deutsch, Dr Alfred Einstein[19] and Professor Erich Hertzmann. Of even longer standing was her friendship with C. B. Oldman, whom she knew and corresponded with for thirty years.[20] Among the internationally known collectors and dealers in manuscripts and autographs with whom she collaborated were Heinrich Eisemann[21] and Stefan Zweig,[22] both of whom would eventually settle in London.

Wherever possible, she visited archives and collectors in person. One such visit was to Bonn in May 1934, to meet Ludwig Schiedermair for collaboration on the Mozart letters.[23] Schiedermair had edited the first complete critical edition of the letters of Mozart and his family. A musicologist and professor at the University of Bonn from 1920 to 1945, as department head for Music History he had founded the Beethoven Archive at the Beethoven House, Bonn, in 1927, on the 100th anniversary of Beethoven's death, and served as its first director until 1945. It is hardly surprising, therefore, that this was one visit which Anderson had to make in person.[24]

In addition to her extensive correspondence, always written on distinctive blue headed notepaper, which featured in turn her two primary addresses – 38 Arkwright Road and, from 1939, 24 Ellerdale Road, Hampstead – Anderson was able to maintain contact with a variety of musicology experts, manuscript dealers and archives via telephone. She even had a telephone installed in her flat at Arkwright Road, which facilitated telephone contact with her various collaborators around the world. It is typical of her efficiency that she ensured continuity of contact by retaining the same telephone number when she moved to her Ellerdale Road flat.[25] Given that much of Anderson's telephone communication was with European or American contacts, time zone differences meant that she could make telephone calls in the evening or early morning, after returning from or before going to work.

*

In January 1931, Anderson's younger sister, Dr Helen Anderson, and her husband welcomed their first child, a son, Maurice Hugh Anderson Lydon (called 'Hukis' by his parents). Then, in 1932, the couple moved to Penistone, West Yorkshire, to take up new medical posts, before, in 1933, Dr Lydon secured a consultant position in King's College Hospital, London, and the family moved to a flat in Portman Mansions, Marylebone, London. As Dr Anderson had also secured a position at Charing Cross Hospital, the couple hired a live-in nanny to care for their son.[26] In 1935, they moved to a flat at Exchange Mansions in Golders Green, not far from Emily's flat at Arkwright Road. The fact that her sister was now living relatively close by afforded Anderson the opportunity to spend time with her young nephew, but sadly, if such was the case, that time was to be cruelly short.

On 4 June 1936, an appalling tragedy befell the couple when Hukis died suddenly, at the age of five and a half.[27] His death occurred at 17 Bentinck Street, London, at that time a children's nursing home.[28] The cause of death was 'intestinal obstruction' and 'mega colon', both the result of the child suffering from a congenital condition known as Hirschsprung's disease.[29] No efforts had been spared in ensuring that Hukis Lydon received the best possible medical care; his doctor, L. E. Barrington-Ward, was the foremost paediatric surgeon in London at that time.[30]

The funeral was private, and attended by close family only, including Emily Anderson. Described in the death notices as 'the darling only child'[31] of the couple, the loss of her son appears to have profoundly affected Dr Anderson. Her husband later described how she was unable to bring herself to return to the flat the family had shared. Instead, she moved into a one-roomed flat alone. She never returned to the family home, nor lived with her husband again.

The death of young Hukis Anderson Lydon was not the only tragedy to blight the Anderson family in 1936. Anderson's father, Professor Alexander Anderson, retired from his position as President of University College, Galway, in 1934, and he and his wife moved to Dublin, where they purchased a house at 7 Pembroke Park. He did not have long to enjoy his retirement, as just months after the death of his grandson in London, he died suddenly on 5 September 1936. Professor Anderson had undergone an operation for acute appendicitis, but diffuse peritonitis had set in and after five days he died of cardiac failure.[32] Emily Anderson travelled from London to attend the funeral. Bizarrely, as was later the case when their mother died some years later, Anderson is erroneously identified in press coverage of the funeral as 'Miss A. Anderson'[33] and her sister as 'Miss E. Rochford', although Elsie was by then a married woman.[34] Sad as the funeral must inevitably have been, the absence of two of the late Professor Anderson's children was a painful reminder that all was not well in the family. Emily's brother Alexander was estranged following the bitter quarrel outlined in the previous chapter, and was living in Liverpool as Arthur Andrews, married and the father of a nine-year-old son (now the Anderson's only grandchild). Alexander – or Arthur – did not attend his father's funeral. Their sister Helen was also absent, as she was still deeply traumatised following the death of her son only three months previously.[35] Professor Anderson's estate amounted to £8,002,[36] a fact that would have a direct impact on Anderson's musicological research.[37] With her brother Alexander disinherited as a result of the family estrangement, Anderson's mother, Emily and her sisters Elsie and Helen were the main beneficiaries of her father's estate. Pragmatic as ever, Anderson would use her share of her inheritance to partially fund the extensive international travel she would undertake in pursuit of Mozart, and later Beethoven, manuscripts.

Anderson was notoriously reticent regarding her private life, and although she does not refer to her relationships with either her parents or siblings in the correspondence that has come to light, it is significant that her respect for her father was such that a story regarding him was one of the few personal anecdotes she shared with her German friends, Dagmar and Friedrich von Busch-Weise. As a young man, Professor Anderson was a cigar smoker. However, in his later years, Anderson recalled that her father gave up the habit completely. As Friedrich von Busch recalls:

> [. . .] for his health, and at the request of his family, he decided to give up smoking. But Emily told us that he kept a box, containing a single cigar, on the desk in his office at the university, to test his resolve. He never wavered, and never smoked again, but Emily told the story with such pride – an exemplar of a man of such resolve that he tested himself every day, but never succumbed.[38]

Such self-control was clearly something in which Anderson took great pride, and always strove to emulate, to the degree that it became the watchword of her entire adult life.

On her return to London following her father's funeral, Anderson threw herself once more into her professional work in GC&CS – work that was becoming increasingly demanding as events in Europe became ever more threatening – and at the same time entered the final stages of work on the Mozart *Letters* collection. Sadly, there was yet more tragedy to come. On 15 May 1937, three weeks before the first anniversary of the death of her son, the body of Dr Helen Anderson was found lying in a clump of bushes in a field off Frith Lane, Mill Hill, Hendon, close to the entrance to Finchley Golf Club. She was just thirty-four years old. Dr Anderson's death was as a result of suicide, with the newspaper report of her death recording that 'by her side was a bottle of chloral hydrate'. The grim discovery was made 'by boys who were bird's nesting'.[39] The death certificate confirmed the cause of death as: 'killed herself by taking chloral hydrate and morphine, while the state of her mind was unbalanced'.[40]

The youngest of the Anderson siblings had never recovered from the death of her son, Hukis. Unable to bring herself to live again in the family home, and by then having moved into the staff quarters at Guy's Hospital where she worked,[41] Helen's husband related at the inquest into her death that the grief of their son's loss had become increasingly difficult for her to bear. She was buried in the same grave as her beloved Hukis in Hendon Cemetery[42] on 19 May 1937.[43] It is not known whether Emily Anderson attended her sister's funeral, but it is inconceivable that she would not have done so, and it must have been an unbearably sad occasion for her, particularly in view of the preceding loss of her young nephew, and her father, in the space of less than a year. The death of Dr Anderson was widely reported in the Irish press, and particularly so in her native Galway, where both she, and her husband's family, the Lydons, were well known and respected.

*

Emily Anderson then did what she always had and always would do in the face of personal crises: she threw herself once more into her work. Events in Europe saw to it that Anderson's work on Italian diplomatic codes increased exponentially in the late 1930s, and, acutely conscious that travel to Europe might soon be rendered impossible, she used up her precious leave in a flurry of travel to places like Vienna, Salzburg, Bonn, Berlin and Florence, where she could access Mozart letters and collaborate with Mozart scholars. While it was still possible, she enjoyed what amounted to working holidays, visiting archives by day and socialising with friends and colleagues in the evenings.

There is only one occasion in the correspondence of that time that survives – written from Treloyhan Manor Hotel,[44] St Ives, Cornwall, in July 1937 – in which she appears to have gone on holiday to a non-archival location. It is significant that this holiday occurred just two months after the death of her sister. Anderson may have sought the solace of a quiet retreat on the Cornish coast to properly grieve the deaths of her nephew, father and sister. Yet the demands of her musicology work were never far away, and complete relaxation was impossible for her. She wrote to a fellow musicologist, Henry George Farmer, from the hotel, as she was in the end stages of preparing the final Mozart letters volume for publication.[45] Her determination to continue with her book-related correspondence, even while she was on a much-needed vacation and recovering from a veritable tsunami of family tragedies, is yet more evidence of Anderson's remarkable dedication and focus.

*

At the same time as she was corresponding with a variety of European Mozart experts, archives and collectors, Anderson's search for Mozart autographs – and in particular the first letter known to have been written by him – led her to what was then one of the finest libraries in the world: the Morgan Library in New York. Established in the 1890s as the private collection of the legendary American financier John Pierpont Morgan, when Anderson first began to consult the library's collections, J. P. Morgan had died, and his son J. P. Morgan Jnr., known as Jack, had, in 1924, transferred its ownership to a board of trustees, along with a $1.5 million endowment. Anderson's point of contact at the library was its formidable director, Belle da Costa Greene.[46] Da Costa Greene was a remarkable woman who ran the library for forty-three years – nineteen years as the private librarian of J. Pierpont Morgan and later his son, Jack, and twenty-four years as the inaugural director of the Pierpont Morgan Library (now the Morgan Library & Museum). Anderson first contacted the library in 1934,[47] requesting copies of Mozart letters in their collection, and must have been thrilled to discover that one of the photostatted* letters sent to her was 'one to his sister,

* The precursor to the photocopier, the photostat, was either a positive (black on white) or negative (white on black) reproduction of printed matter made on a photostat machine, which used photographic paper instead of a transparent negative, and used a prism to render the paper negative readable instead of reversed.

and is the earliest authentic letter of Mozart, written when he was 13'.[48] Anderson asked for, and received, permission to reproduce a facsimile of the letter in the book. Anderson also received permission to reproduce the portrait of Elizabeth and Thomas Linley[49] by Gainsborough, which was in the private collection of J. P. Morgan Jnr.[50]

It is significant that in writing to Anderson in June 1938, acknowledging receipt of Volume I of the Mozart *Letters*, da Costa Greene is uncharacteristically effusive in her praise, stating:

> This important work forms a real addition to our reference division here, and I assure you that it will be carefully preserved, not only for ourselves but for the students who consult the related material here. Mr. Morgan's painting of Elizabeth and Thomas Linley is extremely well reproduced: your own scholarly work speaks for itself and therefore needs no comment.[51]

That Greene felt compelled to refer to Anderson's scholarship at all was comment enough, and the assistance that Greene provided to Anderson was indicative of the significant support she made a point of giving to distinguished women scholars and librarians in particular. However, as was often the case in relation to archives or experts consulted by Anderson, those contacted in turn drew on her acknowledged expertise to clarify specific queries. In the case of da Costa Greene, she enquired of Anderson regarding the earliest Mozart letter:

> The two Mozart letters are written on one sheet of paper, that is, that the letter in Italian to his sister is written upon the reverse of the letter in German to his

mother. It seems a bit curious to me that the signatures
are slightly different. I should be very glad if you would
let me know if, in your opinion, the two letters are of
the same date, and also whether the date 1769 (in
another hand) is the correct one.[52]

Anderson was happy to clarify the situation and replied on
25 October:

[. . .] there is not the slightest doubt on internal evidence <u>alone</u>, that 1769 is the correct date and that the
two letters (really postscripts to a letter of his father,
the autograph of which is in the Mozarteum, Salzburg)
were written at the same time. Mozart frequently did
this, i.e. appended postscripts, one in German and the
other in Italian.[53]

When Anderson could not visit archives in person, she
relied on the goodwill of librarians and archivists, friends
and other scholars[54] to provide her with photostats, photographs or facsimile transcriptions of original autograph
letters. Where this was not possible, she was prepared to
pay for the privilege of having 'eyes on the ground' in the
various international archives. At the Prussian State
Library in Berlin, which contained a number of important
Mozart and Beethoven autographs, Anderson employed
the services of a copyist named Ernst Boucke. Boucke
was at that time a music student of the Sing-Akademie zu
Berlin,[55] but he eventually found permanent employment
as a music librarian at the Prussian State Library. There
was an obvious efficiency in paying for the services of a
trusted collaborator, who could provide her with verbatim
transcriptions of the letters in German (or a mix of German

and Italian, as was often the case with Mozart letters). The system appears to have worked well. In October 1935, Anderson received a letter and enclosures of transcriptions of Mozart letters from Boucke, whose German and Italian may have been flawless, but whose English was slightly imperfect:

> Please excuse that I send only 6 leaves* today I had to work such a lot of different things this week that I could spend [a] total 2 hours with the comparison and copy of the <u>London Leopold Letters</u>.[56]

Boucke was paid a rate of two marks per hour for his work in transcribing the letters in the library's collection.

*

As Anderson's work continued on the Mozart correspondence, the Italian Diplomatic Section at GC&CS were, under her leadership, making considerable strides in book building. However, Anderson's efficiently managed system of friends, academic colleagues and archivists providing her with copies of Mozart autographs was in stark contrast to the casual and almost amateurish nature of interwar GC&CS. One incident, described by Josh Cooper, is revealing in this regard, and relates to the two intelligence sections – GC&CS and SIS – who occupied different floors at 54 Broadway Buildings:

> In about 1932 SIS obtained possession of an Italian diplomatic code-book for a brief period. The book was handed to Italian section GC&CS who were told that

* Six pages.

they could have it for 24 hours only. The book was copied by hand by Bodsworth and myself, working all day and late into the night; we finished at 3.30am! It never occurred to us or to Denniston to ask SIS to photograph the book, and it never occurred to SIS to offer to do so. I suppose they must have had photocopying apparatus at Broadway?[57]

Far more serious ramifications could have resulted from a slack approach to security at Broadway Buildings. Anderson and her colleagues only discovered after the Second World War that the 'blind' match seller who regularly sat outside the underground station opposite the entrance to Broadway Buildings was in fact a German spy, tasked with keeping an eye on the offices of the 'Minimax Fire Extinguisher Company', which in reality housed the staffs of both GC&CS and SIS. The agent took photographs of staff entering and leaving the building, and compiled a dossier that detailed:

[. . .] a floor-by-floor plan naming their departmental heads [. . .] a special wanted list of those to be arrested even gave their home addresses, and in some cases car registration numbers.[58]

In the event, the Sicherheitsdienst (SD), the intelligence agency of the SS and the Nazi Party, never acted on the information.

Volume I of the *Letters of Mozart and his Family* appeared in January 1938, with Volume II published in July 1938,[59] and Volume III appearing four months later, in November 1938.[60] The reviews were universally glowing. Dr Charles T. Harrison, in common with all of his fellow music scholars, acknowledged Anderson's achievement in bringing the *Letters* to the wider public, declaring:

> Miss Anderson's edition is beyond praise. She includes all of Mozart's own letters, and also extensive selections from the letters of his father, mother, sister, and wife. This means that her edition is fuller than the standard German edition of Schiedermair.[61]

In his review, Harrison inadvertently touched on the particular skill set that Anderson had brought to her work on Mozart as a result of her career as a cryptologist:

> Her translation is superb: Mozart writes in doggerel, in macaronics; he writes in reverse and upside down; his high spirits express themselves in broad obscenity. All this Miss Anderson makes idiomatic and credible in English. Her footnotes elucidate every reference; her brief introductory summaries give order to the material; her indexes are extensive and clear. The publishers have issued her work in beautiful form. The three volumes are, therefore, in every sense monumental.[62]

The three volumes were described as being a 'faithful and racy' translation of the letters of this precocious family.[63] Writing of Volume II's release in 1938, the *Daily Telegraph* observed:

> Miss Anderson writes as smoothly as ever. Sentimentalists will miss the flavour of the period, but of what use is period flavour to a knowledge of the living man. You gain nothing by the interposition of 'quaintness'! And lose a sense of actuality. Miss Anderson makes us witnesses of history.[64]

In her home country, praise for Volume II was equally effusive. The *Irish Independent* acknowledged Anderson's 'cleverly edited and fluently translated letters of the Mozart family', and also noted:

> Miss Anderson has done her work admirably, her annotations being exhaustive and informative, while the style reproduces expressively the character and temperament of the various writers of the letters.[65]

In Galway, the *Connacht Tribune* was sufficiently proud of its native daughter's achievement that it reprinted verbatim the extract from the *Daily Telegraph*.[66] *The Times*, in a review, commended Anderson on her fearless and robust translation, stating:

> Miss Anderson has not shrunk from turning into plain English all the smutty passages in the letters from Mozart to his cousin, some of which even Herr Schiedermair veiled under the decency of asterisks. We must be grateful to her for her courage.[67]

In acknowledging Anderson's inclusion of such previously censored or bowdlerised content, another reviewer noted: 'It took great courage in 1938 to present English readers with the first unexpurgated general publication of the "Bäsle" letters,[68] as well as passages of a similar tone in some of the other letters.'[69]

An example of Anderson's deft handling of such material occurs in her translation of a letter sent by Mozart to his mother on 31 January 1778, when he writes:

> *Gefurzt wird allzeit auf die Nacht*
> *Und immer so, dass es brav kracht.*

Doch gestern war der furze Konig,
desen Fürze riechen wie Hönig,
Nicht gar zu wohl in der Stimme,
Er war auch selbsten voller Grimme.

Anderson was no prude, and in her translation the colourful content of Mozart's text became:

At night of farts there is no lack,
Which are let off, forsooth, with a powerful crack.
The king of farts came yesterday
Whose farts smelt sweeter than the May.
His voice, however, was no treat
And he himself was in a heat.

Anderson's translations were lively, eminently readable and remained scrupulously faithful to the original. Almost every review of the three volumes observed that her meticulously researched footnotes provided a hitherto absent contextualisation and understanding of the letter's contents, and as such formed an extremely important aspect of the translations. Following her death in 1962, a review of the 1966 revised edition stated of Anderson's achievement: 'Hers is not a work to be dipped into or kept by as a musicologist's reference source. It should be read page by page, though the pages number nearly a thousand.'[70] It is a testimony to the quality of Anderson's scholarship that hers continues to be the standard English-language version of Mozart's letters to this day.

But 1938 was to prove a landmark year in Emily Anderson's private and professional life. In November, the third and final volume of her *Letters of Mozart and his Family* was published,[71] to universal praise. Anderson, however, did not have long to bask in the approbation. As a direct result of the Munich Crisis of September 1938, with the prospect of war increasingly imminent, the service sections of GC&CS spent a month at Bletchley Park simulating wartime conditions and testing the efficiency of intelligence communication systems. So 1938 was also the year that Anderson's second stint as a wartime codebreaker began as the storm clouds gathered. Crucially, however, with twenty years' experience in codebreaking under her belt, she did not enter the fray as a part-time academic – this time, she was among the most senior codebreakers in Commander Denniston's team, and her experience in building books and breaking codes would significantly change the course of the war.

12

The Gathering Storm: Prelude to War

By the spring of 1938, with the prospect of war looming ever closer, two logistical problems presented themselves. The first was to secure a 'war station' for the intelligence service, ideally somewhere out of London, which would be less prone to the bombing raids everyone knew were likely to come. The second was to find sufficient staff to undertake the inevitable increase in cryptanalytic work. The first problem was addressed when, in May 1938, Admiral Sir Hugh Sinclair purchased, from his own funds, a property comprising a large house and grounds in Buckinghamshire, known as Bletchley Park.[1] Immediately, the GPO* set to work to equip it with suitable lines of communications. Bletchley was an ideal location – a secluded country estate, close to a major telecommunications network, and perfectly placed next to a major railway junction, with connections to the north and the south of England, as well as the so-called 'Varsity line' that connected the university towns of Oxford and Cambridge, where so many of the codebreakers were recruited. Bletchley Park itself was located just 100 metres from the railway station, and could be reached in less than an hour from Euston Station, London, making

* General Post Office.

it accessible but still far enough away to make it unlikely that it would be bombed.

The second logistical problem was something to which Commander Denniston already knew the answer: 'It was often said in the old GC&CS that if we had another war we should have to mobilise the dons again.'[2] Denniston had already begun the process by visiting the universities in 1937, and he continued to do so throughout 1938,[3] sounding out former colleagues from the First World War to establish whether they would be prepared to rejoin in an emergency, and whether they could identify other lecturers, graduates and undergrads who might be useful and would be prepared to come. In the aftermath of the Munich Crisis of September 1938, Denniston was more convinced than ever that an increase in cryptologic staff would be imperative as war appeared no longer avoidable. Years of experience had taught him that the last thing he needed was to take on 'a staff of enthusiastic amateurs of whom one knows little or nothing and who may turn out complete failures'. New talent would need to complement the experience of established cryptologists who had already proved their worth, i.e. a combination of 'old hands and high tables'.[4] Among the 'old hands' brought back were former Room 40 codebreakers Nigel de Grey and Frank Birch. De Grey had worked for the art print company Medici during the interwar years. The man who had deciphered the Zimmermann telegram had been quite forgotten about until the Admiralty wrote to him in early 1939, 'asking if he had any sort of experience in the field of intelligence'. De Grey's sardonic reply 'brought a scramble of apologies and exhortations that he return to the cryptology fold',[5] which he was more than happy to do. To recruit some new blood, Denniston dined at several high tables at Oxford and Cambridge and came home with promises from a number of dons to attend a 'territorial training course'.[6]

The priority was to identify candidates with the necessary skill sets, and ideally brilliance, who would be prepared to give up their academic careers for the duration of the war. In his infamous lecture in Edinburgh in 1927, Ewing had provided a fascinating insight into what distinguished a good cryptologist – those he described as having 'intelligence, assiduity, patience, care' – from those who possessed a special kind of genius for codebreaking. In Ewing's view, this required:

> [. . .] that incommunicable faculty for inspired guessing. To a good many there would come flashes, sometimes brilliant flashes, but two or three, when they had acquired experience, seemed to live in an atmosphere of continuous light. They would leap or fly to conclusions with an agility incomprehensible to my pedestrian wits.[7]

Fortunately for GC&CS, there were sufficient candidates of both categories of cryptanalysts to be found in the universities of Britain.

*

As work progressed on fitting out Bletchley Park as a war station, during the summer of 1938 the British government were receiving from SIS the first reports of Hitler's plans to invade Czechoslovakia, and the necessity of bringing the Bletchley operation into service became more pressing. What amounted to a 'dress rehearsal' for war – the deployment of an advance party of cryptanalysts, technicians and administrative staff to Bletchley to simulate war conditions for a limited period – had been envisaged, but the Munich Crisis prompted the move to Bletchley on a scale that had not initially been planned, with over 150 staff, from SIS and GC&CS, transferred there before moving back to London, a month later, once the crisis subsided. This, then, 'wasn't simply a recce or friendly rehearsal, it was the activation of one of the government's most secret war stations at a time when conflict appeared imminent'.[8]

What came to be known as 'Captain Ridley's Shooting Party' arrived at Bletchley Park on 18 September 1938. Captain Ridley was an SIS officer, and it was SIS that funded the entire operation.[9] Characterising the relatively large numbers descending on the previously unoccupied country house as a 'shooting party' was a necessary ruse to avoid awkward questions being asked. An impression of friends enjoying a weekend at a country house could be maintained, while the installation of telecommunications equipment could be explained by the need to install new telephone lines to facilitate guests. The real purpose, of course, was to see whether Bletchley Park would work as a wartime location. In that respect, the 'Shooting Party' proved a success, and any awkward questions locals may have had were discreetly kept to themselves.

For operational reasons, it was the service sections of GC&CS – Naval, Air and Military – and the Enigma section, led by Dilly Knox, which spent a month at the Park simulating, as far as possible, wartime conditions and direct communication. Mavis Batey's recollection is that for the trial run, GC&CS occupied the lower floor, but 'SIS were in command secretly on the upper floors, in touch with their agents'. Valentine Vivian, the head of Section V counter-espionage, was in overall charge of the trial war site while Captain Ridley arranged the move from London.[10]

The Diplomatic Sections remained in London, as their work was at such a critical stage they could not be spared for the simulation exercise. At the time the 'Shooting Party' was taking place, the real worry for the British was Italy, rendering Anderson's role crucial, and her deployment to Bletchley out of the question in the short term. Anderson's presence as Head of the Italian Diplomatic Section was more critical than even that of the German Diplomatic Section, because at the time, the threat of the Italian navy becoming belligerent in the Mediterranean was of greater strategic importance than what was likely to happen in Czechoslovakia. In advance of war breaking out, it was diplomatic traffic that was critical when it came to discovering the plans of the Italians, and as the undisputed queen of diplomatic intelligence, Anderson 'drove the assault on Italian diplomatic traffic[11] during 1935–38, a leading priority of that time, making her perhaps the central codebreaker in GC&CS for two years'.[12] The specific skill required in working with diplomatic intelligence was to discover not just what the enemy was saying, but the mindset that produced it. Batey described it as 'an intellectual procedure of lateral thinking',[13] and de Grey observed that diplomatic codebreakers needed to be particularly skilled:

> The habit in diplomacy is to use long code phrase books, which the cryptanalyst after having stripped away the concealment keys of varying degrees of

difficulty that may have been superimposed upon the code-book groups, then has to compile laboriously by organised guesswork.[14]

This was work at which Anderson was completely in her element. Expertise in diplomatic intelligence was born of years of familiarity, as:

> [. . .] each section dealt with the entire diplomatic correspondence of a country [. . .] with their representative abroad. The sections therefore became intimately acquainted with the policy of these countries with an experience often extending over many years.[15]

Diplomatic cryptanalysts had to be strong not only linguistically, but also in ensuring that in their translations, they incorporated the correct use of diplomatic phraseology. As de Grey noted:

> It was essential that the English version should leave upon the mind of the reader as nearly as possible the same impression as would be received by its legitimate foreign recipient. To say, for instance, that a Government 'is uneasy about the course of events' conveys a different shade of anxiety than to say that 'it is afraid of what might happen', yet either might render a phrase in another language with rough and ready accuracy. Even a good linguist unversed in the niceties may do a lot of mischief.[16]

But Emily Anderson was not just a good linguist: she was an exceptional one, and one who had honed her translation skills as much in her spare time, working on the letters of Mozart and later Beethoven, as she did while working on diplomatic traffic in her day job. With twenty years' experience, in both war and peace, she was acutely aware of the danger of overemphasis, a particularly dangerous feature in wartime reports.

By the late spring of 1939, plans for a full-scale deployment to the war station at Bletchley were well advanced, and Anderson's seniority and experience meant that she would be one of the first to move. Before she did so, however, sometime in 1939,[17] she moved to her new home, Flat No. 4, at 24 Ellerdale Road, Hampstead. Apart from a few short periods – her time at Bletchley, and in Cairo – she was to live there for the remainder of her life. Since 1924, she had lived in a variety of addresses in Hampstead,[18] and for a woman of Anderson's interests, the choice of Hampstead was an obvious one. Its leafy streets teemed with writers, actors, artists, and, of primary interest to Anderson, musicians, a number of whom became her friends.[19] Anderson's neighbour, Elizabeth Oliver, observed that it was cheap to buy or rent properties there before the war, but prices rose significantly in the post-war period. Anderson's flat at 24 Ellerdale Road, Hampstead, was a short three-minute walk to Hampstead Tube station. The house had previously housed the King Alfred School Society, but the success of the school meant that it finally outgrew its home at Ellerdale Road and moved to a new location, and the house was converted into flats in 1921.[20] Flat 4 was a spacious two-bedroomed first-floor flat, with room to accommodate her beloved pianoforte. In the short term, however, time to practise her piano, or continue with her musicology research, was severely curtailed by the demands of her war work.

Those working within the intelligence community had

witnessed first-hand the apparent sleepwalking into war by what one intelligence officer described as 'a sort of elderly businessmen's government [which] was still unable to jump the gap between 1914 and 1930', and were 'in denial' that a war was looming.[21] Questioning why politicians had 'failed so utterly both in diplomacy and rearmament to deal with the gangsters of Berlin', F. W. Witherbotham[22] observed: 'One thing is certain; it had not been for lack of information.'[23] No one was in any doubt that war was inevitable, and people were resigned to the fact that Hitler would have to be stopped by force. War was finally declared on 3 September 1939, but, as Denniston noted:

> [...] our work could definitely begin on August 1st 1939, when the Admiral[24] ordered the Service Sections to take up their war stations. The Diplomatic and Commercial Sections were ordered to move on August 16th. From then onwards the university recruits began to join, so that by September 3rd when war was declared , GC&CS was in action at its war station already [...] [25]

With an influx of staff about to descend on the Buckinghamshire town, and speculation growing as to what work exactly was taking place at Bletchley Park, GC&CS adopted the name 'Government Communications Headquarters' (GCHQ)*, thereby implying that this was a general communications facility, giving no hint as to its true function as a codebreaking and intelligence centre. This time, unlike with Captain Ridley's Shooting Party,

---

* At this point, as described, GC&CS just adopted the name GCHQ; it wasn't until 1946 that it was formally renamed such.

Emily Anderson did not remain in London, as her skills were too valuable and urgently required at the new war station. As she arrived at Bletchley in August, Anderson, like most of her colleagues, had no doubt hoped for peace, but was nonetheless prepared for war.

Anderson's significant contribution to the cryptographic effort, which would ultimately yield spectacular intelligence, was the result of years of experience and the high regard in which she was held. It also reflected the power she wielded as a Senior Assistant, the only woman of that status within the organisation. She was acknowledged as the leading bookbuilder in GC&CS, but as had been the case since her career began, she expected her own high standards of her colleagues and subordinates, and as a result could be prickly and demanding to work for. Her fellow cryptanalyst at GC&CS, the British army officer Brigadier John Tiltman, noted of Anderson in the period 1936–38: 'she seemed to bully any of my attached officers who worked under her'. But Tiltman also recognised that his officers, and anyone else who trained under Anderson – such as Wilfred Bodsworth and Josh Cooper – got a first-class training in book building and cryptanalysis, training that would ultimately lead to their assuming senior roles at Bletchley Park, and helping Britain to win the war.[26]

13

Bletchley Park

'The Germans invaded Poland on September 1, 1939;
Great Britain and France declared war on September
3. Most of us in England were pretty scared.'

Thus the great Bletchley codebreaker Gordon Welchman
opened the first chapter of his book, *The Hut Six Story*.[1]
Many of those who would come to work at Bletchley Park
undoubtedly were scared; unprepared they were not. The
continuity of intelligence gathering provided by interwar
GC&CS, and the 'dry run' of Captain Ridley's Shooting
Party, had ensured that from both a skills base and a logis-
tics perspective, Britain was fully prepared for the new
intelligence war it would be called on to wage in 1939. It
was a preparation that had been over twenty years in the
making. Denniston, summing up the evolution of SIGINT
from the early days of GC&CS to the outbreak of the
Second World War, observed:

We started in 1919 at the period of bow-and-arrow
methods, i.e. alphabetic books; we followed the various developments of security measures adopted in
every country; we reached 1939 with a full knowledge
of all the methods evolved, and with the ability to read

all diplomatic communications of all powers except
those who had been forced, like Germany and Russia,
to adopt OTP* [. . .] with personal satisfaction
I maintain that GC&CS did during those twenty
years fulfil its allotted function with success, with
exiguous numbers and with an absence of publicity
which greatly enhanced the value of its work.[2]

The continuum of codebreaking activity during the interwar years enabled GC&CS to hit the ground running,
such that Britain did not enter the Second World War
without any codebreaking expertise; it was not the least of
its achievements that 'it gave birth to Bletchley Park'.[3]

Anderson and her colleagues at Broadway Buildings
expected that the order to move to the war station could
come at any time, as and when circumstances demanded it,
and they were instructed to 'keep a suitcase packed, a 10s.
note in their pocket, and await a telephone message that
"Auntie Flo is not so well." '[4] At that point, they were to make
their way to Bletchley, which became known as 'Station
X'.[5] Exactly a month before Hitler's army invaded Poland,
the service stations of GC&CS (military, air and naval)
were ordered to take up their war stations at Bletchley. Two
weeks later, the diplomatic and commercial stations also
moved to Station X.[6] As Head of the Italian Diplomatic Section, Anderson was among those who moved to Bletchley

---

* One Time Pad (OTP) is a system in which a randomly generated
private key is used only once to encrypt a message that is then
decrypted by the receiver using a matching one-time pad and key.
OTPs are practically impossible to break into as each encryption
is unique and bears no relation to the next encryption, so a pattern
cannot be detected by analysing a succession of messages.

Park on 15 August 1939. It was significant that, in that first wave of staff, relatively few were working on German material. Apart from Denniston and his deputy, Commander Edward 'Jumbo' Travis, there were twenty-nine staff working in the Diplomatic and Commercial Sections, none of whom were working on German cyphers. By far the largest number – nine – were working on Italian diplomatic cyphers, the most experienced of whom was Emily Anderson.[7] While most staff travelled to Bletchley by train, Anderson had by then (it is unclear when) acquired a car, and drove herself to Bletchley, an hour's drive north of London. However, once war was declared on 3 September 1939, petrol was the first commodity to be rationed in the UK, and by 8 September, coupons for rationing petrol were introduced.[8] But Anderson, as an individual key to the war effort, continued to use her car for the duration of her time at Bletchley, ferrying both herself and other employees from their billeted accommodation to Bletchley Park each morning and home again each evening.

Those who moved to Bletchley were instructed that letters for them were to be addressed to the official address, which was 'Room 47, Foreign Office'. Post was sent on via a PO number, although, as Cooper humorously observed, 'the system broke down when large parcels were addressed to the Box No;[9] in one case a grand piano was consigned in this way'.[10] Telephone messages could be left at the telephone number 'Whitehall 7947', but no private calls were to be made from Bletchley Park without authority.[11] Staff were also warned against:

> [. . .] any conversations regarding the work with other
> members of the staff while in their billets. If occasion

should arise as to what you are doing the answer should
be that you are part of the aerial defence of London.[12]

In addition, Bletchley staff were under strict instructions
not to discuss their work with their spouses or families.
Patricia Bartley recalled a song, popular with staff, which
was sung to the tune of 'My Bonnie Lies over the Ocean':

> My bonnie is stationed at uh-uh
> And nobody knows it you see,
> Except all the people of uh-uh
> And all his relations, and me.[13]

The logistical task of feeding, accommodating and finding
office space for the staff of Bletchley was daunting. When
Anderson arrived, there were just 186 staff at Bletchley; by
1942, there were 1,600, and by the end of 1944, this had
risen to 8,743. The introduction of female conscription
in 1941 meant that three-quarters of those working at
Bletchley were women. Given such numbers, and the fact
that not a whiff of its crucial intelligence work was ever
revealed during wartime, it is hardly surprising that Winston Churchill described Bletchley staff as 'the geese that
laid the golden egg and never cackled'.[14] And while it was
the case that although General Schellenberg[15] of German
high command had pinpointed Bletchley Park as a communications centre, critically, they never suspected it was a
codebreaking centre.[16]

The move to the war station had significant financial
implications. Staff had to be paid, onsite services such as
canteens had to be provided, and out-of-pocket travel and
subsistence expenses covered for an increasing cohort of
staff. The dry run of September 1938 was to form the basis

of the payments staff were to receive when they moved to Bletchley Park. Staff were paid full subsistence rates, 'and the staff, being in receipt of lodging and food, should pay over two-third, and retain one-third, with a maximum of 5/- a day'.[17] Railway fares were reimbursed and petrol allowances were also paid to those like Anderson who owned a car. Identifying suitable billets was a difficult task given the numbers involved, and the fact that there was a mix of very senior GC&CS 'old hands', such as Anderson, as well as established junior staff and new recruits. The Ministry of Health was charged with finding suitable private accommodation for Bletchley personnel and advised that 'A tactful approach must be made to each householder'.[18] Those with rooms to spare in their homes were encouraged to make them available as a billet to accommodate Bletchley staff, with no questions asked, or answered.

Anderson moved to Bletchley on 15 August 1939, and a billeting list lists Miss E. Anderson immediately below a Miss Brooks.[19] This was Dorothy Brooks, and the fate of these two women would intertwine within a short period of time. Having arrived by car, one of Anderson's first actions was to deposit her luggage at her allocated billet. It was a measure of Anderson's seniority that the first billet allocated to her was one of the largest and most imposing private houses in the district. The Manor House, located eight miles from Bletchley in the village of Swanbourne, was the home of Sir Maurice Henry Weston Hayward, KCSI,* who lived with his wife, Alice, and their daughter, Marjorie.[20] Sir Maurice was a retired barrister and civil servant, and had been the acting governor of Bombay for a short period

---

* Knight Commander of the Order of the Star of India.

in December 1923. The Manor House was a late sixteenth-to early seventeenth-century house,[21] which had been substantially restored in the early twentieth century. The house had been leased to the Haywards in 1927 by Lord Cottesloe, who owned the property. It was a prestigious billet, and Anderson was the only Bletchley employee billeted there.[22] An account written by the Hayward's son, Maurice, may explain why. He noted that when Bletchley Park was established:

> [My] parents were 'invited' to lodge some members of the clerical staff at the Manor House. This proved too much for them, and in 1941 they broke their lease and moved to Hampshire.[23]

The fact that 'invited' is in inverted commas would indicate that providing a billet for Bletchley staff was not something the Haywards were inclined to do voluntarily. It was also the case that, according to an unpublished history of Swanbourne, 'Sir Maurice was not popular in the village. Another ex-Indian Judge. He tried to organise everyone.'[24] Regardless of whether she was welcome or not, on Registration Day for the National Register,[25] 29 September 1939, Anderson was in situ in the Manor House, her occupation listed as 'civil service'. This was hardly surprising. Military personnel were not recorded on the Register, and, technically, as a Foreign Office employee, Anderson was a 'civil servant'. The same 1939 Register shows her GC&CS colleague, Dilly Knox, sharing his home with two fellow codebreakers at Bletchley Park – Hugh Foss and Alan Turing – all three men listing their occupations as 'civil servant'.

Having settled in to her billet, Anderson focused on the

task facing her in establishing an efficient, and much expanded, Italian Diplomatic Section at Bletchley. She was fortunate that in doing so, she could count on an entirely new cohort of cryptographic talent, much of it raw and in need of refinement, but some of it brilliant. With 'old hands' like Anderson, Knox, de Grey and Foss now established at the war station, the recruitment of university candidates previously scoped out by Denniston was activated in earnest almost immediately, and by 1 September, the ranks of GC&CS were swelled considerably by an influx of young, university-educated graduates.[26] In recruiting potential codebreakers, Denniston employed some of the same selection techniques that had been used to great effect during the First World War, i.e. recognising that 'great minds don't think alike'. A lifelong proponent of teamwork and synergy, Denniston had, from the outset, provided an environment that encouraged individuality and harnessed it to enable a disparate team of often quirky individuals to work successfully towards a common goal. Josh Cooper said of Denniston:

> [When] the second war came he had an organisation in being which with all its faults was intellectually honest and formed a nucleus which new staff (recruited by Denniston himself in his visit to the universities in 1937 and 1938) could work with and respect.[27]

Denniston recruited prospective cryptographers and cryptanalysts irrespective of their age, gender or background, valuing talent and potential above all else. Experience had shown that codebreakers had to be able to think laterally. Dilly Knox, for example, brilliant but a noted eccentric,[28] had been known for doing most of his thinking sitting in the bathtub installed in his office in MI1(b). Aside from the bathtub, Knox's eccentricities remained fully in force when he arrived at Bletchley, and he quizzed new recruits to assess their suitability for the subtleties of codebreaking by asking which way the hands of a clock went round. When they invariably answered 'clockwise', he would reply 'Not if you're inside the clock'.[29]

In the early days, before machinery began to be used to help break codes, the complexity of German codes was such that the Germans were supremely confident that they could never be broken. But broken they were, using processes that involved almost unimaginable mental gymnastics on the part of the old hands and their younger university recruits, using little more than pencil and paper or blackboards and chalk. The process by which Anderson and her fellow cryptanalysts received the information they had to decipher was standard across all categories of intelligence – military, air, naval or diplomatic. Firstly, a 'Y' interceptor, or wireless operator, as they were known, would operate short-wave receivers, and find the correct Italian or German frequency. Having done so, as the German or Italian operator began tapping out in Morse Code, the 'Y' operator, armed with just a pencil and specially lined pads, quickly wrote down the letters or numbers as they heard them, at the same time translating what they were writing down in Morse to the ordinary alphabet or numerals. It required intense concentration and speed, and absolute accuracy. Difficult as this aspect of the task was, in truth it was the easy part of the process. The real task began when the completed sheets were passed on to the cryptanalyst, who had to 'break' the cipher in order to make sense of the letter and number combination as they related to the language in which the message was written, and in this way decrypt the content of the message. The ciphers used in transmitting messages in Morse were changed regularly, making the task of the cryptanalyst all the more difficult.

Diplomatic intelligence was, for the most part, gleaned from communications sent from embassies based in London by radio. These were intercepted by a Metropolitan Police intercept station, based in Denmark Hill, south London, and forwarded to skilled diplomatic codebreakers such as Anderson. Intelligence was also intercepted via enciphered telegrams, which were sent via international telephone and telegraph cables. These lines were controlled by the British-owned Cable and Wireless Ltd, which throughout the war facilitated the Foreign Office in the monitoring of enciphered foreign embassy communications, which were printed out and forwarded to Bletchley for decryption.

*

Essential to the nurturing of individuality and creativity was the atmosphere that pervaded at Bletchley, carefully curated by Denniston. Though never at home with the minutiae of administration, and with even less liking for the ways of bureaucracy and hierarchy, Denniston was willing to delegate, to trust his subordinates, and to encourage collaboration. Patricia Bartley[30] noted that: 'Within the organisation, the atmosphere was surprisingly informal. Christian names were the rule – even, sometimes, with commanding officers.'[31] Yet in spite of such informality, when fully operational, Bletchley Park was an intelligence factory that operated 24 hours a day, 365 days a year, and produced remarkable results, with codebreakers such as Alan Turing, Gordon Welchman and Hugh Alexander but a few of those who flourished in this carefully culti-vated atmosphere, and who subsequently became justifiably famous. Far less well known were others like Hugh Foss, Mavis Batey, Patricia Bartley and, most pointedly, Emily Anderson. This intelligence factory was producing the decrypted transcripts of the enemy talking in codes – and, moreover, talking freely, so confident were they that their codes had not, and could not, be broken.

Having acquired a very senior status in pre-war GC&CS, Bletchley had the potential to prove something of a challenge to Emily Anderson. She and her long-time colleagues were used to a certain way of working, and as Bletchley Park evolved, the Diplomatic Sections tended to become a different entity from the Service Sections. For this reason, from late 1939, with increasing pressure on space in the Park, the Diplomatic Sections were moved and accommodated for the most part outside Bletchley at Elmer's School,[32] a former grammar school with accom-modation for fifty boarders and 150 pupils, just a few minutes' walk from the main building. The move made complete sense, for as Nigel de Grey observed:

> They were composed mainly of professional cryptana-lyst linguists, as opposed to the amateur war enlisted staff of the Service Sections and had a professional pride in their work which had little relationship to the use that could be made of it, as distinct from most of the people in the Service Sections who were contented to do almost any work demanded of them so long as they were convinced that it was a help to the war.

Their work brought them into practically no contact with the Service Sections and though by no manner of means dilatory in execution was none the less and rightly conducted at a different tempo.

Elmer's School was acquired at such short notice that the Diplomatic Sections moved in:

[. . .] before the proprietor had had time to remove his furniture. The sight of a professor of some erudition struggling with an unfamiliar task on the blankets of a boy's bedstead in the dormitory is one not easily forgotten.[33]

Just as Anderson had moved from the main building of Bletchley Park within a short period of time, similarly she did not remain long with the Haywards at the Manor House. At some point between the compilation of the register in September 1939 and 23 October that year,[34] Anderson moved billet to the Bartley family, also living in Swanbourne. Their still sizeable but significantly smaller and less prestigious house was a short 300 metres' walk from her original billet. What is significant, however, is that she did not move there alone; she was accompanied by another female Bletchley employee. We are fortunate that an eyewitness to the arrival of Anderson and her younger female companion at the Bartley home survived until relatively recently. Patricia Bartley[35] was then aged twenty-two, and she recalled the family being asked by someone at Bletchley Park to provide a billet for some female staff: 'They asked, and my father agreed, because we had the room.' Patricia could never have imagined that her father's agreement to provide a billet for some Bletchley staff would have a significant influence on her own life, and as a consequence the course of the war itself.

Sir Charles Bartley's willingness to accommodate at least one of the women in question may well have had to do with the fact that, like himself, Anderson was Irish. Patricia recalled: 'Well we knew she was Irish because my mother was very sensitive about the Irish, she didn't like them, despite having married one!'[36] Lady Bartley's misgivings notwithstanding, ultimately the decision to provide billets for two Bletchley staff was the prerogative of Sir Charles, whose will prevailed. Patricia clearly remembered the two women arriving at The Cottage together, and the fact that they were 'very close'. So close, in fact, that she was fairly certain from the outset that they were far more than just work colleagues. Her impression was unequivocal: 'I think they were lesbians.' When asked whether it might simply have been the case that the women were just good friends, Patricia was quite clear: 'Oh no, I don't think so. They shared a room. And it was a very narrow bed.'

Bartley recalls that the other woman was a good deal younger than Emily, and she was struck by the fact that throughout the time the two women lived with the Bartleys they were very open in their affection for each other: 'It was very rare. I mean now people live together and think nothing of it but it was quite something in those days.'

Bartley, who had witnessed such relationships during her time at Oxford, immediately recognised Anderson and her companion as a couple, but her mother, Lady Bartley, was blissfully unaware of the nature of the women's relationship – 'it would simply never have occurred to her that such a thing was possible'. We can surmise, therefore, that Anderson's move from the Manor House may have resulted from the fact that a burgeoning relationship between the two women had developed, and been disapproved of by Sir Maurice and Lady Hayward, as they increasingly wished to spend time together – and Emily Anderson was not a woman to take such disapproval lightly. Whatever the reason, the fact remains that when the two women moved from their respective billets to The Cottage, they did so as a couple, and during their time there, according to Bartley, they were charming house guests and clearly happy to be together, in spite of the intense work pressures they were both subject to at the Park. They went on drives together in Emily's car, and for walks in the surrounding countryside. The presence of a good piano in the Bartley home was an added bonus for Emily, who could play her beloved Mozart and Beethoven for her companion. The women were also fortunate that the Bartleys had a large garden, which in line with government directives had been planted with a variety of vegetables, and they had their own chickens, so those living at The Cottage were well provided for with fresh food.

The identity of the woman with whom Anderson shared her billet – and her bed – has not, so far, been confirmed in any official documents that have come to light. Indeed, Anderson's own move to a billet with the Bartley family is not confirmed by any official documentation, but Patricia Bartley's testimony confirms that it is certain that she moved there, within a month of beginning her work at Bletchley, and most likely at her own insistence. Bartley's description of Anderson – from her nationality to the fact that she was tall, slim and had auburn hair – 'I can still see that golden, almost orange hair'[37] – and the fact that she was a keen pianist, confirms that Anderson was the elder of the two women.[38] The physical description of the younger woman by Bartley, however, appears to suggest that the woman was Dorothy Brooks. Anderson and Brooks had been in the same cohort of staff who had arrived at Bletchley on 15 August 1939, and consistent with her being a more junior member of staff, Brooks had originally been billeted with two other Bletchley staff, all of whom were described on the 1939 Register as 'temporary clerk in the Foreign Office' in Newport Pagnell, some fourteen miles from Anderson's billet in Swanbourne, and seven miles from Bletchley.

Born in Lambeth, London, and then aged twenty-four (Anderson was forty-eight), Dorothy Brooks' family had risen from solidly working-class stock (her paternal and maternal grandfathers were a brass finisher and a baker respectively) to lower middle class. Her father rose to the rank of clerk/telegraphist in the GPO, and by 1939 he had been promoted to 'Assistant Superintendent'. The Brooks family had sufficient income to ensure that their clever and able daughter received a good education, and she graduated in French from University College, London, in 1936. At the outbreak of war, Dorothy was sent to Bletchley, where she worked as a cryptanalyst in the Commercial Section, although for civil service grading purposes, she was designated as a 'translator'. The Commercial Section had moved to Elmer's School at the same time as the Diplomatic Sections, so Anderson and Brooks were working in the same building while they shared a billet.

But idyllic as her new-found happiness in her relationship with a younger woman must have been, it was typical of Anderson that she nonetheless did not fail to spot the potential of the young woman in whose home she was living. Patricia Bartley[39] had studied Philosophy, Politics and Economics (PPE) at Lady Margaret Hall, Oxford. Two years into her degree, however, in 1938, she suffered a nervous breakdown and was recovering at home when the war broke out and Anderson and her companion arrived. Although languages had not formed part of her degree, as a child Bartley had been home-schooled at an abbey in Brittany, where her mother and younger siblings were living while her father worked in India, and she had become fluent in French and German as a result.[40] Almost as soon as she arrived at The Cottage, Anderson recognised the language skills – and sharp intellect – of Patricia,[41] and pounced on the opportunity to recruit a potential new codebreaker to the Bletchley staff. Bartley later recalled how she had become involved in the work of Bletchley Park:

> [A] lady from the Foreign Office, who had been billeted on my family home in the nearby village of Swanbourne, said that people with my knowledge of French and German would be useful down the road.[42] I had just left Oxford. So I went in and was interviewed by the then head of Bletchley Park, a former naval commander named Alastair Denniston.[43]

The 'lady from the Foreign Office' was undoubtedly Anderson, and it is significant that it was Denniston himself who interviewed her, doubtless on the advice of Anderson, who recognised a natural codebreaker when she saw one. Denniston clearly agreed with Anderson's assessment of the young Miss Bartley, and she was immediately:

[. . .] put to work – with nothing more than paper, pencil and her knowledge of the language – on the main German diplomatic code, a system that had largely been ignored during the interwar period because it was deemed too difficult.[44]

Reflecting on her time at Bletchley, Bartley observed: 'There were some very good women there. Much better than the men.'[45]

Anderson was a frequent visitor to Commander Denniston's office in the main house at Bletchley – including when she came to recommend Patricia Bartley to him. There, she would have encountered his PA, Barbara Abernethy (later Barbara Eachus),[46] and as the daughter of an Ulsterman, her keen ear would have recognised an Ulster accent when she heard it. Abernethy was born and raised in Belfast, but like Patricia Bartley, was educated in Belgium, where she became fluent in French, German and Flemish. Remarkably, Abernethy was just sixteen when she joined the Foreign Office straight from school, and within a week had been transferred to GC&CS. Aged seventeen, she formed part of the very first group to go to Bletchley as a member of Captain Ridley's Shooting Party in 1938, and having been initially earmarked as a codebreaker, Denniston, seeing her confident administrative skills, chose her as his PA. Eight years later, in 1946, it was Abernethy who locked the gates of Bletchley for the last time.

*

Bletchley was a melting pot of staff, with the codebreakers, in particular, comprising quirky geniuses such as Alan Turing and Dilly Knox, scatty academics who were brilliant but socially awkward, and an assortment of other misfits and oddballs. The miracle of Bletchley was that such a combination of talent actually worked, to a quite remarkable degree. In stark contrast, the German code-breaking organisations, of which there were seven in total, were all in competition with each other – on one occasion, it was rumoured, even coming to blows with each other.[47] Bletchley was an altogether more cohesive and harmonious outfit, which delivered on its intended purpose to a quite remarkable degree.

As she prepared to spend her first Christmas at Bletchley, in December 1939 Anderson received news that her brother-in-law, John Rochford, husband of her only surviving sister Elsie, had died at the age of forty-nine. A former bank manager, he had retired early on the grounds of ill health.[48] The couple had been married less than ten years. Following Rochford's retirement, they had moved to Booterstown in Dublin, to live with Elsie's widowed mother. Now, aged forty-nine and a widow herself, Elsie remained living with her mother for the rest of her life, and never remarried. Understandably, given wartime conditions and the pressing nature of her work at Bletchley, Emily did not return to Ireland to attend the funeral.

*

With such an enormous weight of responsibility resting on their shoulders, the codebreakers of Bletchley had to find some way of managing that burden, and many of them found that in music. Music and dramatic performances provided a vital pressure valve for staff at the Park, particularly those, like Anderson, for whom intense concentration under time constraint was an integral part of their daily workload. It was also the case that most codebreakers had an instinctive understanding of the structures of music, and a great many of those who served at Bletchley were musicians or singers themselves, or had a keen interest in music.[49] Anderson was one of those for whom linguistic talent and a knowledge of music was intrinsic to their codebreaking ability, and she was not alone. Mair Russell-Jones, who worked in Hut 6, believed her musical training, and consequently her ability to see patterns in passages that needed to be decoded, was instrumental in her success in cryptanalysis. Winterbotham acknowledged as much, noting: 'It struck me at the time how often the art of undoing other people's ciphers was closely allied to a brain which could excel both in mathematics and music.'[50] Nigel de Grey was a keen musician and composer, and his wife Florence Gore was a singer. Oliver Strachey, who had previously served with Anderson in MI1(b) during the First World War, deciphered Abwehr signals and was a classically trained pianist. Jean Alington, who worked on German Army and Air Enigma signals in Hut 3, was a famous opera singer. Gordon Welchman, who played the trombone and sang in choral groups,[51] wistfully recalled some of the younger codebreakers 'singing madrigals on a summer's evening' by the waters of the Grand Union Canal.[52] More ominously, John Cairncross, later revealed to be a Russian spy, was given the code name 'Liszt' by his Russian handler because of his love of classical music. In his memoir, he recalled a highlight of his social life at Bletchley being 'a concert of German Lieder* sung by a colleague'.[53]

---

* German lieder refers to songs performed in German by a solo singer with piano accompaniment.

Concerts by musicians, including performances by staff members with a particular musical talent, or invited professional musicians, such as Myra Hess,[54] were a regular feature of Station X life,[55] and there were numerous musical societies, which all staff were encouraged to join. Bletchley even had its own highland dancing society, led by the codebreaker Hugh Foss. Such musical outlets were invaluable to the mental health of codebreakers and other Bletchley staff, providing both welcome respite from the intensity of the work, and an opportunity to socialise with colleagues, all of whom understood implicitly that speaking about the nature of one's work in one's specific section was strictly off limits.

Such distractions were to become increasingly welcome. The pressure on codebreakers to deliver vital information that would enable British forces to move strategically against the Germans increased dramatically once they invaded Belgium, Luxembourg and the Netherlands in May 1940.[56] Denniston understood from his experiences in the First World War that, if his staff were to be productive, they needed to alternate intense working shifts with sufficient rest when needed. But with many of the newly recruited codebreaking staff still not sufficiently up to speed when it came to producing timely and accurate cryptanalysis, it fell to the more experienced staff, like Anderson, to take up the slack – and the strain was beginning to show on many. Denniston was forced to make a *crie de coeur* to his staff, noting:

> Every member of GC&CS is making her or himself an important cog in a large machine which is producing definite valuable war material and it is now increasingly hard to spare any of you. So I would like

to ask you all, first, to avoid accumulating rest days for the next few weeks. You must have your rest day – you need it. I realise that most of you wish to use it to see your friends and relations in various parts of the country. But I should be very grateful indeed if the habit of 'local leave' could be extended during the present overwhelming crisis. I know this will entail a very great sacrifice for many of you.[57]

Anderson's visits to London for the occasional concert were no longer possible, and there was to be no let-up in the pressure, particularly once Italy entered the war on 10 June 1940. German forces defeated the Allies in Europe on 25 June, France and the Low Countries were conquered, and Allied land operations on the Western Front were effectively at an end. The strain that personnel were under was intense, and could indeed be debilitating. Having trained under Emily Anderson, Josh Cooper was well used to hard work and pressure, but even he was prompted to write to Group Captain Blandy on 2 October 1940 to say:

We are still maintaining a watch in Hut 3 on a staff of 3 men [. . .] A 24 hour watch, on a staff of 3, leaves absolutely no provision for leave or sickness; and consequently these officers do not so much as get a day off, while the rest of the staff of Hut 3 (and of the GC&CS and of other government departments) are now taking their second period of 7 days leave. Apart from being hard on the individuals concerned, this overworking is not in the interests of the show. Under such conditions, the best men would get stale and relapse into a routine of more or less mechanical reporting, instead of being alert to look out for interesting new lines of study.[58]

The increasing need for more staff if a 24-hour round-the-clock watch system was to operate added to the pressure of managing existing staff, and training up new recruits. As the Head of the Italian Diplomatic Section, it was Anderson's responsibility to manage the staff within her section, and she was one of only a handful of women within GC&CS to have this responsiblity. She continued to expect the same high standards of her colleagues and subordinates as she had always set herself, and retained her reputation for being an exacting boss with a sharp tongue. But no one could deny that the formidable Miss Anderson got results. It is also worth considering that the female 'bully' described by Tiltman may, had she been a man, have been more favourably described as a tough and uncompromising boss, deserving of respect. Certainly Patricia Bartley, who having been recruited by Anderson became her counterpart as Head of German Diplomatic Section, was firmly of the view that female heads of sections, regardless of their abilities, were resented and occasionally undermined by some of the male colleagues working under them, and she had first-hand experience to prove it.[59] And it wasn't just women in senior positions who were considered a threat by some male colleagues. William Clarke recalled that his secretary, Winnifred White, had 'the makings of a quite passable cryptographer', and he sent her to work under two men in his section,

> [. . .] both of whom were her enemies and who were jealous of her, realising that she was better at the job than they; in fact she often had had to teach them their job and point out their mistakes [. . .][60]

In February 1942 Miss Clarke moved with the Italian Diplomatic Section to Berkeley Street – where, in May 1943,

Emily Anderson became her boss.[61] Anderson, however, had over twenty years' experience of operating at a senior level in a man's world, and was a woman who never allowed herself to be undermined by anyone, male or female. The perception of her as a 'bully', therefore – whether justified or not – never impacted on her.

It is worth noting that at Bletchley, Anderson's long-time colleague Dilly Knox deliberately hired women exclusively to work in his section, and gave them consider-able responsibility. His talented team of codebreakers included the remarkable Mavis Batey, who explained why:

> Dilly chose people who were language oriented. There was an actress, and some girls who'd been at drama school and they were quite glamorous, but they also understood rhythms and patterns of speech. Dilly was always looking for rhythms and patterns. There were linguists like me, and one girl was a speech therap-ist. We were always referred to as 'Dilly's Girls' or 'Dilly's Fillies', even in places like Whitehall, but he chose us because he liked the fact we were intelligent, made good coffee, and we could pick up his ideas and work on them while he came up with more. It was no use asking the mathematicians because they were too busy with their own ideas. But we could give him the attention he needed and try to pin down his ideas and try them. Some worked, some didn't, but he was never short of them. He was an extraordinary man.[62]

Knox was indeed extraordinary. Aged fifty-five when he moved to Bletchley, he had already worked as a code-breaker, at a senior level, through the First World War and the interwar period. In spite of failing health, he selflessly threw everything he had at his work in The Cottage, the name given to the building in which his section at Bletchley Park was based, surrounded by his army of able women. Crucially, as was the case with Anderson, age and seniority were no barriers to energy, vigour or the ability to adapt to new circumstances and challenges, but not all former GC&CS staff were so adaptable. Frank Birch revealed as much in a letter to Denniston written in May 1940:

> Brandon is leaving. He has been v. nice about it and himself volunteered that he was not the right man for the job, and much as I like him, I must agree. He is too old for a new racket.

Birch went on to say:

> Crawford had better go too. I've tried him in every responsible position, but he has neither the wits nor the will to work, nor the personality for any such position here, where neither seniority nor stripes count, but usefulness only is the measure of importance.[63]

For those who made the grade, and satisfied the 'usefulness' criteria established by old hands such as Birch and Anderson, the work was difficult and demanding, but the commitment of those who signed up was absolute from the outset, as Mair Russell-Jones explained:

> Despite the shift pattern and the exhaustion and disorientation, there was an exhilaration to it all. I remember someone saying to me that we were on the intellectual frontline. Our warfare wasn't with bullets or bombs but a constant battle with encrypted codes and phoney messages. Every day was like looking for a needle in a

haystack, except that the needle was barely visible and the quantity of hay terrifying. This was my war.[64]

The work that the codebreakers did, however, had practical consequences, which occasionally reminded those working at Bletchley that the war wasn't very far away. Gwen Watkins, a codebreaker in the German Air Section, recalls:

> One day, because I could read the schrift,* I was taken to see this code book that had been captured from an airplane that had been shot down. The blood on it hadn't clotted yet. That brought the war very close.[65]

There is no doubting the fact that the work of the codebreakers paid significant dividends. Rozanne Colchester (née Medhurst) who worked in the Italian Air Section, was one codebreaker who saw her work result in an important victory for the Allies:

> I was a decodist at the Park, and one night on duty I was decoding a message freshly arrived on the teleprinter. After many trials and errors [. . .] the groups of numbers began to make sense. Italian bombers were leaving Tripoli to fly to Sicily at 04:00 hours. Imagine the thrill – it was then 01:30. Radio messages were sent to the RAF [. . .] and, consequently, all the Italian aircraft were shot down.[66]

1940 and 1941 were particularly bleak years, when the focus was largely on keeping the enemy from Britain's shores. Germany's ally Italy[67] was becoming an increasing

* The script or writing.

problem, with Mussolini declaring the Mediterranean '*mare nostrum*', a Roman term literally meaning 'our sea'. Bletchley had anticipated the entry of Italy into the war and, as early as March 1939, a Bletchley outpost section – known as the Middle East Intelligence Centre (MEIC) – consisting of a small team of codebreakers, led by Marie Rose Egan, had been set up in Cairo. Their job was to exploit on the spot Italian high-grade traffic,[68] the traffic on which Anderson and her colleagues at Bletchley depended.

There were two problems, however. Firstly, although Bletchley codebreakers had all but completely mastered Italian armed services ciphers by the time Italy entered the war, unfortunately for them, the Italians decided to change all their codebooks at the outbreak of hostilities in June 1940, and the process had to begin again from scratch. British commanders increasingly relied on being fed information from Bletchley, which enabled them to anticipate and forestall enemy operational moves, and until these new Italian codes could be broken – requiring a consistent flow of high-grade traffic from Italian military, air and naval sources on which to work – British armed forces were running blind. If the interception of transmissions was interrupted, vital 'real time' intelligence gathering would grind to a halt. The other problem was that the various 'Y' stations in the region were used by the air, naval and military to intercept traffic, but they only consulted with GC&CS if they needed help with a specific piece of traffic. As a result, there was insufficient and irregular 'joined-up' collaboration between the various arms of the armed forces, something that Anderson found increasingly frustrating. When delays began to be experienced in the interception of Italian traffic from North Africa, resulting in a significant decline in forwarding intercepts to Bletchley via increasingly congested radio links, the situation required a decisive response. At the heart of that response was Emily Anderson.

All told, Anderson spent just under a year working at Bletchley, from August 1939 to July 1940. For the next three years, another crucial phase in her codebreaking career would see her considerable skills deployed on a very specific target: demolishing the Italian military machine in East and North Africa from her new base in Cairo.

14

Cairo and Combined Bureau Middle East

The decision to send Emily Anderson to Cairo[1] in 1940 was as much a matter of push as it was pull. In May 1940, the commander-in-chief Middle East sent a telegram to Denniston that outlined in bald terms the gravity of the situation in the region:

> Establishment in Cairo of sections from G.C.C.S. is now considered urgent. At present Sarafand[2] Cryptography Section already overloaded with Italian military plus Russian [. . .] If war front develops whole situation will become totally inadequate with serious delays and overloading of cables in transmissions to and from London. Recommend you despatch urgently by air two more fully trained Italian cryptographers as nucleus for centre to which additions will be made by locally trained personnel.[3]

Having received such a serious and urgent communication, Denniston's first reaction was significant: at the top of the page, in blue and underlined, he wrote the word 'Emily'. The following day in a cable from MI8[4] to Colonel Jacob, Acting Head of Military Section GC&CS, the need for Italian cryptographers was made even more explicit:

> Strongly urge best solution whole problem send Italian crypto staff Egypt to deal with CA A1 CR6[5] and other material now being wired you.

The word CR6 was underlined in blue, and a line drawn, again leading to one word: 'Emily'.[6]

Sending a group of expert Italian cryptographers who could hit the ground running was only possible if staff such as Anderson were prepared to be transferred, and if they had the support network to allow them to work in collaboration with their military, naval and RAF cryptographer colleagues. Anderson was more than ready to go; in fact, she had insisted on going and, what's more, was prepared to move section and take a demotion to make it happen. She was acutely aware that with the probability of delays and overloading of cables in transmissions compromising the delivery of Italian traffic by the day, something needed to be done, and quickly. Denniston can hardly have been surprised, then, to find Anderson beating a path to his office to request of him exactly what he was preparing to request of her. A report on what transpired noted that:

> Miss Emily Anderson of the Foreign Office who was working on the ITALIAN diplomatic and colonial ciphers, was becoming [disturbed] at the growing possibility of separation from her source of traffic and requested that she and her assistant might be sent out to continue their work on the spot.[7]

Significantly, the original typed report, written by Nigel de Grey, was amended such that the word 'fretful' was crossed out and the word 'disturbed' handwritten in the margin. Emily Anderson was not a woman of such a nervous disposition that she was likely to become 'fretful' about anything, and de Grey, a colleague of many years' standing, would have known that only too well. It is equally significant that Anderson was very specific that 'her assistant', i.e. Dorothy Brooks, should accompany her to Cairo.

Anderson's work on Italian diplomatic and colonial communications was reliant on a steady supply of intercepts arriving by bag (i.e. arriving in paper form and transported via air or sea transport in a special secured mailbag) from Sarafand. By May 1940, she informed Denniston that her supply of bags had dried up almost completely, hence her desire to be closer to her traffic.[8] The answer was clear: there was a need for an inter-service cryptologic and signals intelligence centre for the Middle East, which would handle naval, air and military traffic promptly. The result was the establishment of the Combined Bureau Middle East (CBME), which was based in Cairo and, as the name implied, represented a pooling of cryptanalytical resources. In practice, CBME comprised only an army and RAF section – there was no naval section due to the failure of GC&CS to break the new naval book-ciphers, and the decision by the Navy to concentrate naval SIGINT in Alexandria, not Cairo. CBME became the major Bletchley Park outstation in the region following its opening in Heliopolis, a suburb of Cairo, in late 1940.[9] CBME supported the combined military operation to push the Italian invading force back out of Egypt. It was to achieve this, and a great deal more besides. CBME served a number of important roles, the most critical of which was the sending of Ultra* intelligence from Bletchley Park to officers in the field.

The Italian declaration of war, followed soon after by the collapse of France in June 1940,[10] brought matters to a head. Italy's entry into the war had come about as a result of Mussolini's opportunism, and his ego. In June 1940, when France was about to fall and it seemed that the war was virtually over, Italy joined on Germany's side, with the hope of winning territorial spoils in Africa from the defeated Allies. The British Commander-in-Chief in the Middle East, General Sir Archibald Wavell, highlighted the key role that Mussolini's pride had played in the decision:

> Musso looks to me rather like a man who has climbed up to the top diving board at a swimming pool, taken off his dressing-gown and thrown a chest to the people looking on. I think he must do something. If he cannot make a graceful dive, he will at least have to jump in somehow; he can hardly put on his dressing-gown and walk down the stairs again.[11]

With the need to establish a crack cryptographic unit in Cairo increasing by the day, the army was insisting that a senior person be sent there to handle the military issues. Anderson's metier had always been diplomatic traffic, but Italian military cryptographers were in short supply, and to her credit Anderson was prepared to switch gears, step out of her comfort zone, and deploy her considerable skills

---

* The term 'Ultra' was used to convey the status of the intelligence gathered by breaking encrypted radio communications, which was considered to be above 'Top Secret'.

against Italian military traffic on the ground in Cairo. It was a brave move, which, crucially, she did not have to make. She was sufficiently senior in the organisation that she could easily have sat out the war at Bletchley, working on Italian diplomatic traffic, or any other diplomatic traffic that came her way. She opted instead to go where she was needed most – indeed, insisted upon it – even though this put both herself and her team in the firing line, as it involved a gruelling and dangerous sea journey and traversing the entire length of Africa. Quite apart from the dangers inherent in taking on the assignment, it also transpired that, for procedural reasons, Anderson could not be both Head of the Italian Diplomatic Section and of the Italian Military Section, because these systems were distinct. She therefore relinquished her position as Head of the Italian Diplomatic Section, and never held the role again for the remainder of her career.

The decision to move a large party of codebreakers to Egypt was not welcomed in all quarters at Bletchley. William Clarke of the Naval Section was furious at the decision, and his resentment of how it had come about accounts for the fact that he does not mention Emily Anderson at any point in his extensive memoirs: memoirs which have since coloured much of the history of SIGINT in the First and Second World Wars. A former Room 40 naval man at heart, from the early 1930s Clarke had become frustrated at the degree to which 'codebreakers and intercept operators were increasingly being asked to work on diplomatic material at the expense of service traffic'.[12] Clarke, a man capable of paranoia when it came to work colleagues, may have felt threatened by Anderson's obvious abilities, and he wrote in disparaging terms of 'the stupidity of the detached section in Egypt, which had been established in spite of my protests while I was away for an operation'.[13] Clarke was out of step with the general consensus that victory in the war would depend to a large degree on defeating the Italians by all and every means available as quickly as possible. Given its later success in East Africa, the decision to move the cryptographic unit to Cairo proved to be anything but stupid.

Once the decision had been made to establish CBME, it was a matter of acting as quickly as possible – so quickly, in fact, that Dorothy Brooks had to be paid an advance of £20 to cover her travelling expenses, and neither woman 'left any instructions as to their salaries' or allowances.[14] The official account of what happened next is remarkable:

> Air passage was no longer practicable, and the following set forth for CAIRO by the long sea route, leaving LIVERPOOL on board the 'Windsor Castle' on July 18th, 1940
>
> Capt. C.G. Irving-Bell, Royal Norfolk Regiment
> Lieut E. A. Brooks, General List
> 2/Lieut R.J. Politzer, General List
> Miss E. Anderson
> Miss D. Brooks[15]
>
> In the same party, all from G.C.C.S., there travelled Commander J. Murray R.N., who was to join the naval section at Alexandria; Flight-Lieut A. Vlasto, who was going to SARAFAND to do RUSSIAN; and Messrs R. A. Nicholson and J. Richmond who were to join the RAF cryptographic section being built up at HELIOPOLIS under Miss M. R. Egan.[16]

The *Windsor Castle* was an RAF freight ship, and its ultimate destination was Durban. First-class passage was booked for Anderson and Brooks, per Denniston's instructions.[17] The report, written in August 1940, subsequently records that:

> After an uneventful voyage, but a long and interrupted overland journey from the CAPE to CAIRO by train and plane, the party landed at ALMAZA[18] aerodrome on August 21st and were met by Captain JENNINGS and Lieuts PINK and WESTERN. Within a few days of arrival Lieut BROOKS proceeded to SARAFAND to assist Major WALLACE. Lieuts BOARDMAN and CARR were then posted elsewhere.[19]

'Long and interrupted' was one way of describing the journey to Cairo. The passport of Dorothy Brooks,[20] issued on 27 June 1940,[21] records the odyssey upon which the party embarked following the arrival of the *Windsor Castle* at Durban, South Africa, on 5 August 1940. Anderson and her team's move to Cairo had been eventful to say the least. She wrote to Denniston shortly after their arrival, detailing the various events of their journey, and although not all of her letters appear in the official record,[22] Denniston's response to them does, and indicates that it had been a chaotic and on occasion amusing journey. Denniston wrote:

> I may say these letters are now on their way around the school[23] because they are full of a very amusing story about your trip. I think there is no doubt you got mixed up with another party and you missed your

direct connection which had been arranged for you. From your letters I gather this was a good thing for you saw a lot more than you were intended to. Now you are safely there and I gather hard at work on product-ive subjects.[24]

How the high-profile Bletchley group became 'mixed up with another party' and missed their connection is unclear, but they made the best of it and organised alternative arrangements to get to Cairo. The party travelled through the British-held territories of South Africa and Rhodesia, through the Belgian Congo (courtesy of diplomatic transit visas),[25] and onwards through Anglo-Egyptian Sudan and into Egypt via a combination of trains and planes. Three weeks later, and over five weeks since they had departed Liverpool, they arrived in Cairo on 23 August 1940. One small vignette from their adventures comes from a niece of Dorothy Brooks,[26] who recalls that when the Bletchley party took the train from Cape Town on the first leg of their onward journey, Dorothy inadvertently left her hand-bag on the station platform. The bag was found and handed in to the authorities, a flurry of communications ensued and, with remarkable efficiency, the bag eventually caught up with her at another station. It proved an auspi-cious start to the mission.

CBME was opened in Cairo in late 1940, with an out-station located in Nairobi. As the signals intelligence centre for the Middle East, it comprised army and air force staff working on signals intelligence, and was headed up by Colonel Freddie Jacob of Bletchley Park's army section. The bureau was linked by radio to Whaddon Hall, which served as headquarters of Section VIII (Communications) of MI6, and the 'Station X' wireless interception function had been transferred here from Bletchley Park in February 1940. Colonel Frederick ('Freddie') Jacob had served as a captain in the Queen's Regiment at the battle of the Somme, where he was wounded and mentioned in despatches. Thereafter, he had served in Aden, Egypt and Palestine. He retired as a colonel after service in Egypt under Generals Auchinleck and Alexander. Married to his combat and leadership skills was his familiarity with cryptology – he was a natural cryptologist, who would later make an important contribution to the breaking of the German ENIGMA code while working at Bletchley. Liked and trusted by Denniston, his familiarity with the Middle East made him the perfect candidate to become Director of CBME in 1940, and Jacob proved more than up to the task.

The journey to Cairo made a continuance of normal cryptographic work impossible, and provided Anderson and her team with the first proper rest from their codebreaking work they'd had since the war began. They arrived physically tired, but mentally refreshed and ready for the challenges to come. Moreover, the city to which they had arrived was in all respects a complete antidote to the wartime Britain they had left behind. Denniston inferred as much in a letter to Anderson, in which he was uncharacteristically intimate, something that reflected their long-standing working relationship:

> I envy you your present surroundings, you will remember your drives home on the slippery roads during the Black-out, that is our prospect for the next two months while you regard the pyramids with the moon shining on them.[27]

Denniston clearly envied Anderson her posting in sunnier climes, and in a separate letter to Jacob remarked: 'We are settling down to what I consider a couple of mouldy months and then I hope for a pleasant Spring with real activities.'[28] But it was not just the pleasant weather he envied. The team at CBME experienced nothing of the horrors of the sustained campaign of aerial bombing attacks on British towns and cities carried out by the Luftwaffe from September 1940 until May 1941. Anderson and her colleagues missed the worst of the Blitz, particularly during their first weeks in Cairo when, from 7 September 1940, and for fifty-seven nights in a row, 'the bombing of London was unceasing'.[29] Three weeks after Anderson's arrival in Egypt, the Italians entered the country, occupying Sollum on 13 September. Nonetheless, the Cairo in which Anderson and her colleagues were to spend the next few years was in stark contrast to the London they had left behind. Apart from the sunny weather and the absence of rationing, King Farouk's grandfather, Ismail the Magnificent, had spent lavishly to rebuild the city in the style of Paris. As a result, Cairo was the most Westernised city in the Middle East, well supplied with good hotels, restaurants, country clubs, swimming pools and golf courses offering a vibrant and glamorous social life. Celebrities, including film stars and visiting royalty from the West, constantly passed through Cairo. Raymond Hare, who served as Second Secretary at the US Embassy in Cairo from 1939–44, recalled of his time there:

Life was a sort of mixture of military, political and social. It was a whirlwind sort of place where everything was happening; people were going along having parties and at the same time people were out fighting in the desert. You went to a party and several British officers might approach the hostess and say they were sorry but they were due back to the desert, while a couple of others might show up a bit dusty, and having heard that a party was going on they came along to join in.[30]

Although the CBME had initially established itself in a flat in 'Grey Pillars' (the main GHQ* building), it soon became clear that more space would be needed, and the cryptographic and wireless traffic sections moved to a building opposite the Kasr-El-Nil barracks, where the top floor was fitted out for offices and sleeping accommodation, and masts were erected on the roof. Neither Anderson nor Brooks lived at the barracks until their permanent billet was ready. A letter written by Anderson to the Foreign Office[31] gave her address as 'c/o British Embassy, Cairo', and a subsequent letter written to her by Denniston was addressed to her 'c/o H.M. Embassy, Cairo', so it appears that she and Brooks were temporarily accommodated at the British Embassy. In September 1940, Colonel Jacob arrived to take command of CBME, and act as the main liaison between it and GC&CS. That same month, Commander G. A. Titterton (a pre-war member of GC&CS[32] subsequently posted to the Middle East) wrote to Denniston informing him that he had attended a lunch party in Cairo that included Emily Anderson and Dorothy Brooks, at which they 'drank the health of Absent Friends in various concoctions (Emily A. drank tomato-juice having just been inoculated)'.[33]

* General Head Quarters

It is unclear what disease Anderson had been inoculated against,[34] but she did at one point contract a disease that was practically an occupational hazard of living in Egypt: dysentery. In mid-September 1940, reference is made in a CBME memo to Anderson having been struck down with dysentery to the degree that she had to be hospitalised.[35] Nonetheless, Anderson appeared to be happy with the move to Cairo, and in a letter to Denniston revealed the degree to which her enjoyment of the work, and her happiness at being in Cairo, was not solely professional, but also had a personal dimension to it:

> We are both well and now that the pleasantly cool weather has come we feel very fit and energetic. Major Jacob is a most able and sympathetic head of our company and we are both very happy in our present working conditions. We have not yet heard when we are to be moved to Heliopolis [. . .] Please give my most cordial greetings to my friends at the Park and the School. With kindest regards from us both.[36]

Evidence of just what that personal dimension was is provided in a letter from Jacob to Denniston written on the same day as he forwarded the letter from Anderson. A cheery and upbeat Jacob informed Denniston that:

> We are all in harmony here as far as my own section goes and indeed with the senior and junior service. We look forward to our new [quarters] in early December. Emily & 'family' are doing great work & have some bright lads of mine assisting them.[37]

Jacob's pointed use, in inverted commas, of the term 'family' could only be a reference to Dorothy Brooks, who in addition to the two 'bright lads' Jacob refers to, i.e. Corporals Davies and Petersen, comprised the four-person Italian codebreaking section. The use of the word 'family' in this context has long been a euphemism for the acknowledgement of a same-sex relationship. This, taken in combination with Anderson's familiar and repeated use of the term 'we' in her letter, would seem to infer that the relationship between Anderson and Brooks went beyond the purely professional. Whether Brooks had been the partner with whom Anderson had previously shared her billet in Swanbourne cannot be confirmed definitively, as there is no documentary evidence to support this, and Patricia Bartley, who had met both women, identified Anderson quite clearly but could not put a name to the other woman. However, Bartley's description of a woman much younger than Anderson, and her confirmation that both women left the Bartley home at the same time, and that Anderson's destination was Cairo, would appear to confirm that Brooks was the woman with whom Anderson had been in a same-sex relationship since shortly after her arrival at Bletchley, and during her time in Cairo.

*

Until the advent of the gay rights movement in the late 1960s, being homosexual meant being subjected to a life of secret codes and special rules in one's private and professional life. For men, in particular, it was a criminal offence to have sexual relations with other men, and the penalties for engaging in such activities were severe. Gay women, while they were exempt from prosecution, were nonetheless pressured by society to keep their relationships with other women discreet or face social ostracism, prejudice, or even dismissal from their jobs. Anderson appears to have had no such qualms, believing, it would seem, that her private life was no one's business but her own. As we have seen, she made no secret of the fact that she wished to share a billet, and a bed, with her female partner – indeed, she had insisted upon it by orchestrating the move from the Manor House to the Bartley's home in Swanbourne. Now, in Cairo, it appears that Anderson was sufficiently senior to assume that her relationship with Dorothy would be facilitated, and Jacob's tacit acknowledgement of the same in his comment to Denniston seems to imply that Denniston was also aware of Emily's relationship status, and from a management perspective had no difficulty with it. The women were allowed to enjoy the same freedoms they had had at Bletchley, and, as far as society allowed, they appear to have been happy, and highly productive, in each other's company.

Dorothy Edith Brooks was born on 26 July 1915 in Lambeth, London, to Frederick William Brooks and Ethel Carrie Newman. Involvement with telecommunications was something of a family trait, with Frederick having begun his career as a telegraphist in the GPO. He had served as a sergeant in the Royal Engineers (telephones) during the First World War, and, by 1939, while his daughter was decoding enemy signals at Bletchley and in Cairo, William Brooks was serving as a lieutenant in the Royal Navy Reserve, showing people how to send and receive signals. Having graduated with a degree in French from University College, London, in July 1936[38] with a second class (upper-division) degree, Dorothy had planned to be a teacher, but when there were no teaching jobs available, she sat the civil service exam, and as a result of her language

proficiency was recruited to the Foreign Office, later joining the Commercial Section at Bletchley as a translator.[39]
By 1940, her personal and professional relationship with
Anderson had developed to such a degree that Anderson
insisted that Brooks accompany her on the mission to Cairo.
It is important to note, however, that it was not just a case
of Anderson not wishing to be separated from her partner
for entirely personal reasons. Dorothy Brooks was very
much deserving of her place on the mission to Cairo. At
Bletchley, she had honed her translation skills to become an
excellent codebreaker. The Brooks family were typical of so
many working-class families who had 'bettered' themselves
as a result of education, and by dint of their own hard work
and abilities. They were also made of stern stuff, and Brooks
was not the only member of her family to be subsequently
honoured for their actions during the war. By the time
Dorothy was sent to Cairo, her younger brother, Douglas
Brooks, was a pilot serving as Lieutenant Commander in
the Fleet Air Arm on the aircraft carriers HMS *Indomitable*
and HMS *Victorious*. He was awarded two DSCs[40] in the
course of his career.

*

Emily Anderson was forty-nine when she went to Cairo
(Dorothy Brooks was twenty-five), and it is worth considering that the move there, and the remarkable results that the
team working under her direction achieved, came about at
a time in her life when she was perhaps at her most content.
She had published *The Letters of Mozart and his Family* to
popular acclaim, and was already working on the Beethoven letters. The need for cryptographers expert in
Italian was now paramount, and Anderson, acknowledged

as one of the foremost Italian crypto experts, had assumed the role of Head of the Italian Military Section at CBME. And, finally, she was in a relationship with a woman who was her intellectual equal, whom she could openly partner inside and outside their work environment, and who made her happy. Ironically, it would later transpire that the beginning of the end of the relationship that brought her so much happiness had occurred on the outward voyage to Cairo.

The move from the barracks to the new permanent base for CBME occurred on 10 December 1940.[41] The former Flora and Fauna Museum in Heliopolis was a large, imposing building. Although its proximity to Heliopolis airport made it 'an excellent target for bombing raids', it was 'nevertheless a tough building [. . .] and palatial.'[42] The building had the added advantage that much of its interior was constructed of marble,[43] making it an enviably cool sanctuary in which staff could escape the worst of the searing Egyptian heat.[44] Now that they had a permanent base in which to live, and an operational headquarters, the work of Anderson and her team of codebreakers could begin in earnest.

Denniston's observation that Anderson was 'hard at work on productive subjects' was true. At Bletchley, she had worked on a number of Italian codebooks, but in Cairo, unfolding events made it necessary to prioritise operational traffic within East Africa.[45] Her focus shifted to a number of new books, the most important of which became known as 'CIT'. This book (previously known as CR5c) had been introduced in 1938, and was originally used for colonial traffic between Rome and Addis Ababa. Anderson had broken into it at the beginning of 1939, and she took the book with her to Cairo and resumed work on it in the autumn of 1940. In a stroke of luck, the book was being used by the Italians for high-grade military traffic within East Africa. The repurposing of a colonial codebook (viz CR 5c) for high-grade military traffic was symptomatic of the problems encountered by the Italians in East Africa, owing to their isolation from metropolitan Italy and the distances over which codebooks and tables had to be distributed. Material was not changed as often as it should have been to ensure secure communications, a mistake that was to cost the Italians dearly. It is for good reason that the East Africa Campaign was later described as 'the perfect example of the cryptographers' war'.[46]

Although later overshadowed by British defeats in Crete and Greece, the East African campaign, fought between June 1940 and November 1941, became the first significant victory for the Allies in the Second World War. Also known as the Abyssinian campaign, it was fought by the British Middle East Command[47] against Italy and its colony of Italian East Africa.[48] East Africa was of strategic importance to the British in the Middle East, as it flanked the vital sea-route from the Gulf of Aden to Suez. By November 1940, the Allies had gained a significant intelligence advantage when the high-grade cipher of the Italian Royal Army (Regio Esercito) was broken at Bletchley. With everything depending on defeating the Italians in East Africa, Anderson and her team combined their efforts with their colleagues in the Air Section and threw everything they had at cracking the replacement cipher for the Italian Royal Air Force (Regia Aeronautica). Anderson informed Denniston: 'I have worked up quite an important section consisting of ourselves[49] and two N.C.Os, Davies and Petersen, both of whom are doing first class work'.[50] Her confidence was justified, because by then she and

Brooks had identified and solved three reciphering systems all using the same book – CR5c – which had first been introduced in November 1938. Anderson described two of the variants as 'exceedingly simple' and the third 'quite manageable',[51] and she renamed this book CIT.[52]

It was now a race between code-maker and codebreaker, but breaking into CIT was no easy matter. CIT code was transmitted in 'reciphered' form, affording greater protection by adding an additional step to the encryption process. After the plain language text had been replaced by five figure groups obtained from the codebook, the coded message was then disguised, or 'reciphered' by combining each code group with another group of five figures, known as a key group, taken consecutively from a reciphering table. Reciphered codes and their solutions were nothing new; Anderson would have been very familiar with them, and Dorothy Brooks became so. This was old-school pencil-and-paper cryptography at its most basic and most intense; there was no tabulating machinery at CBME, and there is no indication that data was sent back to Bletchley for processing. Notwithstanding the intense pressure Anderson and her team were under, Jacob jauntily wrote to Denniston, informing him that:

> Emily A. is doing great work (as is everyone here), and we are having a great time with cribs, between the book CIT (CR5C) which she is working on and the old Air Force book in East Africa.[53]

Looking for cribs in recycled code groups (a common enough practice as part of the pressures of wartime cryptography) was Anderson's speciality, one at which she was particularly adept following her years working in diplomatic SIGINT, and as a result she was in her element. It soon became clear that CIT 'contained very important operation (air and land) material'. Anderson reported that she and her team were 'working full tilt at it (running three ideas) in order to bring it up to a readable state in the shortest possible time'.[54] They were not working in isolation. CBME was in regular contact with colleagues in the Air Section at Bletchley. The Head of the Air Section was a former protégé of Anderson's, Josh Cooper. Primarily a Russian expert, he had subsequently served for a time in the Naval Section, and in 1936 he had been appointed as Head of the new Air Section at GC&CS. His early Italian training under Anderson stood him in good stead, and although faced with competing demands on all sides, and with limited interceptor sets and operators available to him, he nonetheless provided a steady supply of Italian intercepts to her in Cairo. Such collaboration proved critical, and although, in her usual blunt manner, Anderson reported to Denniston that '[t]he Rome outward material taken in England and wired out to us is quite insufficient for the purpose of solving a daily subtractor',[55] it was enough to help in the process of so doing, and the breaking of CIT in record time proved that.

The Air Section had been in existence in Cairo since March 1939, and while Anderson's team arrived refreshed and rested in August 1940, the pressures of the work were beginning to tell on those who had been there a good deal longer. A memo sent to Denniston in October 1940 advised him that the section's head, Marie Rose Egan, had been 'overworked for months' and was 'urgently requiring a rest'.[56] Egan had been sent to Cairo in 1939 for exploitation of on the spot of Italian air force high-grade cipher traffic.[57] Born in France in 1914 to a French mother, a member of a notable French family, and an Irish father from a wealthy family of wine merchants, Egan's family later moved to London, where she grew up. She graduated with a BA in French, German and Italian from University College, London, in 1935 – the year before Dorothy Brooks graduated from the same college with the same degree, so they may well have known one another. Through some unknown connection, Egan joined GC&CS just after graduation and, much as Anderson had done in 1918, she soon impressed her colleagues with her abilities, and Denniston quickly appointed her as a Junior Assistant to keep her in the service. In March 1939, Egan, another Junior Assistant, Flying Officer Fischer-Sobell, and two women translating plain language Italian voice for Air Intelligence, moved to Cairo and established a SIGINT base for the RAF under Egan's direction. This deployment was a significant development, as it abandoned GC&CS's older view that women could not serve in combat areas, and Whitehall knew that war with Italy was a distinct possibility. Anderson, similarly, was sent to the Middle East to take a post that many in that theatre would have expected a man to fill. Yet both women more than measured up to the challenge, and Egan and Anderson – two women with Irish roots – subsequently 'ravaged Italian cryptosystems, an underrated triumph stemming from female prowess',[58] and oversaw the attacks on Italian air and army traffic during the desert campaign, which approached Ultra in value during 1941 and much of 1942.[59]

Italian dependence on wireless communications yielded vast amounts of crucial information, and, working in tandem, CBME and the Air and Military Sections at Bletchley

Emily's mother, Emily Gertrude, is seated with Emily standing on left, and her sister Elsie seated right. Standing behind is Elisa Curtet, the children's Swiss governess.

Emily, aged 9 or 10, pictured on Queen's College, Galway's grounds, on the banks of the River Corrib.

Emily's father, Professor Alexander Anderson, President of Queen's College, Galway.

Arthur Andrews, also know as Alexander Anderson, with his wife Lilian.

The female staff of MI1(b) on the roof of their offices at Cork Street, London, 1919. Major Hay is pictured centre, and Emily Anderson is seated in the second row on the left, leaning against the chimney. Miss Carleton is seated immediately to the left of Major Hay, and Claribel Spurling is seated to the right, with her back to the chimney.

Commander Alastair Denniston, Anderson's long-time boss, colleague and friend.

Patricia Bartley (later Brown), Head of German Diplomatic section at Bletchley Park at the age of just 24.

Bletchley Park, also known as 'Station X'. Commander Denniston's office was the room with the bay window to the left of the main door.

Emily Anderson pictured in Cairo. On the extreme right is Colonel Jacob, commanding officer of CBME Cairo. The officer pictured centre may be Major George Wallace, head of 5IS at Cairo.

The British Embassy at Cairo, where Emily and Dorothy Brooks stayed during their time in Egypt.

Dorothy Brooks, visiting the pyramids at Mina, with Colonel Jacob on the right, and another officer, possibly Major Wallace, on the left.

The offices of GC&CS at 8 Berkeley Street, London, 1942. The offices were located above a dress shop (pictured with an awning) on the ground floor.

The staff of the German Diplomatic Section at Berkeley Street. Seated at the front, wearing glasses, is Ernst Fetterlein; Patricia Bartley stands to his left.

Dr Dagmar Weise pictured in 1952, shortly before she began working with Emily Anderson on the Beethoven Letters.

A musical soirée in the home of Gerald Gover and his wife in Hampstead. Anderson is seated in the front row, third from the left.

Hans Conrad Bodmer, Emily's good friend and owner of the largest and most significant private collections of Beethoven material. Bodmer later donated his collection to the Beethoven Haus Archive in Bonn.

Emily's piano, currently in the care of Timothy and Elena Sidwell.

The only studio portrait of Emily Anderson known to exist. The photo was taken at the behest of Macmillan publishing to help promote the publication of Anderson's *The Letters of Beethoven* in 1961. Here, it is inscribed to her friend Dagmar.

were accessing enemy intelligence 'of a spectacular nature'.[60] In the last three months of 1940 alone, Bletchley provided 2,600 solutions of Italian army traffic in Libya; Anderson's team produced 8,000.[61] Having cracked one Italian cipher after another, Anderson and her colleagues were able to read Italian battle plans in Libya and Ethiopia. Daily reports sent by the Italian viceroy in Addis Ababa to Rome were intercepted by CBME, read, and the information forwarded to the British military, often before their intended recipients received them. As a result of such intelligence, British armed forces were able to anticipate and subvert Italian plans such that Britain defeated and captured an Italian army of 140,000 men (five times larger than its own forces) in Libya, and an Italian army of 370,000 men in Ethiopia (three times larger than British forces there). If RAF and army commanders had ever doubted the importance of SIGINT and 'Y' information, the East Africa campaign put an end to any such doubts.

It was later noted:

> The flood of intelligence was not confined to any one sector or level of command, but was general throughout the whole area of operations and throughout the whole chain of command from the Viceroy down to the commander of the smallest garrison detachment. Never, indeed, can the commander of an army have had such an unfailing access to the plans of his opponent, or such precise particulars of the disposition or intended movements of the opposing forces.[62]

Intercepts of Italian signals revealed operational details, such as order of battle plans, troop numbers and the supply situation, as well as messages from Prince Amedeo, 3rd

Duke of Aosta, Commander-in-Chief of all Italian military forces in East Africa.[63] The speed and accuracy with which the 'Y' signals being intercepted were used to great effect in operational plans is made clear in a letter sent by the Director of Intelligence in November 1940.

> It is not a time to give or receive bouquets, but Fighter Command has put in writing the statement that there have been several recent instances where information provided has proved of immediate practical value to the Command, including the successful interception and infliction of loss upon the Italian Squadron and the German dive-bombers the next day. I think you will like to let your people know how very grateful we are for all their hard work and efficiency.[64]

The following month, the operation in Cairo suffered something of a setback when the CIT codebook and reciphering tables were captured in a raid. Knowing that their cipher had been compromised, the Italians introduced new reciphering tables.[65] Fortunately for CBME, all was not lost, as due to time restraints and a lack of cryptologic resources, they did not replace the underlying codebook itself. As a result, two variants of the new reciphering tables were solved by Anderson, albeit 'with difficulty' due to the lack of raw material available to work with.[66] Anderson and her team made the reading of the new reciphered CIT their priority and, by early 1941, CIT was once again beginning to yield valuable operational intelligence.[67]

In early December 1940, Commander Denniston wrote to Anderson 'to wish you and Miss Brooks and the rest of the party a very cheerful Christmas and every success in the job in which you are now engaged'.[68] A remarkable souvenir of that first Christmas spent in Cairo survives.[69] Dorothy Brooks' family, who in spite of security protocols were clearly aware that her destination was Cairo, recorded a message to her via a phonograph record. The recording features Brooks' parents, uncles and aunts singing a specially composed song performed to piano accompaniment. The song is a cheery ditty wishing Dorothy a happy Christmas and New Year in Cairo. Beginning with the salutation 'We send good wishes from over the sea', the song acknowledges that Dorothy is going 'such a long way'. Family members identify themselves in the chorus at the end of each verse: 'your mother, your father, Aunt Edith, Uncle Charlie' . . . etc, before the entire group sing 'and the rest of the family' together. It is a plucky, touching and poignant recording, which must have meant a great deal to Dorothy when she received it, and no doubt she would have played it for her friends and colleagues, including Anderson. The recording ends with some personal messages, including from one of her aunts – 'God bless you, Dorothy, have a ride on a camel for me whilst you're out there!', and one of her uncles – 'Cheerio Dorothy, give my love to the Sphinx!'

Denniston's letter to Anderson of 4 December 1940[70] contained more than Christmas greetings to herself and Miss Brooks. In veiled terms, he enquired of her regarding:

> [. . .] certain books which were thought to be in your possession, on the subject on which you were engaged about 1933 and I am hopeful that we shall hear that they are in some safe place though I shall not be surprised to hear that they are no longer available. We are trying to start that subject again and the researches of K. and yourself would have been useful.[71]

The 'K' referred to was undoubtedly Dilly Knox, and the 'subject' on which he and Anderson had been working back in 1933 was made clear in a subsequent wire sent to Jacob: 'Ask Emily if she knows what she did with the HUNGARIAN books.' Having done so, Jacob replied: 'Tell Commander Denniston that Emily left HUNGARIAN books in strongroom.'[72] While we know from Cooper's account that Knox was working on Hungarian codes during the interwar period, this is confirmation that Anderson's skills during the same period had not been limited to Italian diplomatic traffic. It is highly significant that it was those he considered his two top cryptologists – Knox and Anderson – who were tasked by Denniston with working on codes in a language that is acknowledged as the most difficult of all European languages for an English speaker to master.[73] Hungary was one of the Axis powers, but at the same time as it was supporting Germany's efforts against the Red Army, Hungary was also initiating secret negotiations with the Allies, as it was fearful of what would come if the country was overrun by the Soviet Union and Bolshevism. Interest in Hungarian SIGINT increased significantly as a result. It is also worth noting that the ease and familiarity with which both Denniston and Jacob repeatedly refer to 'Emily' in correspondence conducted at the highest levels of the intelligence community is quite striking, and unique in official correspondence of the period. Denniston's high regard for Anderson's abilities is evident throughout the correspondence related to CBME. He wrote to her frequently, always addressing her formally as 'Miss Anderson', but when writing to Jacob often referring to her as 'Emily', a trait that Jacob reciprocated. Denniston greatly valued her codebreaking instincts and extensive experience, and in December 1940 sent an urgent telegram to Jacob and Anderson, enquiring: 'Have you ever seen any Italian book that answers the following description?' Anderson provided a definitive one-word reply: 'No'. Based on over twenty years' experience of working with her, that would have been enough for Denniston.[74]

By March 1941, Anderson's team had reconstructed the reciphering tables to the point that CIT could be fully exploited at the main point of interception. The intelligence gathered was immediately put to great effect in the field. In March 1941, for example, two signals drafted by the Commander-in-Chief of the Italian forces, the Duke of Aosta,[75] were intercepted, decrypted and sent to British military HQ on the same day. The signals contained a military situation report from the Italian perspective, and indicated their future operational plans, at the very moment they were being communicated to Italian field commanders. Aosta was planning to regroup his forces and form a new front at Gondar and at Amba Alagi.[76] As it transpired, the latter was astride the route along which General Wavell, Commander-in-Chief in the Middle East, planned to withdraw forces urgently needed to halt Rommel in Cyrenaica. Thanks to the intelligence received from CBME, Wavell's priority was to clear Italian forces from this road as swiftly as possible. By April 1941, Amba Alagi became the site of a 'last stand' on the part of the forces of the Duke of Aosta, who had withdrawn his forces to the mountain stronghold. British forces began an attack on Amba Alagi[77] on 4 May and, by 14 May, Amba Alagi was completely surrounded. The Italian commander began ceasefire negotiations two days later, and surrendered his garrison to Lieutenant-General Sir Alan Cunningham on

19 May 1941, an event recorded in a Pathé newsreel, marking the end of any significant Italian control in East Africa.[78] Colonel Jacob was well placed to appreciate the immediate impact the intelligence produced by Anderson and Brooks was having on the conduct of the East Africa campaign. Writing to Denniston, he noted: 'their work had been of the very greatest assistance to the Military and I may truthfully add had actually influenced the conduct of the campaign'.[79]

Back in Bletchley, the significant role played by women codebreakers in smashing the Italians mirrored that of Anderson, Brooks, Egan and their colleagues in Cairo. The Italian Naval Enigma machine had been broken in late March 1941 by Mavis Batey (née Lever), who, along with an all-female team of codebreakers, worked under Dilly Knox in The Cottage at Bletchley.[80] Batey deciphered a message that indicated the Italians were planning an attack on a Royal Navy convoy carrying supplies from Cairo to Greece. Convincing the enemy that their codes had not been broken and their plans discovered was essential, and Admiral Cunningham,[81] Commander of the Royal Navy's Mediterranean fleet, while secretly preparing his fleet to attack the Italians at Matapan, came up with a plan. Knowing that the Japanese consul in Alexandria, a keen golfer, was sending the Germans reports on the movement of the Mediterranean Fleet,

> Cunningham ostentatiously visited the clubhouse with his clubs and overnight bag, giving the impression that he was taking the weekend off to play golf. The Japanese consul conveyed this information to the Germans, who passed on to their Italian allies that their naval mission could proceed.[82]

Admiral Cunningham slipped out of the clubhouse under cover of darkness and resumed command of his forces. The subsequent Battle of Cape Matapan[83] saw the Royal Navy ambush an Italian convoy, resulting in three heavy cruisers and two destroyers, carrying 3,000 sailors, being sunk. On the evening of the Cape Matapan victory, Rear Admiral Godfrey, Director of Naval Intelligence, telephoned Dilly Knox at home and left a message: 'Tell Dilly that we have won a great victory in the Mediterranean, and it is entirely due to him and his girls.'[84] Mavis Batey recalled that, following the Matapan victory, Knox wrote the following 'epitaph to Mussolini':

> These have knelled your fall and ruin, but your
>   ears were far away
> English lassies rustling papers through the sodden
>   Bletchley day.[85]

Less sodden, but no less productive, were Anderson and her CBME colleagues, sweltering in the heat of Cairo. In comparison with the North Africa campaign, the use of SIGINT in the East Africa Campaign has, undeservedly, received very little attention. Anderson's achievements in breaking into and reading Italian ciphers, and the use to which information so gleaned could be put to work in the field of combat, was largely responsible for convincing the Commander-in-Chief in the Middle East, General Wavell, of the crucial strategic importance of SIGINT. Born in 1883, Wavell had served in the Second Boer War and the First World War, during which he was wounded at the Second Battle of Ypres, losing an eye.[86] On his appointment as Commander-in-Chief of the Middle East in February 1940, he was originally a cynic when it came to

SIGINT and its usefulness in battle. The breaking of Italian codes at Bletchley, and the intelligence thereby acquired, quickly convinced him. He came to recognise the value of codebreakers like Anderson as they began to produce SIGINT that enabled his forces to anticipate Italian moves in real time. His subsequent engagement with CBME was undoubtedly the decisive feature that brought about Allied victory in the East Africa Campaign, the first significant Allied victory of the war. Wavell was suitably grateful, and paid Anderson a remarkable compliment, which until now has not been recognised. In December 1940, Wavell decided that the 4th Indian division[87] – a crack force of experienced troops – would begin to move from the Western Desert to the Sudan, where they would be replaced, brigade by brigade, by the 6th Australian division. The name given to this special force was 'Force EMILY'.[88]

Wavell's victory in the Western Desert over numerically far superior Italian forces significantly boosted morale at a time of disaster in Europe. But in 1941, early successes against the Italians in Libya, Italian Somaliland and Ethiopia turned into costly failures in Greece and Crete, and a belief on the part of Churchill that Wavell was reluctant to act decisively. As a result, Wavell lost Churchill's confidence and his fate was sealed – he was replaced by General Auchinleck in June 1941. The change in personnel did not result in any diminution of the important role being played by CBME, however, and the team continued to provide essential intelligence to the Eight Army, such that by the summer of 1941, the integration of SIGINT with COMINT* and intelligence in formulating operations

* Communications Intelligence.

plans became the norm for British armed forces until the end of the war. Intercepts taken in the Middle East were transmitted to Bletchley, and solutions sent from Bletchley to Cairo. RAF Commanders also acknowledged that 'Y' information 'forms our most important source and is of direct operational use to us'.[89]

Their military colleagues were equally appreciative of the crucial role played by SIGINT in the victory in East Africa, with General Cunningham, acknowledging:

> [. . .] there can seldom in the history of war have been a campaign in which the Commander was so continuously served with accurate information of the enemy's movements and dispositions. The bulk of this information was received from 'Y' sources.[90]

Back at Bletchley, the system was under increasing strain as a result of tensions between civilian, service and intelligence staff due to the organisation's rapid growth, which had implications for the allocation of resources and manpower.[91] In January 1942, an inquiry had been launched, and its recommendations were put into effect the following month. Administration of GC&CS by the Joint Board of Control was abolished, and the civilian sections (i.e. those dealing with diplomatic and commercial cryptanalysis) were withdrawn from the Bletchley Park site and placed under the control of a deputy director (civilian). The service sections were also placed under a deputy director (service), who was responsible for all work carried out at Bletchley Park. In practical terms, it marked the end of Denniston's tenure as the operational head of what has become GCHQ. He and the Diplomatic Sections moved back to London, to Berkeley Street, and Commander

Edward 'Jumbo' Travis assumed overall command at Bletchley.

As head of the civilian sections, Denniston remained Anderson and Brooks' administrative boss. In recognition of the significant impact their work on the East Africa campaign had had it was recommended that Emily Anderson receive the OBE and Dorothy Brooks the MBE. Although the document making the original recommendation has not come to light, there is no doubt that it was submitted by Lieutenant Colonel Jacob. In October 1942, he wrote to Denniston to see if the latter could establish whether or not the necessary paperwork had been received in time. In this letter, Jacob confirmed that the nomination was in recognition of both women's work during the campaign against the Italians in East Africa:

> In April 1942 the names of Miss A & Miss B were submitted by me on Major Wallace's recommendation to DMI* for recognition of their very great services to the Military in doing quite invaluable work on S.I.† during the E.A. campaign [. . .][92]

The SIGINT for which Anderson and her team had been responsible had been instrumental in making possible the first Allied strategic victory in the war, but it had accomplished a great deal more than that. The East Africa campaign cost the Italians an army of around 220,000 men, and an empire in East Africa. The losses inflicted on the Italian forces also meant that very few Italian units had escaped the region to be used in other campaigns, and the

---

* Director of Military Intelligence.
† Signals intelligence.

Italian defeat significantly eased the flow of supplies through the Red Sea to Egypt, removing a major impediment to the Allied war effort going forward.

Back in England, Anderson's instincts regarding Patricia Bartley were being confirmed in spectacular fashion. By the spring of 1942, Bartley had been appointed Head of the German Diplomatic Section, and she and her team – which included the former Russian Tsar's personal cryptanalyst, Ernst Fetterlein, who had worked with Anderson in MI1(b) – were focused on breaking into Floradora, the German diplomatic code, and sister code to the better-known German military code, Enigma. Floradora was a double-additive cipher, which had been a notoriously difficult problem for GC&CS to break during the interwar period. During wartime, German diplomats developed lax practices in using Floradora, which Bartley was able to exploit, as she explains:

> Something did strike me. It was a repeat, which they should never do, repeat verbatim something that they have signalled. What we got was merely the menus for the seamen, that they thought they weren't getting enough [. . .] so it didn't give us any vital, exciting [information] but . . . [93]

The simple act of sailors complaining about the quantity and variety of food they were being fed – which necessitated a repetition of the contents of the menus – was sufficient for Bartley to make the initial break into Floradora. This was achieved through traffic intercepted between Berlin and the German Embassy in Dublin. After months of intense work, and due largely to the crucial repetition Bartley had identified, by May they 'were reading a small number of messages between the embassy in Dublin and Berlin. By August 1942 they were able to read every one.[94] Much as Anderson's ravaging of Italian codes had enabled allied commanders to know the enemy's plans, often before they were communicated to officers in the field, Bartley, when asked what the practical implication of breaking Floradora was, replied: 'It meant we were reading messages meant for Hitler before he read them.'[95] It was an astonishing achievement for a then twenty-four-year-old. Unsurprisingly, in October 1942,[96] Secretary of State and future prime minister Anthony Eden was moved to write to Bartley and her staff in the German Diplomatic Section on their success in breaking Floradora.[97] Eden wrote:

> It is a very remarkable achievement on the part of the Code and Cypher School to have broken this cypher. I have heard something of the months, and indeed years, of labour which the school have put into their task and I am more than delighted to know that their efforts have at last been rewarded with the success which they deserved. Will you please convey my warmest congratulations and thanks to all concerned?[98]

Bartley also received personal letters of commendation for the breakthrough from MI5 and the British Cabinet Secretary, Sir Edward Bridges.

*

Back in Cairo, by July 1942 the prospect of the Axis forces taking Cairo was becoming all too real for the staff of CBME. During the first Battle of El-Alamein, the German army under Rommel came to within 150 miles of Cairo.[99] As the threat of Rommel's forces breaking through grew, plans were made to evacuate Anderson and her team from Cairo swiftly to avoid their possible capture. The military section in CBME, 5IS,[100] wanted to enlist Anderson and Brooks in the ATS*[101] in July 1942 to ensure that, if Rommel's forces broke through, and 5IS had to evacuate, they could take Anderson and Brooks with them.[102] As it happens, this proved unnecessary, as British forces halted the Axis armies at El-Alamein in late July. But the battle was not yet won. A memo in August 1942 discussed the possibility of Anderson's team having to evacuate, and a plane was on standby to evacuate them to Sarafand.[103] In the event that air travel was not possible, provision was to be made to move CBME, complete with its intercept sets, to Advanced Air HQ in the Western Desert, then located with the 6th Army. Air Command concluded that there would 'inevitably be some danger' involved in attempting to move the section from Heliopolis, with possible 'enemy action impeding get-away of party in [an] emergency'.[104]

These were tense times for the staff of CBME. Marie Rose Egan's family recall her telling them that 'all the staff were living out of suitcases ready to evacuate when the Germans were rapidly advancing'. Some of the codebreakers were prepared to defend themselves in the event of any attempted capture by German forces; Egan recalled that 'she drove a car with hidden machine gun pointing backwards for a while'.[105] Rommel's forces were finally defeated at the second Battle of El-Alamein in November 1942, and the danger for Anderson and her team abated somewhat, but did not disappear completely.

* The Auxiliary Territorial Service was the women's branch of the British Army during the Second World War.

The beleaguered British contingent received a welcome boost when Churchill visited Cairo in August 1942.[106] Perceived weaknesses in the leadership of the British 8th Army facing Field Marshal Rommel's formidable AfrikaKorps[107] had convinced Churchill that it was 'urgently necessary for [him] to go there and settle the decisive questions on the spot'.[108] This he did at a meeting of all the senior officers of GHQ on 21 August. Prior to this meeting, however, there are accounts,[109] including from Anderson's boss, Lieutenant Colonel Jacob, of morale-boosting lunches and dinners he also attended. Churchill's engagement diaries are blank for overseas trips,[110] but we know he attended a dinner 'of notables' at the Cairo Embassy on 10 August, which included Jacob and senior members of his CBME staff. Although the names of those who accompanied Jacob are not provided, the list certainly would have included Anderson, given her seniority, her work on the successful East Africa campaign and Churchill's own keen interest in diplomatic SIGINT, of which he was known to be 'a prime user'.[111]

*

In spite of its remarkable successes, it was not until the summer of 1942 that SIGINT came to truly be regarded as 'an integral part of the conduct of war [. . .] and field SIGINT came to be fully integrated with other intelligence sources.' Prior to that, the SIGINT provided by Anderson and her colleagues was viewed by officers in the field as 'interesting rather than valuable'.[112] The pioneering work of CBME – and in particular Anderson's work on the East Africa Campaign – changed all that. Years of experience were finally paying dividends. As Wing Commander John Mapplebeck observed, 'A whole host of "intelligent beginners" will not replace one or two old hands,'[113] and Anderson was by then one of the oldest and most experienced hands in the business.

By the spring of 1943, with the German menace increasing just as the Italian threat was in decline, Anderson's time in Cairo was coming to an end. Denniston informed Jacob that: 'HG (high grade) key cracking in Cairo should be discontinued and key crackers repatriated <u>now</u>.' All the women in the Italian Section, with the exception of Egan, were to be repatriated as 'we are in urgent need of good key crackers'.[114] Colonel Jacob agreed that Anderson and Brooks 'should be repatriated as soon as possible as there is now nothing for them to do here'.[115] With the Italian threat in Africa dealt with, every available body with experience of book and subtractor systems was now needed to work on the new priority: Japanese traffic.[116] On 30 April, Anderson was given a letter of passage from the British Embassy in Cairo, which stated:

> [T]he bearer, Miss E. A. Anderson, a civil servant employed by the FO, is urgently required by her department in the UK. If you have any difficulty in obtaining for her a priority sufficiently high to guarantee that she is not held up anywhere along the route please let me know [. . .][117]

Dorothy Brooks might have been expected to return to the UK with Anderson, but by then she did not wish to do so. Brooks' desire to remain in Cairo reflected the reality that her affections now lay elsewhere, and her relationship with Anderson had been over for some time. Dorothy had met Lieutenant Thomas Bowring Carr on the boat journey from England to South Africa in July 1940. On arrival,

Lieutenant Carr proceeded to his posting in Sarafand, to work on Italian intelligence. Carr was, by all accounts, something of a charmer, who 'looked like Noel Coward and was very wealthy'.[118] Born in Genoa, Italy, in 1893 into a family of prosperous shipping agents, he had served as a 2nd Lieutenant in the Intelligence Corps during the First World War.[119] Fluent in several languages, Carr's profile was typical of many of those recruited to the Junior Intelligence Officer Corps, and he had the added advantage that he had travelled widely in Europe, given the nature of the family business, and could fit in anywhere. His military record was punctuated by periods of sick leave, likely due to the fact that he was gassed at some point during the war. After the First World War, he was awarded a 'reserve commission' in 1921, a move designed to keep intelligence officers such as Carr 'on the books', and was called up as a reservist in 1939 at the outbreak of war.

When they met in 1940, Dorothy was twenty-five and Carr a forty-seven-year-old who had already been married twice. He first married in 1916, while serving as a 2nd Lieutenant with the Worcestershire Regiment. That marriage ended in divorce in 1928, on the grounds of his adultery. He subsequently married an Italian woman in Italy, and had two children. That marriage had also ended, acrimoniously,[120] by the time he met Dorothy. In spite of her relationship with Anderson when they set out from England, within a few months the beginnings of a relationship had developed between Brooks and Carr. Certainly, by January 1941, Carr had visited Brooks in Cairo (there are photos of them riding camels and visiting the pyramids) and Brooks' passport confirms that she visited Palestine, where Carr was based, for a week in August 1941.[121] The relationship developed to the point that, when it came to leaving Egypt, Brooks was reluctant to do so. Details of Carr's career following his posting in Sarafand are hazy, but he did appear in the *London Gazette* in 1944, getting a 'mention' for services in Italy. It appears, therefore, that he had been transferred back to Italy after the Italian armistice of September 1943, where he would have been a real intelligence asset to the Allied forces, given his familiarity with the country.[122] Shortly thereafter, he reached the age limit for reserve officers, retired from service and resumed work with the family shipping business.

*

There is no way of knowing how Anderson reacted to the ending of her relationship with Brooks, the time frame in which it unfolded, or what had prompted it. It appears that Brooks simply fell in love with a handsome, mature and successful man, who swept her off her feet, and that she wanted the happiness and respectability that marriage and the prospect of children would bring. Whatever the circumstances, it is a measure of the professionalism of both women that the change in their personal relationship appears not to have impacted on their working relationship, as there are no indications in the official CBME files of personnel issues arising within the unit. Dorothy Brooks and Thomas Bowring Carr eventually married in July 1947 in Genoa, Italy,[123] and their only son, Peter, was born in 1950.

But whatever Brooks' personal wishes, the decision to stay or go was not hers to make. Jacob had advised Denniston that 'Miss Brooks is anxious to remain here if possible', and that he had sufficient work for her on

German and Italian traffic,[124] but Denniston's response was unequivocal: 'Miss Brooks should return as she is urgently wanted.'[125] Consequently, the letter of passage of 30 April was amended to apply to both women.[126] A similar letter issued in respect of Marie Rose Egan, described her as 'An Air Ministry Civil Servant proceeding to the UK, who was to be "given every assistance on her journey"'.[127] As events rapidly unfolded, the original plan for Egan to remain in Cairo had been superseded by the more pressing demands for codebreakers back in the UK, and arrangements were made to transport all three women back to the UK on board a Boeing Short-S26 airboat via Algiers.

*

The Italians paid a heavy price for their defeat in Africa. Their war there had been an unrelenting succession of military disasters in which a fatal decryption of their signals intelligence by CBME had played a very significant role. By the time Anderson and her colleagues left Cairo, Italy's position was hopeless. They had lost Northern and Eastern Africa, and three days after the surrender of the Axis powers in North Africa on 13 May 1943, the Allies bombed Rome. Sicily was successfully invaded on 10 July, and preparations began to land Allied forces on the Italian mainland. But there was worse to come. The Armistice of Cassibile in September 1943, between the Kingdom of Italy and the Allies, prompted a swift reaction from Germany, which began attacking Italian forces in Italy, southern France and the Balkans. The demoralised Italian forces were quickly defeated, and most of Italy was occupied by German troops.

Just as Anderson was preparing to return to the UK, after the fall of Tunis on 12 May 1943, Fred Winterbotham[128] was ordered to Cairo, and his account of the Cairo of the summer of 1943 provides us with a fascinating insight into the world in which Anderson was operating – which, pressures of work aside, was far different to those being experienced by her colleagues in the UK:

> After the black-outs and cold of England it was absolutely heaven. I had many old friends there, but the first thing to do was to have a swim at the Gezira Club pool, then lunch in town with Tom Mapplebeck [. . .] Tom had a lovely flat looking out over the Nile. Just to feel the warmth of Egypt and to see everyone in gay summer clothing was a tonic; dinner out of doors at the Club under the stars, fairy lights strung between the graceful palms, good food, soft-footed waiters; the sound of music and gay girls – it was rather hard to leave, was Cairo in 1943.[129]

Hard it may well have been, but it was also absolutely necessary. With her work in Cairo done, and demand for her skills in the UK, arrangements were made to bring Anderson back to London as soon as possible. The war was not yet won, and as she left Cairo to begin the next stage of her codebreaking career, a host of new challenges, personal and professional, awaited her.

15

Berkeley Street

By the time Emily Anderson returned to the UK in May 1943, she had been away for over two and a half years and, flushed with CBME's success, she was assured of a senior position at the heart of GC&CS's operation. But it was not Bletchley to which Anderson returned when she arrived back from Cairo. In February 1942, the sidelining of Denniston, and his replacement by Sir Edward 'Jumbo' Travis, had resulted in the sections previously based in Elmer's School, Bletchley, i.e. the Diplomatic and Commercial Sections, being moved to London under Denniston's command, while the Military Sections, under Travis, remained at a much-expanded Bletchley. The success of the Bletchley operation and its contribution to the war effort was by now recognised in all government and service quarters, and:

> [. . .] there were less scrupulous and more ambitious men on hand to skim off much of the credit. Denniston left Bletchley and came back to London to escape the back-biting and get on with the job; he disliked the in-fighting more than he feared the Luftwaffe.[1]

Denniston was given the title Deputy Director (Civil), with a reduced salary, and, shamefully, no knighthood.[2] The

Diplomatic Section, for which Anderson was destined, moved to Berkeley Street, near Piccadilly. Although no longer Head of the Italian Diplomatic Section, having relinquished that position when she moved to Cairo, Anderson would at least be working directly under her long-time colleague and mentor, Commander Denniston. Known officially as Government Communications Bureau, the section was always known informally as 'Berkeley Street' to those who worked there.[3] No. 8 Berkeley Street was a large office building, with a ladies, dress shop, Madame Riché, *couturière des dames,* located on the ground floor, and a small side entrance leading to six floors of office space above.[4]

Dorothy Brooks, by now in a relationship with Thomas Bowring Carr, rejoined the Commercial Section, which had also moved from Bletchley and was now located on an upper floor of Aldford House on Park Lane.[5] Dorothy was able to make good use of her degree in French, as she was working on French decrypts of the Free French under General de Gaulle and the communications of the Vichy government.[6] Unlike Anderson and Brooks, Marie Rose Egan did not return to her pre-Cairo section, but was sent on a crash-course to learn Japanese before joining the Japanese Forces Section at Bletchley.[7] Emily Anderson was too long in the game at that stage (she was then aged fifty-two) to have any desire to retrain in a new language, and she was also sufficiently senior that Denniston knew he could not, and would not, force her to do so. She returned to take up her previous specialism in diplomatic intelligence, working on Hungarian and German diplomatic codes. Though less well known than Bletchley Park, Berkeley Street is nonetheless deserving of recognition for the fact that 'under Denniston, they had a good war, outmatching any other diplomatic Comint agency in the world'.[8]

At the heart of that agency was Emily Anderson, whose return to the UK came about at a time when the practice of cryptology was experiencing a renaissance as a result of technological advances precipitated by the war. The development of Hollerith machines, and the groundbreaking work on Enigma, which culminated in the development of the BOMBE machine,* inevitably led to codebreaking becoming more strongly aligned with the pure theory of mathematics, whereas it had previously been the realm of classicists and linguists. The Bletchley of 1943 was a hive of activity, as the volume of intercepts, and the speed at which they could be deciphered, had increased significantly with the development of the BOMBE. From late 1942 to early 1945, there was a rapid expansion of the workforce, and GC&CS transformed 'from a "cottage industry" into an industrial-scale intelligence operation'.[9] Berkeley Street, in comparison, was a much smaller show, with just 250 staff employed in its Diplomatic and Commercial Sections by March 1944. But what it lacked in numbers, it more than made up for in the quality of its output.

Other changes had also taken place in Anderson's

---

* Settings on Enigma machines changed every twenty-four hours, and with 159 quintillion possible combinations every day, a mechanical method to speed up the process of identifying the keys was required. Alan Turing designed, and Gordon Welchman perfected, the BOMBE, a machine consisting of 100 rotating drums that searched through different possible positions of Enigma's internal wheels looking for a pattern of keyboard-to-lamp board connections that would turn coded letters into plain German.

absence, which were to significantly impact the outcome of the war. Denniston's secretary, Barbara Abernethy, recalled the first American visit in 1941:

> 'I've got something important to tell you,' he said, 'at twelve o'clock there are going to be four Americans coming to see me and I require you to come in with the sherry. You are not to tell anyone who they are or what they are doing.'[10]

Anderson's return to the UK, as it turned out, coincided with the secret, tentative beginnings of a UK–USA collaboration on SIGINT, which had advanced significantly following the Japanese attack on Pearl Harbor on 7 December 1941, the event which had brought the Americans into the war on the side of the Allies. While the Americans had made significant advances in the use of machines to break codes, there was still a lot for them to learn from their British counterparts when it came to organisational structure and information chains, and a number of senior officers in the US intelligence service visited the UK in 1943 to evaluate the operations at both Bletchley and Berkeley Street. A valuable insight into how that mission played out is provided in the McCormack Report, written in 1943 by Colonel Alfred McCormack, the deputy head of the US Army's Special Branch, which supervised signal intelligence in the US War Department. In April 1943, he had led a high-level delegation, consisting of himself, Colonel William Friedman[11] and Lieutenant Telford Taylor[12] to Bletchley, followed by a lengthy visit to Berkeley Street in May and June of 1943. His report consisted of a series of signals sent for the attention of General George Strong, the US Army's Military Intelligence chief. McCormack was impressed by

Berkeley Street, observing that the US War Department would be 'absolutely astonished' by the 'resources of intelligence [. . .] here in Denniston's show, waiting for somebody to tap them'.[13] He observed of Berkeley Street that it had:

> [. . .] none of the hectic atmosphere of [Bletchley] Park but rather gives the impression of a well established operation that goes along through wars and peace. Whole organisation is very simple and they seem to accomplish a great deal with quite limited personnel. Whole outfit consists of 200.[14]

McCormack noted that '[e]verything that is circulated goes to the Foreign Office, and Director', and also to the War Office and Admiralty, the exception being where service ministries were not passed on material, which indicated that 'some British diplomat abroad has "dropped a brick".'[15] McCormack acknowledged that Denniston had continued his policy of cooperating fully with the Americans and 'more than anyone else has turned his people over to us for questioning and given us a free run of his place'.[16] McCormack's earliest cables reporting on Berkeley Street in May 1943 provided an initial assessment of the various language sections, and in his overview he recorded that although Hungarian was not being read, 'Berkeley Street is expecting the return of someone who will soon undertake it'. That 'someone' was Anderson, who was at that point en route from Cairo.[17]

The Americans recognised that 'the long term interest of the United States requires the greatest possible self-sufficiency in the field of signal intelligence',[18] and in order to achieve this had posted staff at Bletchley to familiarise themselves with all forms of mechanised attack, and sent others to Berkeley Street to acquire 'every diplomatic system the British cryptanalytical effort at Berkeley Street had mastered'.[19] Both sides recognised that diplomatic signal intelligence would be at a premium once the war ended – and that the time was coming when there would inevitably be a parting of the ways when it came to sharing such intelligence. In the interim, it was imperative that they learned as much as possible from each other.

There was plenty for Anderson and her diplomatic team to do. Some 150,000 diplomatic decrypts generated by the section between 1943 and 1945 are held in the National Archives at Kew,[20] and these decrypts cover not only enemy traffic but also that of neutrals, governments in exile and some allies.[21] John Croft, who was transferred to Berkeley Street from Bletchley in September 1943, observed: 'Traffic was intercepted by the Radio Security Service but a good deal was passed through the telegram and cable services run by the General Post Office and Cable and Wireless.'[22]

The manner in which information and resources between the UK and US cryptologic agencies were to be exchanged provides us with a remarkable window into Anderson's time at Berkeley Street. Regene 'Jean' Lewis,[23] then a young married woman, worked under Anderson on Hungarian codes in the Diplomatic Section. The following anecdote, recorded in a series of oral history interviews of Bletchley Park veterans, is revealing in a number of respects.

I was moved to the Hungarian section to help break the diplomatic code because the section was headed by a woman, whose name I have forgotten, who had

had distinguished service in the Middle East; she had an OBE or some decoration as a result of it. I don't know what she had been doing there but it certainly wasn't codebreaking, it may have been translating, or something. She landed up with the Hungarian section but was unable to read the Hungarian diplomatic code, so I ended up there temporarily. When I was in the Hungarian section there was an amusing incident. We had close relations with the Americans and an American officer who had done a tour of everything at Bletchley arrived to tour the Diplomatic Section. The Americans had something which must have been an early form of mainframe computer, but we just called them the machines.[24] I never saw these machines so I have no idea what they looked like. We knew that they handled the material faster than we could by hand; I mean they sped up the codebreaking. As far as my head of department was concerned, and she was quite right from our point of view, the most important thing in the world was the Hungarian codes. The moment the American had left the room, and remember, I was about twenty-two years old at the time; she looked at me, this wizened old spinster, and said, 'you know, if you offered to sleep with him I am sure he would let us use their machines!' I just told her that we didn't need them because the work was almost done, and it was. I don't know if any of the Diplomatic Section had access to the machines. As far as I know, all of my colleagues just used pencil and paper.

A number of points in Lewis's account are striking. Why, for example, did she conclude that whatever Anderson had been doing, 'it certainly wasn't code-breaking'? Was it so inconceivable that 'a wizened old spinster' – Anderson would have been fifty-two or fifty-three at the time – could have been a senior codebreaker, especially considering her recently awarded OBE, and the fact that she was senior to Lewis, and a former Section Head at Bletchley? What Lewis would not have known was that as one of the best bookbuilders, if not *the* best bookbuilder in the intelligence service, Anderson's prowess stemmed from her ability to both translate and decrypt at the same time. Nigel de Grey observed of Diplomatic cryptanalysts that:

> [B]ookbuilders should also decrypt and translate the tasks upon which they were working [. . .] for the reason that they were able, especially where the bookbuilding had not advanced to near completion, to produce a much better decrypted text than anyone else could do and by force of the intense study to which the text had been subjected to produce a translation which more nearly reflected the sense of the original, especially in the finer shades of meaning so important in a diplomatic despatch.[25]

De Grey was acknowledging that linguistic and cryptanalytic skills had to be particularly in tune with one another when working on diplomatic ciphers, which were full of nuance and a higher level of linguistic sophistication than would normally have been the case with service ciphers. The objective in diplomatic intelligence was not just to discover what the enemy was saying, but the mindset that produced it – what Mavis Batey described as 'an intellectual procedure of lateral thinking'.[26] This required great skill and took time to develop, and Anderson had more than served her apprenticeship in that regard. Lewis was, without knowing it, completely outclassed by a woman with decades of experience, who did not feel the need to waste time justifying or explaining her methodology to a relative novice. And she was wrong in concluding that Anderson was unable to read Hungarian codes. As we have seen, prior to her departure for Cairo, she had been working on Hungarian codes with Dilly Knox; her apparent unfamiliarity with Hungarian codes was more likely to do with the fact that during her time in Cairo, her focus had been solely on Italian codes, and she needed some time to refamiliarise herself with the notoriously difficult-to-crack Hungarian ones.

Finally, Anderson's decidedly un-prudish, even risqué, attitude to the Americans, and her desire to embrace the new Hollerith machine methods of codebreaking, is remarkable. Many of the First World War and interwar codebreaking veterans – such as Knox and Clarke – were suspicious of the new generation of codebreakers who were transforming cryptanalysis with machines, yet Anderson had no such qualms. Her comment to Lewis reflected the reality that the world of cryptanalysis was changing fast, and codebreakers would have to adapt or become obsolete.

Anderson, then, was as far from a 'wizened old spinster', stuck in her ways and struggling to keep up with her younger subordinates, as it was possible to be. But Lewis was not alone in perceiving 'Miss Anderson' as something of an oddity. In common with many of her contemporaries who had seen service in the First World War and interwar period, Anderson was viewed as a dinosaur by some of the younger staff. This is confirmed by the following account, written by P. W. Filby, a cryptologist based in the German Diplomatic Section, who provides us with a rare glimpse of Anderson following her return from Cairo:

> Some of the older staff fitted in excellently, but there were others who still demanded recognition of the status that they had acquired, with little thought that war had made a change for everyone [. . .] I shared a room with four others, but one lady, recently returned from Egypt, demanded her own room, and refused to come to work until she was given it. How Denniston mollified her I will never know, but after a week's absence she meekly asked me if she could have a table and chair. She was an excellent translator, but with her status as the senior lady of the Foreign Office, she insisted on translating only messages less than a week old! When there was nothing to her liking she brought from her drawer her manuscript of a definitive biography of Beethoven, which later became a classic.[27]

Filby's description of the 'senior lady of the Foreign Office' is clearly Anderson, and it is astonishing to think of a senior codebreaker working on the letters of arguably Germany's greatest composer at her desk at the heart of British intelligence when she had nothing else to do. But given the volume of traffic with which codebreakers were being consistently bombarded, it is unlikely that there were many such occasions in either the German or Italian Diplomatic Section, and it must be remembered that Filby was viewing Anderson through the eyes of a younger man (he was thirty-two) evaluating an older woman. Filby's assertion that Anderson was working on a biography of Beethoven is clearly wrong, but other shortcomings in his account are more revealing. The account was written in 1988, yet it is striking that he didn't take the trouble to identify Anderson by name – although at the time he met her she was Head of the Hungarian Diplomatic Section at Berkeley Street, had been awarded an OBE for her intelligence work in Cairo, and significantly outranked him both in status and experience. Anderson was far more than just an 'excellent translator', and that must have been clear to him, yet he at no point refers to her as a codebreaker. And whether Filby knew it or not, the degree to which Denniston had sought to 'mollify' Anderson was far less significant than the fact that he felt compelled to do so at all. Denniston troubled to do so because Anderson was one of his most valued code-breakers, someone with whom he had worked since 1919, when she had been one of the first women recruited by him to GC&CS. Filby did not appreciate that, in insisting 'on translating only messages less than a week old', Anderson was merely being strategic. As one of the most experienced codebreakers at GC&CS, it made sense for her to use her skills to decrypt the most up-to-date mes-sages as quickly as possible so that the intelligence gleaned could be put to immediate use in undermining and outwit-ting the enemy.

Unlike Filby, in an interview given to the NSA in 1978, one of cryptology's leading figures, John Tiltman, one-time Assistant Director of GCHQ, the successor to GC&CS, did not hesitate to identify Anderson. In a brief but revealing vignette that formed part of his account of the operation at Bletchley Park during the war years, Tiltman confirmed that Anderson's musicological work was as important to her as codebreaking – if not more so. Tiltman recalled:

We had a very famous lady, Emily Anderson, who wrote the standard books *The Letters of Beethoven* and *The Letters of Mozart*. And I never worked with her, but the story was that she got into an argument with Denniston, and she said 'You don't seem to understand, Commander Denniston, that my work starts when I leave your office.' She was very good. She lasted through the war. She was in Cairo for a bit.[28]

Tiltman's observations are revealing. The fact that Anderson got into an argument at all with Denniston, who was at the time the man in overall command of Bletchley Park, and gave as good as she got, speaks volumes for just how senior she was in the pecking order. Tiltman's anecdote also confirms that, throughout her time at Bletchley, Anderson continued to spend whatever free time she had working on the Beethoven letters. Tiltman, at least, acknowledged that Anderson was 'very good' at her job as a codebreaker.[29]

Filby acknowledged the problems faced by Denniston in integrating his older established staff with newer and significantly younger recruits:

Although they had worked in the organisation for several years between the wars, systems had changed considerably, and by now Denniston had recruited several younger experts and translators – yet jobs had to be found for these civil servants.[30]

He noted that 'these "civil servants" came in at 9 a.m. and left at 5 p.m., but others still appeared at 10 and left at 4.' What Filby would not have known was that his boss, Patricia Bartley, Head of the German Diplomatic section, and responsible for cracking the German diplomatic code Floradora, had been recruited by Anderson in 1939. By late 1943, Anderson's skills were much sought after, not only by her own section but also by Filby's German Diplomatic section,[31] as Bartley was then on sick leave following a breakdown brought about by her work on Floradora.[32]

Filby was right in one respect: the war had changed everything, and in wartime it was inevitable that the Diplomatic Sections would be overshadowed by the development of the Service Sections, i.e. those at the sharp end of the conflict, whose work was given priority. Nigel de Grey noted that:

> The Service Sections had the pick of the office space, the pick of the war enlisted staff and the administrative side of the organisation, insofar as it provided at this time any convenience at all, was directed towards the convenience of the 24-hour shift workers of the Service Sections. The Diplomatic Sections, manned principally by established civil servants with fixed hours of labour in the normal way, and other Civil Service privileges, were forced to conform.[33]

Anderson was not particularly out of step with her fellow 'old hands', but in surrendering her senior position as Head of the Italian Diplomatic Section in 1940, and undertaking a posting in the field in Cairo, she had gone above and beyond what would normally have been expected of someone of her age and seniority. It was typical of Anderson that she never referred to this fact, or played on her achievements in Cairo. As a consequence, the younger generation of codebreakers were unaware of her abilities and achievements, and treated her accordingly.

McCormack's report refers on a number of occasions to Patricia Bartley, who greatly impressed him:

> The G* section is primarily Floradora. It started out
> as strictly an amateur show under the present section
> head, the attractive 25 year old Patricia Bartley, whom
> Tiltman took at the beginning of the war fresh from
> Oxford and trained in his school.[34]

Anderson's role in the recruitment of Bartley is completely unacknowledged, and Tiltman was happy to take credit for having spotted her potential. The Americans were smitten with Bartley, whose 'brains, beauty and vivacity swept senior Siginters off their feet'.[35] Friedman's diary makes reference to taking 'the delightful Miss Bartley' to lunch and dinner on a number of occasions. It is unlikely that Emily Anderson received any such invitations.

A month after the Americans visited Berkeley Street, the announcement that Anderson had been awarded the Order of the British Empire (OBE) appeared in *The Times* on 17 July 1943. She was described as 'Miss Emily Anderson, senior assistant, Foreign Office, GHQ, Middle East'.[36] Anderson was conferred with her OBE by King George VI at Buckingham Palace, the man who, as Duke of York, had conferred on her brother Alexander the Distinguished Flying Cross in April 1920. While Anderson received her OBE 'For services to the forces and in connection with Military operations',[37] Dorothy Brooks was awarded the MBE in the same conferring ceremony, as was Major George Wallace, Commanding Officer of 5IS.[38] Deservedly, the Divisional Manager of Cable & Wireless Ltd, Middle East, H. T. Bennett, was also awarded an OBE 'for services in provision of cable communications'. The speed at which

* The 'G' stands for German.

the awards were conferred was a recognition of the strategic importance of the SIGINT work undertaken by all those associated directly with the East Africa campaign – Lieutenant Colonel Jacob was not awarded his OBE until 1949. It was also the case that the achievements of Anderson and her team were of a different order to the reciphering challenges that faced their colleagues at Bletchley. Well placed to appreciate that was their overall boss, Commander Denniston, who had worked on similar cipher systems in the interwar period. Of their achievement, Denniston observed:

> I think she & Miss Brooks earned their honours when one thinks of the speed required to obtain the keys in time to produce the operational intelligence which played such a vital part in the campaigns.[39]

Marie Rose Egan would be awarded the MBE in January 1946.

Recognition aside, a challenge faced by women in the intelligence service was having credit for their work taken by male colleagues. No woman was immune to such treatment, and Patricia Bartley discovered that her subordinate, William Filby, was claiming credit for the critical breakthrough she had made with Floradora. Bartley was sufficiently senior – and sufficiently furious – that she marched into Denniston's office to take up the matter with him directly. Denniston fully supported her but, as we have seen, the strain of the work, and Filby's brazen attempt to claim credit for her breakthrough, caused Bartley's health to break down, and Filby subsequently became Head of German Diplomatic Section in Bartley's stead. As had been the situation from the beginning of her career, Anderson appears never to have suffered from such flagrant jealousy or misogyny, because she simply would not have stood for it. Filby's characterisation of her as 'meekly' asking for a chair when her demand for an office was not met should not be seen as a capitulation, but rather a desire on Anderson's part to get on with the task at hand as quickly as possible.

Such gendered discrimination aside, the potential for advancement of women codebreakers had changed considerably as the end of the war loomed. Just as 'skills with languages or work in key stripping once opened the door for women as code breakers, it closed with the emphasis on machines and mathematics'.[40] Languages and classics graduates, who had formed a large component of the codebreaking staff of the First World War and the interwar period, were becoming increasingly irrelevant in a world that was rapidly changing:

> Gordon Welchman,[41] equally responsible for the breaking of Enigma as Turing [. . .] wrote that Dilly Knox, one of the most senior men in GC&CS 'did not seem to like me'. After a week or so, Knox gave him some sort of test and was annoyed, it seemed, when he passed. Knox saw the breaking of Enigma as an academic problem akin to solving the Rosetta stone and resented any outside intrusion into his little world – particularly from a mathematician.[42]

The advance of machinery and computing changed everything. Women were less represented among the mathematicians who dominated the new machine-driven cryptanalysis than men. Female mathematicians who did break through, such as Joan Clarke and Margaret Rock, achieved real status within GC&CS, with Clarke becoming Deputy Head of Hut 5 and Rock becoming the most senior cryptographer in Dilly Knox's team working on Enigma. There remained, however, a need for cryptographers skilled in the creative art of book building and cipher-stripping, largely the forte of linguists, and this shift in specialisms is reflected in the fact that Anderson, Bartley, Clarke and Rock – two linguists and two mathematicians – became the ranking female British SIGINTers of the war.[43]

Machinery of another kind proved a serious danger to the staff at Berkeley Street, and the population of London, in the summer of 1944. On 13 June 1944, one week after the successful Allied landings in France, the first of a new type of bomb was launched on London by the Germans. The V-1 was a mechanically guided, pilotless rocket, launched from a metal ramp using a catapult slingshot and powered by an Argus pulse jet engine. Difficult to combat as it flew at 3,000 feet at speeds up to 400 mph, each rocket travelled a set distance pre-programmed into an air log in its nose. On reaching its target, it suddenly stopped and dropped. This was the feature that made what became known as the 'Doodlebug' or 'Buzz Bomb' such a menacing threat, as people would see the fire of the rocket crossing the sky, hear its distinctive sound, and know that when the engine cut out, in exactly fifteen seconds 2,000 lb of explosives were set to go off close to them. For those who experienced the high-pitched wail of the Doodlebug bombing of London, the silence that followed the engine cut-out was the most terrifying aspect of the war. Anderson's time at Berkeley Street coincided with London becoming a target for V-1[44] and later V-2[45] bombing raids, and Rommel's tanks notwithstanding, the contrast with her relatively safe posting in Cairo must have struck Anderson forcefully as air-raid sirens became a regular feature of the lives of Londoners. Nancy Winbolt, who worked at Berkeley Street in late 1943, recalled:

> One Sunday[46] a bomb fell in Berkeley Street but on the other side of the road where there were casualties. Our building was not damaged. Later one girl had a miraculous escape when a V2 landed on the house next door and left her in bed hanging on a partition wall. We had regular warnings of an approaching V1 from a pair of watchers on the roof of the Strand Palace hotel visible from our sixth floor window half a mile away. They raised a warning flag.[47]

Berkeley Street staff were advised to hide under their desks in the event of an air raid, 'in order to avoid glass shattered by blast'.[48] The first bomb had landed just 100 yards from the Berkeley Street operation at a 'secret Air Force establishment' located at Lansdown House. The top floor of the building was completely destroyed.[49] The worst of the V-1 attacks had ceased by September 1944, but it was not until 29 March 1945 that the last rocket hit Suffolk.

*

Regardless of what happened outside, inside, the work of Berkeley Street continued to deliver impressive results under the direction of Commander Denniston. Always more of a technical man, and a reluctant administrator, the reorganisation of GC&CS in February 1942 that him in charge of a staff of *c.* 250 may have wounded him professionally, but ultimately played to his strengths. His longstanding professional relationship with Emily Anderson meant that she was one of the few who fully appreciated

Denniston's unique talents, and he respected hers. Berkeley Street assumed many of the characteristics of the old interwar GC&CS operation at Broadway Buildings, and both Anderson and Denniston thrived there. Another of the 'old school' cryptographers who thrived at Berkeley Street was Ernst Fetterlein. Born in 1873, he had been Tsar Nicholas II's chief cryptographic officer, holding the rank of 'General-Admiral'. Ironically, British codes were among those he deciphered. Following the Russian Revolution of 1917, he and his wife walked out of Russia across the Finnish frontier, and fled to Western Europe on board a Swedish ship, narrowly evading capture. Fetterlein contacted the British and French intelligence organisations, offering his services to the highest bidder. When the British made him the better offer, he was recruited to the Admiralty's Room 40 in June 1918 to work on Georgian, Austrian and Bolshevik codes. When the war ended, he was recruited to GC&CS, eventually retiring in 1938. But Fetterlein's career was not yet over. In 1939, he was recalled from retirement to work at Bletchley, but moved with the German Diplomatic Section to Berkeley Street to work on Floradora under Patricia Bartley. Fetterlein was a brilliant cryptographer, and highly regarded by his colleagues. Filby observed that: 'On book cipher and anything else where insight was vital he was quite the best. He was a fine linguist and would usually get an answer no matter the language.'[50] Patricia Bartley remembered him fondly, recalling his plaintive, heavily accented cries as they worked together on breaking Floradora: ' "Oh Patreesha, zis is awful!" he would say, and that was our catchphrase.'[51]

Berkeley Street's success was due to the fact that it was comprised of some of the 'old hands' of Room 40 and

MI1(b) – Denniston, Anderson, Fetterlein – and those recruited and mentored by them, such as Bartley and Filby.[52] Away from the frenzy of Bletchley, they got down to doing what they did best – cracking codes and providing top-level diplomatic intelligence. It is to Denniston's credit that, having been ousted from Bletchley, 'once established at the Berkeley Street office [. . .] he never missed a day's work until retirement. He accepted demotion and settled down to make the new job work.'[53]

Anderson, similarly, settled down to her new task of breaking Hungarian codes, and assisting with German diplomatic codes as and when required. Filby recalled, 'we worked like beavers [. . .] 18 hours a day seven days a week'.[54] This punishing work rate may indeed on occasion have been necessary, but a more likely work schedule is provided by Nancy Winbolt, who recalled, 'We worked an average 52 hour week (6 days) with one day off per week.'[55]

Yet the work done and results accomplished were not something for which the staff of Berkeley Street could claim credit. For many of the male codebreakers especially, the fact that their work at Bletchley and Berkeley Street had to remain secret proved something of a strain in the post-war period, as had been the case following the First World War. As they watched friends and family wear their medals and speak about their war service, the thousands who had worked in intelligence had to continue to steadfastly observe that secrecy.[56] For some, the strain was too much, and as early as 1945, articles appeared in *Time* and *Life* magazines hinting at what had been going on at Bletchley Park.[57] Such breaches of security – always by male employees – were the rare exception, and in general, the adherence to secrecy regarding the work that codebreakers, particularly female ones, had engaged in was quite remarkable. Apart from receiving a personal letter from Anthony Eden,[58] Anderson's protégée, Patricia Bartley, received no public recognition for the work she did in breaking Floradora, the German diplomatic code, until she was 102 years old, and her contribution was finally recorded in *Behind the Enigma: The Authorised History* of GCHQ by John Ferris.[59] She died a mere five months after the book was published. But in 2010, in a review of a book about Bletchley, she referred in veiled terms to what she had achieved:

> The work was extraordinarily long and hard [...]
> I remember only one small triumph. We were working
> with five-figure subtraction cyphers, where it was
> necessary to subtract one group from another to get
> at the result which could, with luck, be decoded.
> I noticed some regularities in these that no one else
> had seen, which vastly reduced the number of groups
> that needed to be decoded. I never knew the lasting
> significance.[60]

The repeats that Bartley identified were, as we have seen, related to sailor's complaints regarding menus, but were sufficient to provide Bartley with a 'crib', which enabled her to break into Floradora. Bartley's family never knew of her wartime activities, her children merely observing that 'Mummy was very good at solving crossword puzzles'. It is ironic that it was the cryptologic talent of Bartley – first talent-spotted by Anderson – which was to become 'the acme of Berkeley Street's success', second only to the breaking of Enigma at Bletchley Park.[61]

Like most of her colleagues in the Diplomatic Section, Anderson did not seek the limelight, or seek to take credit for work done. It is for this reason that the work she did is not better known about in the wider intelligence community, and why it doesn't feature in the historiography of the period. Robert Cecil observed that, at Bletchley, 'Heads of sections, each armed with a choice tit-bit of intelligence, used to carry it to "C"[62] as if it was all their own work, in the hope of basking in the sunshine of vicarious success.' This was not the case at Berkeley Street, and instead a 'selection of the most telling diplomatic intercepts [. . .] were always sent to "C" in a locked box by hand of messenger'.[63] In Anderson's case, the lack of recognition was not something that troubled her. Although cognisant of the value of the work she did – the East Africa campaign having provided incontrovertible evidence of this – it suited Anderson's purpose to draw a discreet but impenetrable veil over the work she did for the 'Foreign Office'. The reasons for this are clear: outside of her cryptologic work, Anderson had a second career, as a musicologist, a fact emphasised by Tiltman's recollection of her statement to Denniston that 'my work starts when I leave your office'.[64] It is also telling that Tiltman described Anderson as 'a very famous lady', yet apart from this small aside, he, nor any other codebreaker other than Josh Cooper, ever mention her in their memoirs of the First or Second World War – or interwar – codebreaking. While this was an unfair reflection on her undoubted abilities, the fact that she was not on anyone's radar as a leading practitioner in the art of secret, high-level cryptanalysis suited Anderson's purpose, as it meant she could compartmentalise her work at Berkeley Street and her work in her 'Beethoven workshop' at Ellerdale Road.

One of the benefits of that duality in her life, and likely the reason Anderson never succumbed to any sort of mental breakdown, was her love of music, which provided a much-needed safety valve from the pressured environment of GC&CS, and later GCHQ. When she returned to London, she could once again play her precious piano, and reconnect with her musical friends. She was also fortunate that classical music concerts continued to be held at the Wigmore Hall, a ten-minute walk from Berkeley Street.[65] But the venue she is likely to have attended on a regular basis was the National Gallery in Trafalgar Square. The celebrated pianist Myra Hess – who had performed at Bletchley – had the idea of using the gallery as a venue for classical music concerts. From October 1939, Hess and her friends from the world of classical music staged daily lunch-time[66] performances from Monday to Friday, even during the Blitz. Performers were a mix of famous names, a number of whom were personal friends of Anderson, such as the concert pianist Denis Matthews, and unknown faces, including musicians drawn from the ranks of the armed forces. The concerts did much to boost the morale of ordinary Londoners at a time of 'cultural black-out', with over 750,000 people attending over six and a half years, the last concert taking place in April 1946. Trafalgar Square was a fifteen-minute walk from Anderson's office in Berkeley Street, and with a programme featuring works by Beethoven, Mozart, Bach and Brahms, the concerts would have been a natural draw for Anderson, and provided a welcome respite from the intense work in which she was engaged. The ability to 'switch off' was essential, but Anderson was unique among her peers in that the interests she engaged in in her private life – her musicological research – was as intense as her 'day job'. Yet it gave her enormous pleasure and allowed her to escape into a completely different world: the world of the great composers. More than anything else, it ensured that she remained working in GC&CS (and later GCHQ) longer than any other woman in the service, and a good deal longer than almost all her male colleagues.

One of those colleagues, Commander Denniston, left government service on 1 May 1945 after a career spanning thirty-one years, during which he had been involved in the establishment of Room 40 in 1914, and subsequently the establishment of both GC&CS and Bletchley Park. It was typical of the man that there was no fanfare surrounding his departure – he cleared out his desk, 'put on his hat and walked out of Berkeley Street to the Green Park Underground station, saying nothing to his fellow workers'.[67] There was no official thank you or goodbye from GC&CS or the Foreign Office, although Denniston hosted a dinner for the senior staff, which would have included Emily Anderson, his colleague of some twenty-seven years.

A week after Denniston's retirement, on 8 May 1945, the Second World War in Europe came to an end. As news of Germany's surrender reached the UK, joyous crowds gathered to celebrate in the streets. For many of the GC&CS staff, the elation they felt that the war had finally ended was matched by a sense of relief that they could finally move on with their lives and leave the world of code-breaking behind, never to be spoken of again. This was especially true of the women, who had steadfastly adhered to the 'Loose lips cost lives' mantra to a quite remarkable degree, such that the 'geese that laid the golden eggs and never cackled', as Churchill had put it, would go on preserving their secrets, even from their own families, for decades to come. On VE Day, a congratulatory message from Stewart Menzies, MI6 chief and Director-General of GC&CS, was sent to all staff, thanking them for their contribution in helping to win the war. Menzies, memo read:

> On this ever memorable day, I desire that all who are doing duty in this organisation should be made aware of my unbounded admiration in the way in which they have carried out their allotted tasks. Such have been the difficulties, such has been the endeavour, and such have been the constant triumphs that one senses that words of gratitude from one individual are perhaps out of place. The personal knowledge of the contribution made towards winning the War is surely the real measure of the thanks which so rightly belong to one and all in a great and inspired organisation which I have the privilege to direct. This is your finest hour.[68]

The day after the war had officially ended, Filby recalls that his entire section, including Anderson, walked the quarter of a mile from their offices to Buckingham Palace, where, to cheering crowds, the Royal Family appeared on the balcony. Churchill also spoke, announcing the end of the war in Europe, yet reminding everyone that 'the Japanese still had to be beaten'. In a joyous frenzy of happiness, 'hats flew in the air and in the evening lights in Piccadilly were turned on for the first time for five years'.[69] It had been a hard-won victory, requiring immense sacrifice and engendering a determination and stoicism that had ultimately prevailed. Those who had played a part in that victory were determined to savour every moment of it; those who had played a significant part in it, including the staffs of Bletchley Park and Berkeley Street, could justifiably consider it ample reward for a job well done.

For Anderson, it was the end of an era as she bid farewell to the man who had recruited her to GC&CS in 1920, and had been a friend and colleague throughout that time. But it was not the end of her career. Emily Anderson's codebreaking skills had hastened the end of the war, and saved countless lives due to the part she played in the defeat of the Italians in East Africa. Unlike Patricia Bartley, she had, at the very least, received an OBE for her trouble, but there was to be no elaboration on what she had done, how she had done it, and what its impact had been. But, in truth, that is as she wished it to be. For, with the war now over, she could resume the work that gave her the greatest pleasure and satisfaction – her work on translating the letters of arguably the world's greatest composer. Once again, she could become Miss Anderson of the Foreign Office, who by day continued to work in diplomatic intelligence-gathering, and outside of office hours could tackle the correspondence of the complex musical giant that was Beethoven. She had another six years of service left before she retired, and, just as in the interwar period, although military SIGINT was no longer a priority, diplomatic SIGINT had become ever more important. This had always been Anderson's metier, and, for the now-fifty-four-year-old, the next six years would be very much business as usual. But crucially for Anderson, she was also now free to take up the threads of her pre-war research, travel freely and resume old friendships in the great archives of Europe, and with international collectors. The resulting work would take her fifteen years, draw on all of her cryptologic and linguistic skills, and become an unrivalled classic in the canon of musicological research.

16

Eastcote and Beethoven

At the end of the war, the majority of Anderson's colleagues at Berkeley Street and Bletchley Park reverted back to their former careers in academia and other spheres. For most, it was a welcome return to normality once their wartime duty was done. Single women were expected to work in respectable jobs before eventually settling into marriage, domesticity and motherhood. Dorothy Brooks left GC&CS and went to work in the British consulate in Naples, in order to be closer to her fiancé, Thomas Bowring Carr, who was working in the Italian consular service. The couple married in July 1947. Marie Rose Egan retired from the by-now renamed GCHQ in 1946, and in 1950 married Peter Palmer, whom she had met at Bletchley, and who went on to assume a senior role within GCHQ. Patricia Bartley joined the Foreign Office, and during her time there met Denys Brown, whom she married in 1954.

Not so Emily Anderson. Marriage and domesticity were never going to feature in Anderson's plans, and she was by that stage sufficiently well established not to consider any other career. She was also fast approaching retirement, and would see out the final years of her career in Berkeley Street, under its new boss,[1] Captain Eddie Hastings, before one final move, to GCHQ's new home at Eastcote, near

Pinner in north-west London, in 1946. She retired, just three months shy of her sixtieth birthday, in November 1950.

At war's end, GC&CS had made the decision to consolidate its by now scaled-down operations in London, Bletchley Park, and the other outstations at Eastcote. A former wartime outstation established in the autumn of 1943 and used primarily to house BOMBEs, the devices used to find the daily key settings of the Enigma machine, by 1945 over 100 machines were located at Eastcote, along with over 800 Wrens and RAF technicians, and a group of American GIs.[2] In the spring of 1946, the remaining staff at Bletchley began to move to Eastcote. That same year, in June, GC&CS was officially renamed the Government Communications Headquarters (GCHQ). In the post-war years, the advent of the Cold War and the subsequent need for signals intelligence, particularly of a diplomatic nature, saw to it that GCHQ continued to expand. By 1948, the search was on for another, more permanent home, at a safe distance from London in the event of any future wars. The new permanent home of GCHQ was established in Cheltenham in 1951, but by then Anderson had already retired.

*

In a world no longer at war, portents of future trouble were likely to be found via diplomatic intelligence. Fittingly, it was Nigel de Grey, the man who had decrypted perhaps the most significant secret diplomatic communication of the First World War, the Zimmermann Telegram, in January 1917, who came up with the prophetic maxim of how a post-war SIGINT service should work: 'In this brave new world we have got to be prepared to follow trouble round the globe – vultures ready to take to wing at the merest indication of corpses.'[3]

Anderson was sufficiently experienced to take her place at the heart of any such diplomatic intelligence agency. Her work at Berkeley Street and later Eastcote returned to a more regular nine-to-five routine, affording her more time to re-engage with her musicological work. Anderson continued to live at her flat in Ellerdale Road, using her car to commute to Eastcote daily, a journey of approximately forty minutes.[4] Once back in her flat, she was free to resume her Beethoven research each evening, and at weekends.

Details regarding the SIGINT work Anderson was engaged in at Berkeley Street and Eastcote are difficult to come by, as much of GCHQ's post-1945 history remains closed to researchers. Nonetheless, a report by the Joint Intelligence Sub-Committee of the Chiefs of Staff had considered the question of post-war organisation of intelligence, and was of the view that 'there is a valuable source of information which offers a wide field, but which, before the war was little exploited'.[5] The 'valuable source' referred to was diplomatic SIGINT and COMINT,* the former being Anderson's metier. It was also significant that, at Berkeley Street – and, as far as is known, at Eastcote – it was primarily Hungarian (and occasionally German) SIGINT that Anderson was tasked with breaking into. The advent of the Cold War rendered acquiring an insight into

---

* COMINT was the acronym used for Communications Intelligence, and refers to the interception of communications between two parties, e. g. telephone communications, which comprise speech or text in an un-coded format.

Russo-Hungarian relations absolutely crucial. Soviet military operations in Hungary officially ended on 4 April 1945, when the remains of the German army were finally expelled, although Soviet troops and political advisers remained, and Hungary eventually became a member (albeit an unwilling one) of the Soviet Eastern Bloc. The secret 'percentages agreement' signed by Churchill and Stalin at the Fourth Moscow Conference divided Eastern Europe into British and Soviet spheres of interest, with the Soviet Union granted 80 per cent of influence in Hungary. Russia's consolidation of its power in Hungary resulted in an estimated 600,000 Hungarians being captured and deported to labour camps in the Soviet Union. In light of such developments, it was essential for the West to know as much as possible about Russia's expansionist plans, and Hungarian SIGINT would provide an invaluable source for such intelligence.

*

Welcome as peace and the changes it brought about were, there is evidence that Anderson found some post-war changes challenging. Her friend Dr Friedrich von Busch recalled a story Emily told him when she visited him and his wife Dagmar in Bonn in 1962:

> In 1945 when the government in the UK changed, and Churchill lost the election[6] and was replaced by Clement Attlee, when she came downstairs to the milkman he called her 'my dear' or 'darling', and put his arm around her shoulders, and she said this was like [. . .] it was a revolution, this was like the French Revolution. And it reveals, to my mind, quite a lot

about her upbringing and how she felt. She felt
attacked, that was my feeling.[7]

Such familiarity from an obviously elated Labour supporter was clearly jarring for Anderson. For a woman who
valued her privacy above all else, and always employed
discreet politeness when dealing with those outside her
immediate circle, the brave new world of post-war Europe
would provide many further challenges.

Anderson was one of Britain's best codebreakers, and
throughout her career in SIGINT, music had always been
a vital pressure valve that sustained her. One former
cryptanalyst summarised the skills required by a codebreaker in the following terms: '[T]he cryptographers main
requisites are probably patience, accuracy, stamina, a rea-
sonably clear head, some experience, and an ability to
work with others.'[8]

He might just as well have been describing the skills
required of a musicologist undertaking the task of collating
and transcribing the correspondence of one of the world's
greatest composers. Anderson had already used her cryptanalytic skills to great effect in her work on the Mozart
letters. Beethoven's letters presented an even more formidable challenge, but she was now older and more experienced
than she had been when she tackled Mozart during the
interwar years. And the friends, academics, antiquarians
and archival specialists with whom she worked on her
musicological research held her in very high esteem. They
also appear to have genuinely liked her, enjoyed her company, and were happy to reciprocate the generosity shown
by her in sharing her expertise and research material with
others in the field. Anderson, then, was primed to take full

advantage of her less onerous work commitments at GCHQ, and wasted no time in getting to work.

Anderson had begun her work on the Beethoven letters even before her *Letters of Mozart and his Family* had been published in 1938. Her first letter to the Beethoven archive in Bonn is dated 28 November 1938 – two months after 'Captain Ridley's Shooting Party' had begun their trial run at Bletchley. Following the outbreak of war, the correspondence ceased, and did not resume until November 1952. She would visit Bonn many times once the war ended, but such visits might not have been possible were it not for the brave actions of one man on 18 October 1944, during a heavy aerial bombardment of the city by the RAF. While much of the Beethoven archive had been moved to safe locations outside the city,[9] the building itself, in the city centre, was highly vulnerable. During the bombing raid, in a remarkable display of courage, the caretaker of the building, Heinrich Hasselbach, remained on site and climbed on to the roof. With his bare hands, he threw an incendiary bomb that had landed on the roof into the courtyard, where it was extinguished before it could do any damage.[10] His actions saved the birthplace of Beethoven and its invaluable archive for future generations, and he was later honoured with the same award that Anderson would receive for her work on the Beethoven letters – the Order of Merit, First Class – from the government of the Federal Republic of Germany.

Anderson's visits to the various archives did not begin in earnest until after the war had ended, but, understandably, she did not immediately rush to visit Germany, instead planning a much-anticipated visit to Hans Conrad Bodmer in neutral Switzerland in June 1947. Bodmer, however, was committed to being in the United States at the time, and the visit was postponed, and rearranged for the following year, when she began by visiting Frau Floersheim-Koch[11] in Switzerland in June 1948.[12] Maria Floersheim-Koch and her sister Martha had inherited the extensive collection of their father, Louis Koch, and had kept it safe from Nazi looters during the war, when, as Jews, their lives were in constant jeopardy. Following her visit to view Frau Floersheim-Koch's Beethoven manuscripts, Anderson arrived in Zürich on 13 June 1948, and met Bodmer for the first time. Bodmer had, over the course of four decades, succeeded in putting together the largest private Beethoven collection there has ever been. His remarkable collection had first come to public attention at the International Music Exhibition held in Lucerne, Switzerland, in the summer of 1938. The Beethoven section of the exhibition included over 100 items loaned by Bodmer from his collection. The quality of the exhibits was breathtaking, and included some of the earliest portraits painted of the composer, a lock of his hair, his hearing trumpets, numerous personal letters, and original annotated scores of his most famous musical compositions. The resulting publicity in the international press ensured that Bodmer's collection became known around the world, and not just in specialist circles. Bodmer's collection might well have been looted during the war had he not lived in Switzerland, but it survived intact, and it is hardly surprising that Bodmer's home was one of the first places Anderson chose to visit once the war ended, and visited many times thereafter.

A visit to Bodmer's house was akin to being granted access to the 'Holy Grail' of Beethoven scholarship.

Bodmer had set up three rooms in his large house at Bären-gasse 22, Zürich, to house his valuable collection. Wary of damage to his collection of artefacts (which included Beethoven's writing desk), Bodmer allowed very few guests to view them, and this was strictly by invitation. Those allowed access were those he considered 'morally justified', usually musicians such as the German pianist Wilhelm Backhaus, the Swiss-French pianist Alfred Cortot, and the Spanish cellist Pablo Casals, whom Bodmer believed would be inspired in their performances of Beethoven's works, hav-ing viewed items belonging to the great composer and experienced the atmosphere of his collection rooms. Fewer still were given access to the Beethoven manuscripts them-selves, and Anderson was one of the very few granted this privilege. Her reputation as a music scholar preceded her, her written and spoken German was impeccable, and in her extensive knowledge of Beethoven's correspondence, Bod-mer would immediately have recognised a kindred spirit. An exhibition on the Bodmer collection at the Beethoven-Haus noted that: 'Few researchers enjoyed the privilege of studying the manuscripts. Erich Hertzmann[13] and the Englishwoman Emily Anderson [. . .] achieved this.'[14]

It is not surprising that Anderson was considered an 'Englishwoman', instead of the Irishwoman she actually was, by those international scholars, collectors and anti-quarians with whom she met and collaborated. She appears to have had no sentimental attachment to the country of her birth, and rarely visited Ireland after she had moved to London in 1919. By the time the war had ended, she had spent almost half her life living in England.

*

Anderson's delight in being afforded access to the finest private collection of Beethoven autographs in the world is palpable in the various accounts she provided of the experience. As she later noted, Bodmer's collection:

> [. . .] comprises many musical autographs of exceptional interest, such as, to name but a few, the pianoforte sonata Op.53, (the Waldstein), the Eroica Variations for pianoforte, the C minor Violin Sonata, the last string quartet Op.1135, cadenzas for the pianoforte concertos and numerous sketches. It contains, also, more than a quarter of all the extant letters of Beethoven either in holograph or signed by him.[15]

But it was not just access to the manuscripts themselves that Anderson cherished. Following Bodmer's death in 1956, Anderson was compelled to write a letter to *The Times*, which reflected on both the man himself and his collection. Clearly moved by the sense of Beethoven's presence, which Bodmer's collection brought to the space it occupied, she observed: 'Entering this small but unique museum the visitor immediately feels that something of Beethoven's spirit has come to settle there.'[16]

Her visits to Bodmer's house were 'a memorable experience not only in virtue of the task itself but also because of the infectious enthusiasm displayed by their owner. And his warm welcome and friendly hospitality I shall always remember with heartfelt gratitude.'[17]

Following her visit in June 1948, Anderson wrote to Bodmer thanking him for granting her access to his 'magnificent collection' and requesting that she be allowed to return to Zürich the following spring 'for a longer stay during which I could complete my work on the collection of

Beethoven's letters if you will allow me to do so [. . .]'[18] Bodmer was happy to oblige, and the following year Anderson did return, in June 1949. Afterwards, she wrote to Bodmer, providing come clarification on the dating on some of the letters, which she had checked against her own vast archive of material.[19] The warm friendship between Bodmer and Anderson was born of mutual respect and a shared love of the great composer and the preservation of his legacy. Their relationship was also mutually beneficial, as Anderson's encyclopaedic knowledge of the entire corpus of Beethoven's letters allowed her to provide clarification for Bodmer on issues related to the letters in his possession, and she was also happy to seek answers from her network of existing collaborators around the world in relation to questions that she herself could not answer.

Anderson's international study of Beethoven manuscripts was a costly exercise, involving travel, accommodation and subsistence costs, not to mention the cost of having copies of various letters and other documents made, and her post-war career as a musicologist was to a large degree made possible by the fact that she had amassed quite a bit of money during the war. Working as a senior codebreaker was a relatively well-paid job. She was paid travel and accommodation allowances while she lived away from home, and she still earned enough to retain her flat in Ellerdale Road and run her car. Anderson's Foreign Office rank was Senior Assistant, and by the time she went to Cairo, the salary for male SAs was £600 for men and £480 for women, but it was noted that 'a few posts' (three in total) were set at £800.[20] In a letter to T. J. Wilson of the Foreign Office, Denniston confirmed that Anderson was one of those three SAs, and paid 'at max of scale,

£738–12–£905–3 pa'.[21] While she was in Cairo, she was also paid an additional allowance of £205 p.a.[22] When she returned to Berkeley Street, and later moved to Eastcote, she retained her Senior Assistant grade and associated salary. Anderson had also inherited some money from her late father's estate, and there were royalties from sales of her Mozart *Letters* collection, so, until she retired, it was not cost but rather time that curtailed her international travel.

Anderson's dual lives overlapped to a significant degree when it came to the people she worked with. This is evidenced in both *The Letters of Mozart and his Family* and *The Letters of Beethoven*. In the introduction to the Beethoven *Letters*, for example, she expressed thanks to Professor W. H. Bruford, who held the position of Schröder Professor of German at the University of Cambridge from 1951 until 1961. This was the same Walter Horace Bruford who had served as a codebreaker in Room 40 during the First World War, returned to academia after the war (as a lecturer and then reader in German at the University of Aberdeen, and later Professor of German at the University of Edinburgh) and, from 1939 to 1943, worked at Bletchley in the German Naval section.[23] Harold Macmillan was the publisher who commissioned both the Mozart and Beethoven *Letters* collections. Macmillan had also been privately coached by one of Anderson's colleagues, Dilly Knox, at Cambridge in 1910, and in 1942, during Anderson's time with CBME in Cairo, he had been appointed as British Minister Resident in North Africa, based at Allied Headquarters in Algiers.

Beethoven himself was something of a cryptologist. As increasing deafness made communication more difficult, Beethoven resorted to carrying notebooks with him and conversations with others were conducted in writing.[24] John Russell, who met Beethoven in 1827, recorded another use for his notebook:

> In this, too, although it is not lined, he instantly jots down any musical idea which strikes him. These notes would be utterly unintelligible, even to another musician, for they have no comparative value; he alone has in his own mind the thread by which he brings out of this labyrinth of spots and circles the richest and most astounding harmonies.[25]

Here, then, was a composer who, like Mozart, wrote in codes. But the challenge did not end there. Beethoven's notoriously bad handwriting, particularly in the latter stages of his life, was practically illegible to all those but the very few who had spent sufficient time intensely studying the original manuscripts, and thereby identifying patterns and repetitions that would make the deciphering of it possible. In other words, it was a code that needed to be cracked, if the sense of what he was saying, and why he was saying it, could be accurately discerned. As we have seen, Anderson was one of only a handful of people in the world (her friend Dr Dagmar Weise of the Beethoven-Haus being another) who could do so. Anderson had spent years at the task, and the widely acknowledged quality of her translations of Beethoven's letters, in which many previous errors of translation were corrected, owes much to the fact that they were being 'decoded' by one of the best code-breakers in the world, had the world of musicology but known it.

*

Deciphering handwriting was but part of the enormous task that Anderson had undertaken. To decipher the letters, she first needed to access them, and just as she had done when working on the Mozart letters, she employed copyists to work for her in archives she could not visit herself. Her professional association with Ernst Boucke in Berlin survived the war; by the time the war had ended, Boucke had been appointed as a music librarian in the Prussian State Library, now in Soviet-controlled East Berlin, and he continued to be an important source of copied material for her.[26]

Anderson's circle of friends and associates was a close-knit one. One of her best friends, and an esteemed music collaborator, was Alexander Hyatt King, who worked in the British Museum,[27] where he was appointed as Superintendent of the Music Room in 1944. Anderson's friendship with him had begun when King had been appointed as a cataloguer at the museum in 1934, but he was also a musicologist, and a Mozart expert, and Anderson would have first encountered him during her research on the Mozart letters. Interestingly, King had spent the first six months of 1943 working at Bletchley Park, in the Italian Military Section. His Cambridge double first in Classics certainly fitted him for that position, and as Head of the Italian Diplomatic Section, Anderson is likely to have been aware of his language capabilities, and may well have played a part in his recruitment. However, the nature of the work at Bletchley did not suit King and had a negative impact on his health, such that he left Bletchley and returned to his post at the British Museum.

Also at the British Museum was Douglas Eric Barrett,[28] who was appointed Deputy Keeper in the Department of

Oriental Antiquities[29] at the same time that King became Deputy Keeper of Printed Books there.[30] As Captain Barrett, he had been appointed as the British officer for art protection in the post-war period, and in that capacity had been the one who worked with the Beethoven-Haus and 'oversaw the restitution of Beethoven's piano to its owners'.[31] Captain Barrett was also involved in the recovery of a number of works of art that had been hidden during hostilities, and he developed a good relationship with Theodor Wildeman, Acting Director of the Beethoven-Haus, who had replaced the pro-Nazi Professor Schiedermair in January 1945. In 1947, Barrett wrote to Wildeman to thank him for his hospitality, stating: 'The summer of 1945 was quite the happiest time of my life and I came to regard the country and the people there as my own and I am still very homesick for them.'[32]

For a man who had had a distinguished career in the war as a British Army Commando, taking part in a number of landings, this was a remarkable admission. Similarly, the irony that a woman who had made a significant contribution to the defeat of Germany in the war was now turning her attention to the works of Germany's greatest composer would not have been lost on Anderson. Undertaking research in Germany and Austria, in particular, was going to be challenging, and it would be necessary for her to tread a delicate path in order to resume her Beethoven research. But not only was Anderson prepared to tread this path, she was also sufficiently skilled to do so in such a way that those she would work with never suspected that, in dealing with Miss Emily Anderson, civil servant with the British Foreign Office, they were in reality dealing with Britain's foremost female codebreaker, and a woman who had been eavesdropping on their country's secret communications for almost three decades.

The quandary regarding how all things German would be received both during and after the war was, nonetheless, a difficult one for lovers of German music. For example, the following occured prior to one of the scheduled lunchtime music concerts organised in the National Gallery in May 1940:

> [A]s news reached London of the German advance on the Netherlands, the celebrated German Lieder singer, Elena Gerhardt, telephoned Hess to cancel her appearance at the Gallery. 'Myra,' she told her friend, 'I cannot sing today. Nobody will want to hear the German language.' Hess reassured Gerhardt this wasn't the case and offered to accompany her. As the two women walked on stage, Gerhardt was still concerned, when the audience, sensing her nerves, responded with an ovation warm enough to dispel any doubts that music was what mattered.[33]

For Anderson, similarly, with the war over and victory secured, music was once again what mattered, and her 'real work' could recommence in earnest.

*

Anderson's approach to acquiring information for her musicological research was as methodical as one would expect of a codebreaker of her calibre. Not only had she assembled a virtual army of music collaborators and friends throughout the world, but she also made it as easy as possible for these collaborators to respond to her queries or supply her with information. She provided stamped

addressed envelopes to those from whom she was requesting information. It was a highly effective strategy, albeit a
costly one. The British musicologist Cuthbert Girdlestone,[34]
for example, writing in response to a letter of Anderson's in
July 1934, clearly felt compelled to do so, noting: 'I must
use up one of your stamped addressed envelopes, so here is
some information which you are almost certain to possess
already.'[35] Her determination to chase down every owner
of a Beethoven letter was also time consuming. She wrote
to all of the owners of Beethoven letters in the US – over
thirty of them, as identified by Sonneck in his *Beethoven Letters in America*[36] – and in 1949 put out an additional call, via
the music journal *Notes*, to 'institutions and private individuals possessing Beethoven letters' that had been acquired
since the publication of Sonneck's book, asking them to
contact her at her home address.

Anderson's reliance on copyists and collaborators eased
once she retired and was free to undertake the travel
involved in accessing archives and private collectors, like
Bodmer, herself. She formally retired in November 1950,
after thirty years' service with what had become GCHQ.[37]
Whether any sort of retirement event took place is unknown.
She may, like Alastair Denniston, have simply picked up
her coat and left her office in Eastcote for the last time,
without any fanfare. Alternatively, she may have had some
sort of low-key informal event with former colleagues of
long standing to celebrate her more than three decades
working for the British 'Foreign Office'. We may never
know for sure, but it was the nature of the woman to avoid
drawing any attention to herself, so a quiet, fuss-free transition into retirement is the most likely scenario. However,
it is unlikely that there was any degree of sadness or regret

on the part of Anderson that her exciting life at the highest echelon of the British codebreaking community was coming to an end. Quite the contrary. With a healthy bank balance and a good pension, Anderson was now free of the nine-to-five routine and could finally embark, full-time, on the work she had begun almost as soon as her work on the Mozart letters had ended. It would prove to be a daunting task, and it would take her more than fifteen years to complete. It has been said: 'Music is above all other things a language, and since no one used that language more daringly than Beethoven the more of it you speak, the more of it you feel, the more you will find in his Music.'[38]

Few music lovers would deny that Beethoven used the language of music 'daringly'. Although he communicated his processes, thoughts and motivations in his letters, Beethoven's use of coded notes to himself – and his notoriously bad handwriting – made the task of understanding him extraordinarily difficult. It would require a person of exceptional skill, dedication and patience, and someone capable of performing feats of intellectual gymnastics, in order break into the enigma that was Beethoven. No one was better suited to that task than Emily Anderson.

17

Retirement and Beethoven

During the war, Beethoven's music had been shamelessly appropriated for propaganda purposes by the Nazi regime, but a remarkable coincidence, and some creative thinking, ensured that the Nazis did not have everything their own way. The famous four-note motif of the opening of Beethoven's Fifth Symphony – three short notes followed by one long note – was similarly appropriated by the British propaganda machine and equated with the Morse Code for the letter 'V' – dot-dot-dot-dash – and so became a defiant aural representation of Churchill's famous 'V for Victory' sign. Every wartime BBC broadcast to Europe began with the famous four notes, played on the timpani.[1] The irony would not have been lost on Anderson.

Unlike those who approached retirement with a sense of dread as to how they would fill their time, Emily Anderson had a plan. She had the time and financial resources to fully immerse herself in her Beethoven research, as she had always intended to do. A description of Anderson in the years following her retirement comes from one of her neighbours in Ellerdale Road. Mrs Elizabeth Oliver moved to the house next door in 1958, and remembers Anderson as a pleasant lady, who very much kept herself to herself, was uninterested in idle chatter, looked somewhat frail, and 'probably looked older than she was'.[2] Although knowing nothing of Anderson's career in intelligence when interviewed, Mrs Oliver recalled that she and the lady in Flat 4 would sometimes chat to each other in passing, but that Miss Anderson was:

> [...] very self-contained. She wore loose clothes, she had dark hair and it was cut rather simply. My house adjoined no. 24 and I think at some point my house and 24 was one building.[3] The roof caught fire and the top floor was demolished,[4] and then it was divided. So Ellerdale Court became 24 and my bit of it became 22.

By the time Anderson resumed her Beethoven research in Germany, there had been a change in personnel at the Beethoven-Haus. Professor Joseph Schmidt-Görg had replaced the Acting Director Theodor Wildeman. Anderson was also fortunate that by then, Dr Dagmar Weise had begun working at the Beethoven archive. Thereafter, it was primarily Dagmar with whom Anderson corresponded in relation to her queries and requests for photocopies of autographs. Dagmar recalls meeting Anderson with a great deal of respect, as her reputation preceded her. Hans Conrad Bodmer had already met Anderson by the time Dagmar first met her in 1953, and 'spoke about her in warm terms'. Dagmar recalls of Anderson that initially 'she was shy and distant', but over time, a warm and genuine friendship developed between the two women, which lasted until Anderson's death. The correspondence between them regarding the Beethoven letters was frequently punctuated by exclamation marks, an indication of the excitement and joy being experienced by both women at the discoveries they were making. But it was typical of Anderson that the correspondence refers also to money orders sent to cover the cost of photocopies, and drawn on Emily's bank, Coutts & Co., of the Strand in London.

Anderson spent much of the summer of 1952 visiting archives and friends in Europe.[5] She spent May and June in Vienna, transcribing Beethoven letters (*c.* 250 of them) held in the Gesellschaft der Musikfreunde, and attended the International Music Congress and Festival in May.[6] In June, she went to see Bodmer in Zürich.[7] In one of her letters to him, she remarked how moved she was by being so close to personal items belonging to the great composer, noting: 'The proximity of Beethoven's own desk just overwhelmed me.' Anderson was compelled to cut short her visit to Bodmer in late June/early July, the most likely reason being the sale of the house that contained her flat at 24 Ellerdale Road. In May 1952, the house containing Anderson's flat, and the adjacent property, No. 22, were put up for sale, likely following the refurbishment work undertaken as a result of the fire Mrs Oliver describes.[8]

In the years following her retirement, from 1952 to 1955, Emily Anderson did something that she had never done before: she shared her home with another woman. Little is known about Josephine Morrissey, other than that she was a nurse who worked in a number of hospitals in the London area over the course of her career. For many years, Josephine Morrissey lived in the nurse's home of the various hospitals in which she worked,[9] but from 1952 to 1955, she shared Anderson's flat in Ellerdale Road. The precise nature of their relationship cannot be confirmed, as Anderson did not leave any personal correspondence, and only rarely did she refer to personal or family matters in her correspondence to her friends and music collaborators. It is impossible to know precisely how the two women came to meet. She may have been a friend in need of accommodation, whom Anderson decided to help out. But for that sort of arrangement to have existed for four years, particularly in the case of a woman like Anderson, who relished her privacy and the time it afforded her to focus on her musicological work, is unlikely. Any guest would have had to stay in the spare bedroom, which had always been used as an office by Anderson – she called the one in Ellerdale Road her 'Beethoven workshop'. What is certain is that Anderson did not need to let her spare room to a tenant for financial reasons. Given her salary, and later pension, her share of her late parents' estate, and the profits from the sales of her books, she never needed the money. Only two possibilities therefore present themselves. Either Anderson was simply lonely and wanted a flatmate, or she was in a relationship with Josephine Morrissey.

The evidence would point to the latter. Her relationship with Dorothy Brooks, which had played out in the high-octane atmosphere of Bletchley in the early days of the war, and subsequently in the balmy setting of Cairo, was something that Anderson undoubtedly missed once Dorothy began a relationship with Tommy Bowring Carr. Now retired, Anderson had more time to devote to her personal life, but her fiercely independent personality saw to it that this aspect of her life was still something that would have to take a back seat to her 'real work', her musicological research. The years during which Anderson shared her flat with Josephine Morrissey were the years in which she travelled extensively in her efforts to track down each and every Beethoven letter, and she always travelled alone. Now in her sixties, Anderson's feelings for any new partner are likely to have been significantly less intense than had been the case when she was a younger woman, and they certainly were not sufficient to restrict the amount of travel she undertook, nor the time she was prepared to devote to her scholarly research. But all of this we must surmise. Anderson herself does not at any stage refer to Morrissey in any of her correspondence, and the women were no longer living together when Anderson's friend Dagmar visited her flat in the late 1950s. No correspondence from Morrissey herself has come to light that would speak to the nature of the relationship between the two women, nor why they stopped living together sometime in late 1955 or early 1956. What is clear is that, by 1956, Anderson was again living alone, and did not share her flat with anyone else in the remaining years until her death in 1962.

But if personal relationships do not appear to have been at the top of Anderson's agenda in the 1950s, her scholarly work on the Beethoven letters undoubtedly was. Her determination that every letter would be translated with absolute accuracy, and previous errors eliminated from her edition, was laid out in an article she wrote for the music journal *Notes* in 1952.[10] Her approach was forensic, but, for Anderson, whose entire professional life had been spent finding the precise and possibly crucial detail in diplomatic codes, everything mattered, no matter how small it might appear to be to the casual reader, and it all contributed to making sense of the letter as a whole. One example of her approach will suffice. Anderson notes that:

> [In] the autograph of a short note to Zmeskall, dated 13 November 1802, the beginning sentence runs as follows: 'Sagen Sei Ihra *Musik bei Förster* ganz ab . . .' (Cancel definitely your *music making at Förster's*). All the editors, without exception, merely reprint the copy made by Thayer [. . .] who first saw the autograph. His version reads *"Ihre Musik bei(m)Fürsten" (Your music-making at the Prince's)*.

Thayer, author of the first scholarly biography of Beethoven, had misread the name Förster for the word *Fürsten*, and in her footnote Anderson noted that E. A. Förster (1748–1823) was a distinguished musician and teacher of music, at whose house chamber music and particularly string quartets were performed. Anderson knew, as a result of her research, that 'Zmeskall usually played the 'cello in these quartets'. So there was no unidentified 'Prince' – it was simply a reference to musical soirées among friends, the detail of which Anderson was happy to provide because she knew it, something that Thayer did not. A small detail it may have been, but detail mattered, as much in musicology as codebreaking, and nothing escaped Emily Anderson's critical eye. Identifying the errors of previous transcribers, and potentially putting scholarly noses out of joint, was not something that worried Anderson – it was all about accuracy, and professional pride did not enter into it.

Anderson was aware that the task facing her was considerable. In her introduction to the *Letters*, Volume I, she stated:

> The present editor realized from the outset that nothing should be taken on trust; a clean sweep would have to be made of nearly all the editorial work hitherto

presented, and no effort should be spared to trace the
original of each letter; whether written by Beethoven
or merely signed by him.

The reason that nothing could be taken on trust was down
to the fact that the authors of previous collections had, of
necessity, relied on copyists, many of whom were unfamiliar with the difficulties of Beethoven's script 'and the
eccentricities of his orthography'.[11] Errors and critical
omissions were the result, and Anderson was determined
to work, wherever possible, from original manuscripts or
photographed material, which she had the necessary skills
to interpret correctly; in doing so, she could avoid the errors
of previous editions. She drew on the assistance of friends,
antiquarian booksellers and dealers, exhibition and sale
catalogues, and appeals in English, American and foreign
journals to identify letters that had not been included in
any published works. Her eye scanned every possible publication to track down any possible lead. She notes in her
introduction to Volume I, for example, that:

> [A] stray paragraph in a London evening paper
> revealed the hiding-place in England of an unknown
> letter from Beethoven to the poet H. J. von Collin; and
> a short notice in the Paris *Figaro* produced an unre-
> corded one in Belgium.[12]

Anderson's debt to antiquarian dealers was often repaid
with the expertise she could offer in identifying the work of
forgers. The increasing prices paid for Beethoven autographs encouraged forgers to try to pass off imitations,
particularly of his later letters, when his handwriting was
hieroglyphical and, as Anderson observed, 'readily lends

itself to imitation'. No such forgeries could get past Emily Anderson. Her persistence was at play in chasing down the opportunity to view original manuscripts in the hands of private collectors, even, as she noted, 'at the risk of being unpleasantly importunate to private owners'. Few could resist her entreaties, and she noted that 'in nearly all cases [. . .] the applications have been courteously received' and access was granted.[13]

Visits to Bodmer continued as she worked her way through his collection of Beethoven autographs, something she considered 'a great adventure, and a privilege'. In the summer of 1954, Anderson informed Bodmer that, with the help of the Foreign Office and the British Museum, she was 'launching an attack' on archives in Stuttgart, Romania, Czechoslovakia and Russia, in the hope that they would provide her with access to copies or microfilms of their Beethoven autograph collections.[14] This statement confirms that Anderson was not afraid to use her contacts in the Foreign Office if it would help in progressing her research. She was bold enough to inform Bodmer that she was drawing on such resources because, as far as he and others were concerned, her work in the Foreign Office was that of any other retired senior civil servant – he certainly never suspected that her career had had anything to do with codebreaking or intelligence work.

There were inevitably some challenges in accessing archives that, in post-war Europe, were now in the hands of the Russians. In his review of *The Letters of Beethoven*, the music critic Colin Mason observed that 'the only sizeable number of them that she has not been able to consult are some of those in the Deutsche Staatsbibliothek in Berlin, for which she has been obliged to take over versions already published – mostly from the German edition of Thayer'.[15] It had not been for the want of trying. In 1955, she contacted the then-Foreign Secretary's office to request assistance with accessing Beethoven letters that had previously been in the Berlin library, but which the Russians had removed to the Soviet Union.[16] While the original letter in response from the Foreign Secretary's office does not survive, Anderson provided a handwritten copy of it for the Beethoven-Haus archive. The response from the Foreign Secretary – Harold Macmillan, who also happened to be her publisher – read:

> I am directed by Mr. Secretary Macmillan to acknowledge receipt of your letter of September 15th concerning your wish to obtain Her Majesty's Government's assistance in approaching the Soviet authorities for microfilms of Beethoven manuscripts which you have reason to believe are at present in the Soviet Union. I am to state that this Department consider it inadvisable to make the approach which you requested to the Soviet authorities without more definite information that the documents are in fact in Soviet keeping.
>
> I am to advise you, therefore, first to communicate with the Custodians of the Prussian State Library, which formerly housed the collection of autographed letters in which you are interested. If the Custodians are able to confirm that the relevant documents are at present in the Soviet Union,[17] this Department will be glad to assist you by making an approach to the Soviet authorities on your behalf requesting them to supply microfilms of these documents.[18]

The implication was clear: the Foreign Office was not prepared to ask the Russians for something that they could deny they had, unless there was evidence that they did, in fact, have the items, thereby compelling them to comply with the request. Anderson was familiar enough with Foreign Office language that she immediately made contact with a colleague in the Berliner Bibliothek, Dr Virneisel,[19] who was able to confirm that the Russians had removed the letters from the former Prussian State Library, and that they were now in Soviet hands. She wrote to Professor Schmidt-Görg of the Beethoven-Haus, explaining that she had informed 'a colleague in the Foreign Office' of this fact, and an official letter had been sent to the Russians requesting copies of the autographs. Anderson later received the necessary microfilms of the letters in question.[20]

She was equally tenacious when it came to defending her translations of Beethoven's letters. In advance of the publication of the *Letters of Beethoven*, she published a number of articles in academic journals, providing a 'taster' of what was to come. One such article appeared in the July 1953 volume of *Music and Letters*,[21] which prompted a letter from a leading authority on Beethoven, who identified a perceived error in one of Anderson's translations.[22] Her response was unequivocal:

Mr. Ludwig Misch[23] maintains that in my transcription of Beethoven's letter of July 11th 1825, which is facsimiled in the July 1953 issue of your review (p. 223, line 11) 'mir' should be substituted for 'nur'. He is wrong. By kind permission of its present owner I have again consulted the autograph letter, in which Beethoven's 'Bogen' or, rather, his characteristic oblique stroke over the 'u' is far more definite than in my photograph and, consequently, in the facsimile. Moreover, a prolonged study of the originals of Beethoven's letters based upon an application of the inductive method enables the reader eventually to distinguish between his 'nu' and his 'mi', which are formed quite differently. In this instance there is no shadow of doubt that 'nur' is the correct reading.[24]

Anderson's stout defence of her own scholarship is understandable, but it is the manner in which she approaches it that reveals her formidable character. Firstly, she wrong-foots her critic by referring to the original document, to which she had had access; she knew he had not. She then treats Misch to a tutorial on letter shapes in Beethoven's handwriting, confidently referencing her own long experience of dealing with the same. Finally, she is sufficiently confident in her own abilities that she leaves her critic in absolutely no doubt that her identification of the word is correct. This was not a music scholar to be taken on lightly. The fact that Anderson's response was published in the April 1954 edition of *Music & Letters* would indicate that she had gone to great lengths to track down the original autograph letter for the second time so as to refute Misch's assertion that she had made an error.

Anderson was generous with her expertise and the extensive archive of Beethoven resources she had assembled at her 'Beethoven workshop' in Hampstead. The American conductor, musicologist and Beethoven scholar Eliot Forbes[25] was one of the many scholars whom Anderson assisted in their research work. In his introduction to his revised *Thayer's Life of Beethoven*, published in 1967, Forbes observed:

> [I]t was the privilege of this editor to work with the
> late Miss Anderson in her home in Hampstead, Eng-
> land, in the Spring of 1953, and she most kindly
> allowed the checking of the letters translated by
> Krehbiel against her reading of the original Ger-
> man text.[26]

Anderson's expertise in reading Beethoven's handwriting
meant that she was the acknowledged Beethoven authenti-
cator in London, and her services were often called upon
to confirm the provenance of letters or other Beethoven
manuscripts. In July 1954, she was asked by Sotheby's auc-
tioneers[27] to authenticate some Mozart and Beethoven
manuscripts coming up for auction.[28] Similarly, in 1956,
what was described as a 'treasure trove' was discovered at
the Royal College of Music. In a brown paper parcel discovered in a safe were letters from the private collection of
George Grove, first director of the Royal College of Music.
Among a host of other correspondence[29] were two original
letters from Beethoven, one of which, a letter to Diabelli,
was previously unknown. The Beethoven letters were
described as Grove's 'cherished possessions'. Anderson was
asked to authenticate the letter, which she happily did –
she was among the first to see it – and subsequently
prepared a translation of it, which was published in 1956.[30]

Some years into her retirement, Anderson revealed that
she had not entirely left her former career behind. In January 1955, she sent a scrupulously polite yet subtly rebuking
letter to Rupert Erlebach, Secretary of the Royal Musical
Association:

> I hope you will forgive me for raising what might
> seem to be a very small matter. In the latest issue of

the *Proceedings of the Royal Musical Association 1953–1954*
I notice that in the list of members (to whose names
their honours, though not their academic degrees and
distinctions are attached) my name appears without
its accompanying honour (O.B.E). As this honour was
offered to me for services in the Middle East during
the last war, and as I accepted it, I feel it is my duty
not to discard it.[31]

The letter is highly revealing of Anderson's response to
the awarding of the OBE for her work at CBME. She
had neither sought nor expected it, but had sufficient
respect for the honour bestowed that she felt it her duty
'not to discard it'. There is no sense of Anderson being
miffed, from a sense of pride, that her honour was omitted from her name. She was, however, unwilling to have
it disrespected by seeing it omitted in the company of
others who had their honours recognised. Erlebach made
the change to the membership list, and the omission
of the OBE was corrected in the 1954–55 listing of
members.[32]

Anderson attended the July 1955 Congress of the International Musicological Society held in Oxford, where
Professor Schmidt-Görg gave a lecture on one of the great
mysteries of Beethoven scholarship: the identity of the
'immortal beloved'. The event turned out to be something
of a damp squib, as Schmidt-Görg, largely based on an
examination of letters in the Bodmer collection, 'restored the
"immortal beloved" to her former anonymity'.[33] Anderson
subsequently attended the reception marking the end of the
Congress hosted in London by the Royal Musical Association on 5 July,[34] having written to Erlebach requesting

'two cards of admission to the reception'. It is not known who accompanied her.[35]

*

The 1950s was a time of intense interest in new or redis-covered Beethoven letters, for which there was a healthy and competitive market among private collectors, anti-quarians and archives. For Beethoven scholars and collectors, 'every bit of paper touched by the hand of Beet-hoven [was] precious'.[36] With such a resurgent interest in Beethoven letters, in the winter of 1952–53, some of the foremost Beethoven collectors, antiquarians and scholars united in what promised to be a formidable collaboration. Bodmer and August Laube[37] in Zürich, and Heinrich Eisemann in London, established a contact network among those to be involved in a proposed collaboration to pool resources in order to produce definitive collections, in Ger-man and English, of the Beethoven letters. Invited to contribute were Max Unger, Otto Erich Deutsch, the Beethoven-Haus – and Emily Anderson. With competition intense among international scholars, a number of reputa-tions (and egos) were at stake and, shockingly, Schmidt-Görg, Director of the Beethoven-Haus archive, in an ill-considered memorandum sent to all of the above, suggested that Anderson's English translation of the *Letters* should not include a detailed scholarly commentary, presumably because he considered Anderson insufficiently qualified to undertake such as a task. It was an insensitive and unwar-ranted snub, but, unruffled, Anderson herself suggested that a German version edited by Otto Erich Deutsch should be published before her English edition, and she generously offered to make all of her material available to

Deutsch for his proposed German edition of the complete correspondence. It was a remarkable offer – the fruit of countless years of chasing down Beethoven autographs around the globe, over 230 of which she personally had discovered for the first time, freely handed over to a rival. As it transpired, the much-anticipated collaboration came to naught. A battle ensued between Unger and Schmidt-Görg, with Bodmer unwillingly drawn into the fray, and as a result, Unger's edition of Beethoven's Letters never appeared. Deutsch squabbled with publishers over his commission for undertaking a German collection, and refused to produce a German version of Anderson's letters for the same reason, although he promised to assist Anderson as much as he could. In the end, Bodmer gave up, and donated money and pledged his precious collection, to the Beethoven-Haus. It is significant that, of all the key players involved in the initial collaboration, it was Anderson alone who delivered on her publication project, producing a collection of the Beethoven letters that remains to this day a classic. That she did so without the financial support of any institution renders her achievement all the more remarkable.

*

By 1956, Anderson was once again living alone. There was no further trace of Josephine Morrissey in Anderson's life – like Dorothy Brooks, she did not feature in Anderson's will, which was drawn up in 1959. Anderson, therefore, was unsupported when, that same year, she suffered two major losses. Her mother, Emily Gertrude Anderson, died on 21 May. In the years following her husband's death in 1936, Mrs Anderson had moved to a house at 84 St Helen's

Road, Booterstown, Dublin. As her health began to fail, she moved to a private nursing home, where she died of 'cardiac degeneration'. Emily, her eldest daughter Elsie, and her estranged son Alexander and his family survived her. It is typical of the intensely private nature of the family that the death notice for Mrs Anderson stipulated 'Funeral private. No flowers, no letters, please.'[38] Bizarrely, once again Anderson's name was incorrectly noted in the death notice, which read 'dearly beloved mother of Elsie and Amy', not Emily, and there is no mention of Alexander, or his wife and son. Mrs Anderson left an estate of some £6,178 to be divided between her two surviving daughters. No bequest was made for Alexander.

Anderson's relationship with her family was a complex one. No correspondence to or from her family in Ireland survives, and her friends Dagmar and Friedrich were not even aware that she was Irish, as she never spoke of Ireland, and to their ears spoke with an upper-class 'English' accent. Throughout her career, her precious annual leave was devoted to travel in pursuit of Mozart or Beethoven research, and she rarely returned to Ireland once she had moved permanently to the UK in 1920 – the funerals of her parents being the rare exceptions when she did so. Dagmar recalls that Anderson never spoke of her family, other than sharing the story regarding her father, and the cigar he kept on his desk to test his resolve to give up smoking. Her relationship with her mother, however, came sharply into focus following her death, in a way that surprised her friend. Anderson had informed Dagmar of her mother's death in a letter, and Dagmar had responded with what she considered the appropriate degree of sympathy. To her surprise, Emily responded in a way that made it clear she found the condolences expressed by her friend Dagmar to be deficient. It was a rare, and telling, show of sensitivity on the part of Anderson, and suggests that her apparent lack of any sentimental feelings for the country of her birth belied an attachment to her family that was very real, if unspoken. The absence of any surviving Anderson family correspondence renders it impossible to know what the family dynamics were between the Anderson parents and their offspring, or between the Anderson siblings. However, what we do know suggests that Anderson and her mother had much in common. Mrs Anderson had shown courage and spirit in marrying Alexander Anderson in defiance of her parent's wishes. Her involvement in the suffrage movement, her forthright personality, her independent spirit, were aspects reflected in her feisty, auburn-haired middle daughter. It is significant that, five years after her mother's death, *The Letters of Beethoven* was dedicated 'In Memoriam E. G. A.', a reference to her mother, Emily Gertrude Anderson.

The second blow to Anderson occurred just a week after her mother's death. On 28 May 1956, Anderson received word that her friend Hans Conrad Bodmer had died at the age of sixty-five, 'after a serious illness, which he endured with great bravery'. Anderson delighted in the company of her fellow Beethoven enthusiasts, but in Bodmer and his wife Elsy she had found kindred spirits. They became good friends who enriched the early years of her retirement, and in whose company and home she experienced genuine joy. Following his death, Anderson recalled her first visit to Bodmer's house, and the impression created on her by his collection:

The owner had arranged these treasures with devoted care in two rooms, the larger of which houses the writing desk and other relics of the composer. Entering this small but unique museum, the visitor immediately feels that something of Beethoven's spirit has come to settle there.[39]

It is a measure of Anderson's reputation, and bona fides as a Beethoven scholar, that she had been afforded remarkable access to one of the finest collections of Beethoven material then in private hands. The warmth of the welcome afforded her is also indicative of the fact that she appears to have had a facility for forming friendships with those whose interests very much mirrored her own. Anderson noted of her visits to Bodmer:

I had the privilege of examining and copying the originals of Beethoven's letters [. . .] it was a memorable experience not only in virtue of the task itself but also because of the infectious enthusiasm displayed by their owner. And his warm welcome and friendly hospitality I shall always remember with heartfelt gratitude.[40]

Anderson had paid one final visit to Bodmer in January 1956, but by March of that year, his illness had progressed and he was confined to bed. Even from his sickbed, he was issuing instructions to Anderson's London-based art-dealer friend Heinrich Eisemann[41] to act for him in acquiring two Beethoven letters that were being auctioned at Sotheby's in London. The letters were purchased by Bodmer for a combined price of £1,120 plus commission.[42] Two months later, he was dead. Under the terms of his will, Bodmer bequeathed his entire Beethoven collection, including items of furniture such as Beethoven's desk, to the Beethoven-Haus. This bequest is recognised as one of the greatest acts of patronage in the world of music. There is a considerable case to be made that his personal friendships with both Anderson and Dr Dagmar Weise were instrumental in convincing Bodmer that the Beethoven-Haus was the most appropriate home for his precious collection. Anderson had been visiting Bodmer since 1948, and while, as we have seen, she considered it both a privilege and an honour to be afforded access to such a remarkable collection, lovingly curated by a passionate Beethoven-lover whose motives were entirely altruistic, it was also the case that Bodmer was equally happy to spend time in Anderson's company. Here was a woman whose knowledge of the minutiae of Beethoven's life, acquired over years of intense study of his letters, enabled her to provide Bodmer with contextualisation for many references in the letters he possessed, and provide answers to many of his unanswered questions. They clearly delighted in each other's company, but Bodmer was equally impressed with the young and gifted scholar Dagmar, who visited him on many occasions to examine his collection. It is a measure of the trust and friendship that developed between Dagmar and the Bodmers that she was invited to stay in their home during her later visits. Bodmer had, in 1952, allowed copies of his collection, running to some 4,800 pages, to be placed at the disposal of the Beethoven-Haus archive at Bonn. He was awarded an honorary PhD by the University of Bonn for this act of extraordinary generosity,[43] but it was the bequest in his will that really established the

Beethoven-Haus as the leading centre for Beethoven scholarship in the world.

Having recovered from the twin losses of both her mother and her friend Bodmer, the following year, 1957, was a time of great productivity for Anderson on the Beethoven letters. Bodmer's death in particular appears to have really galvanised her determination to finish the *Letters* and begin work on her next task, a revised edition of her *Letters of Mozart and his Family*. She continued her correspondence with other musicology scholars, and it is in one letter to an American Beethoven enthusiast, subsequently published by its recipient, Louisa Cagwin, that Anderson revealed much about her approach to her craft and the challenges she faced. Dated 1 March 1957, the letter was written by Anderson in response to what amounted to a 'fan mail' letter sent to her by Cagwin,[44] which also featured a number of specific queries regarding her work on the Beethoven letters. Anderson responded as follows:

My dear Miss Cagwin:

How very kind of you to send me such a long and appreciative letter about my work. Such encouraging remarks help me over the dull portions of the task. Because though a great deal of it is fascinating and thrilling – a marvellous adventure and a wonderful privilege, I consider – there has been, and still is, a good deal of dreary spade work to be done – rather like what Beethoven felt when faced with those mountains of publishers' proofs to correct . . . I need hardly tell you that I am greatly indebted to kind friends and well-wishers in the U.S.A for helping me to discover the whereabouts of Beethoven letters, so that I might have a reliable text in each case to translate and annotate. How strange it is that we nearly met in Bonn in the summer of 1953! My good friends Professor Erich Hertzmann of Columbia University and his wife were working there too and we had many pleasant outings together. He is one of the foremost Beethoven scholars. They have been to London since and very often to the Beethoven 'workshop' in my flat.

Now to your questions which I am delighted to try to answer. Apart from decyphering Beethoven's characteristic handwriting, which anyone can learn to do by studying it for a sufficiently long time, I have not found any difficulty in <u>translating</u> his letters as such. Every translator is faced with the same problem, which consists of two processes: 1) discovering the exact meaning of what the writer was saying, 2) rendering that meaning in lucid English, so that the reader forms in English the same idea as the German reader of the original. The English reader should never have to refer to the German text in order to find out what Beethoven or Mozart did say! That is the real test of a good translation.

Beethoven's letters are totally different from those of Mozart. One can't compare them, no more than one can compare their different musical compositions or their personalities. They were born in different circumstances and surroundings. Mozart died very young. Beethoven lived to be 57 and most of his letters <u>which have been preserved</u> begin at the age of 31. So we don't know what kind of letters Beethoven was writing during the years when Mozart was writing reams to his father. Again, Beethoven was far more interested in human nature than Mozart and in the events of the world; he read more too (but then he lived longer!). What is of interest is that Mozart, so far as we know, hardly ever wrote to anyone outside his family, whereas my card-index of recipients of letters from Beethoven runs to over 230! . . . [45]

Anderson concluded the letter by stating that the Beethoven *Letters* would appear 'sometime in 1958'. As it transpired, that target date was overly optimistic, and a combination of personal matters and health issues delayed progress for another three years.

*

One family matter that distracted Anderson from her Beethoven work was the death, on 22 October 1957, of her sister Elsie in Ireland. One year older than Anderson, she died, aged sixty-seven, at her mother's former home in Booterstown, Dublin. Elsie was described in an obituary as 'one of the very highly accomplished daughters of a former President of University College, Galway' who was 'survived by her sister, who is in the service of the British Foreign Office in London'. No mention is made of Anderson's sole surviving sibling, Alexander Anderson, who was now living as Arthur Andrews in Liverpool. Elsie's short marriage to John Rochford, who had died in 1939, had produced no children, but had been a very happy one, with Elsie 'intensely devoted to her husband'.[46] She was laid to rest in her husband's grave at Dean's Grange cemetery, Dublin. With both parents dead, and her brother estranged from the family, it fell to Emily to resolve out-standing financial matters, deal with wills and probate issues, and arrange the sale of the Booterstown property. It was time Anderson could ill afford away from her research and writing, but it was nonetheless necessary, and much of it could be done via correspondence from London.

By the following year, most of the estate matters were resolved, and Anderson had a visit from her friend and col-league Dagmar to look forward to. Dagmar visited London in October 1958, prior to her forthcoming marriage to Dr Friedrich von Busch. Anderson subsequently wrote to thank her for the visit and send her good wishes for a happy married life. The warmth of the sentiments expressed to her friend reflects Anderson's somewhat wistful recogni-tion of what she herself had missed out on in having never married: '[. . .] in my heart I wished and do wish to you always, everything a happy marriage may give to a person – a secure existence – a lifelong deep friendship'.[47]

This statement is one of the most personal and reveal-ing in all of Anderson's correspondence. Conscious that her young friend had embarked on a lifelong partnership that would – and did – provide her with not only love but the security of a deep and lasting friendship, there is an acknowledgement of what might have been, had Anderson chosen a different path. There is also a telling indication that the one marriage Anderson had first-hand experience of – that of her parents – had been exactly that which she wished for her friend. Anderson's sexuality, however, cou-pled with her single-minded determination to pursue a life of intellectual stimulation unencumbered by family com-mitments, had decided her path for her, and that path would never include marriage. It was a sacrifice she was willing to make. And the commitment of marriage aside, Anderson did cultivate deep personal friendships, and was valued as a generous and thoughtful friend, remembered for many acts of great kindness, usually dispensed quietly and without fuss.

When Dagmar visited Anderson's flat, she was shown the 'Beethoven workshop' in her spare bedroom. She recalls that the flat was well furnished, and the furniture was of the dark, heavy, Victorian variety, with pride of place given to her beloved pianoforte. Dagmar recalls of Anderson: 'She was a very warm person. Panda bear was a sensation in London Zoo and I had to work in the British Museum, and she insisted that I had to go to the Zoo to see the panda.'[48]

On a subsequent visit to Bonn, Anderson brought with her a stuffed panda bear toy for Dagmar's child as a memento.

Shortly after Dagmar's visit, Anderson's health suffered a setback. In a letter to Alexander Hyatt King in November 1958, she noted that she had just shaken off 'a rather horrid attack which turned to pleurisy and kept me in bed for a fortnight'.[49] But she rallied quickly, as barely two weeks later she wrote to Dagmar informing her that work on her Beethoven *Letters* had finally been completed, saying: 'My entire material, letters and documents, is now with Macmillan.'[50] Following the years of effort, extensive travel and copious correspondence she had undertaken in order to bring together the most complete collection of Beethoven's letters ever assembled, the action of handing over all of her material to her publishers was undoubtedly a moment of triumph, but it must also have been something of a wrench. *The Letters of Beethoven* was undoubtedly Anderson's magnum opus, and surrendering the extensive collection she had amassed over the course of more than two decades, and through a World War, was a great act of faith on her part. But Anderson clearly trusted Macmillan, and that trust was not misplaced.

Anderson saw in 1959 with renewed good health, satisfied that her Beethoven volumes were now in the hands of her publishers, and with a much-anticipated trip to Austria in late January ahead of her. Later that year, on 27 November,[51] she was awarded the Mozarteum Foundation's Mozart Medal in Bronze, '*[i]n Aner kenning ihrer besonderen-Verdienste um die Mozart-Forschung*'.* Awarded two decades after the publication of *The Letters of Mozart and his Family*, this was a significant award and a great honour, the first of two major international awards she would receive for her music scholarship. The awarding of the Mozart Medal reflected the fact that, although her primary focus at that stage was seeing her volumes of *The Letters of Beethoven* published, the Mozarteum Foundation was aware that she had already begun work on a revised and updated collection of the Mozart letters. It was also the case that:

> [O]f late years an intensive search for autograph letters of Beethoven, with a view to producing an up-to-date English edition, has occasionally led me into untrodden paths, and brought to light some interesting

* Translates as 'In recognition of her special services to Mozart research'.

documents whose existence had not been hitherto suspected.[52]

One such document was a short letter from Mozart to his father, but its significance was clearly seen by Anderson by virtue of the fact that it cleared up 'a slight obscurity surrounding the composer's and his librettist's collaboration on *Die Entführung aus dem Serail*'.[53] Anderson was the first musicologist to bring the letter to public attention, and was in a position to do so because its then-owner, knowing of her reputation, was prepared to share it with her. Anderson had contacted Sir Stephen Lewis Courtauld[54] regarding two Beethoven letters in his possession, which were already published. Courtauld, however, made her aware of a Mozart letter, which Anderson said 'to the best of my knowledge is unedited and has so far been overlooked'.[55] Courtauld provided Anderson with the provenance of the letters, which had been acquired seventy years earlier by his father, Sydney Courtauld. The Beethoven letters were put on public display at an exhibition in 1904, but Sydney Courtauld had decided to keep the Mozart letter private. It was a major coup for Anderson, and afforded her the opportunity to remind the world of music scholarship that a revised edition of the Mozart *Letters* would be her next project once the Beethoven *Letters* had been published.

*

Matters of a more personal nature occupied Anderson in the summer of 1959, when her recent brush with ill-health prompted her to put her affairs in order. On 3 June 1959 she made out her will at the offices of her solicitors,

Farrers & Co. of Lincoln's Inn Fields, London. As might have been expected, her will was highly detailed and specific in its bequests, but it was one bequest in particular that would leave a significant legacy. Anderson had been in negotiations with George Baker,[56] Secretary of the Royal Philharmonic Society, regarding her intention to endow an annual prize for violin-playing. She wrote to Baker confirming this:

> The portion of my will which relates to the prize for violin playing has been worded in the paragraph a copy of which I am enclosing for you and the Committee. The Society will not be put to any expense in connexion (sic) with the awarding of this Prize as the fund earmarked for the purpose will be quite sufficient to cover the costs (advertising, hall, adjudications, fees etc.)

The paragraph confirmed that Emily Anderson was making provision for:

> [. . .] an annual prize for violin playing, such prize to be awarded to the best competitor at an annual competition to be held in London and open to international entry and to be called 'The Emily Anderson Prize for violin playing'.[57]

The honorary Treasurer of the Society subsequently confirmed that 'the Royal Philharmonic Society will gladly undertake the management of your prize for violin-playing', but, significantly, also stated 'and we fully understand that the competition must be on an international basis'.[58] Anderson had stipulated that there be an international dimension to the prize, something very much in line with her view that music belonged to, and should be enjoyed by, everyone, regardless of nationality. She was anxious to have the matter resolved before she departed on her next international trip, to Vienna.[59]

International travels aside, with just corrections to proofs remaining to be gone through – a not inconsiderable task given that the combined volumes ran to some 2,900 pages, with over 100 pages of endnotes – Anderson had a good deal more time on her hands. This she filled with attendance at concerts and recitals with friends. In October 1959, she wrote to Nigel Fortune, the Secretary of the Royal Musical Association (RMA),[60] informing him that she had 'already invited two guests to the lecture recital to be given on October 21st by Paul Badura-Skoda[61] (who is a friend of mine)' and asking his permission 'to invite another (i.e. a third) guest [. . .] I do not drink sherry and am therefore several glasses to the good which can be drunk by others!'[62]

The reference to not drinking sherry is an interesting one. Anderson appears to have been abstemious when it came to alcohol. She did drink wine on occasion, but not to excess.[63] This may have been a matter of personal choice, or it may have been the case that, like many in her profession, Anderson had to be constantly on her guard when it came to the possibility of persons, intentionally or innocently, trying to elicit information from her regarding her work. She was careful regarding her consumption of alcohol in public settings, much like her colleague Dilly Knox, who in 1936 stopped attending the annual Founders' Feast at King's College, Cambridge, 'as the wines were so good that he feared he might be betrayed into some slight indiscretion about his work'.[64]

Apart from attending concerts, Anderson was invited

to do something she had never done before: deliver a public lecture on Beethoven to members of the Royal Musical Association. As early as November 1959, she was already in discussions with Fortune regarding a paper to be delivered during the 1960 series of events organised by the RMA. Submitting articles to journals was something she had done on more than one occasion; presenting a paper in person was entirely another, and marked a significant stage in Anderson's transition from her scrupulously guarded professional life to a more public one as an acclaimed musicologist. Anderson indicated that she was willing to accept the invitation of the RMA:

> [. . .] provided I am allowed to defer the choice of subject (relating to Beethoven of course) until the Spring or Summer. For I should like to base the paper on new material or on an original point of view; and this would require some thought and more preparation. At the moment I am faced with the imminent arrival of page proofs; and you probably know what a deadening effect this can have.[65]

The proofs for the Beethoven *Letters* took a great deal longer to go through than had been expected, as Anderson experienced another health setback during 1960. In a letter to Fortune in early 1960, Anderson stated:

> A few weeks ago I left hospital after a rather serious operation and since then I have been trying to finish indexing of my edition, which Macmillan would like to bring out in May or June. So far as I can say at the moment, I shall be quite prepared to read the paper I proposed in the Autumn.

The nature of her illness is not specified, but may have been related to the heart problems she later experienced, which ultimately brought about her death. Anderson's health problems delayed publication of *The Letters of Beethoven* far longer than either Anderson or her publishers would have liked. In January 1960, she suggested to the RMA that the paper she would give would be:

> [. . .] on Beethoven's operatic plans (excluding Leonore, Fidelio, of course). As to suggested dates, I shall have to think this one, because Macmillan & Co hope to bring out my edition of Beethoven's letters in October–November, and may not wish me to use unpublished material in a lecture beforehand.[66]

But her health problems persisted, and three months later, she wrote again, deferring her paper 'until the Autumn of 1961' and noting:

> At the moment my proof readers and I are involved in the heavy task of getting three or four fat volumes ready for the press; and my publishers are not at all certain whether this can be done before the end of the year, as they would like it to be 'owing to various factors'.[67]

Anderson's health remained precarious during 1961, and the waning of her powers must have come starkly into focus on New Year's Day, January 1961, when her long-time boss, Commander Denniston, died and was subsequently buried in Burley in the New Forest. No official representative from any of the three intelligence services attended his funeral, and his death went unreported in national newspapers.[68] It is impossible to tell who attended the funeral, but given that they were colleagues of long standing, who held each other in high regard, it would have been remarkable if Anderson had not done so. In many respects, both Denniston and later Anderson were perhaps fortunate in that they did not live to see the revealing of secrets that began to trickle out as more and more codebreakers started to write books and give interviews regarding their classified war work at Bletchley and other places. Mavis Batey was not alone in being horrified at the cavalier way in which those who had worked in intelligence were prepared to reveal the secret nature of their work when the war had ended, noting that 'many of us brought up in the Denniston ethos of protecting secret sources shudder at the way "secrets" now become "stories" for the day's events on *Newsnight*.' [69]

Anderson worked steadily on the corrections to the Beethoven *Letters* proofs until the summer of 1961, when, editing work completed, she did something that she had almost never done: she took a vacation in her home country. Anderson rarely visited Ireland unless it was on the occasion of a family funeral. Her annual leave was too precious to use on anything other than visits to music archives or collectors. Now retired, and with the Beethoven letters ready to go to print, in May she wrote to her friend Cecil Oldman regarding the revised edition of her Mozart *Letters*, and noted: 'I am off to Ireland on the 23rd for about three weeks, a really lazy holiday with cousins who have moved to a charming house on the Irish Riviera.[70] Wonderful scenery I hear.'[71] There is no indication as to who these cousins were, or what part of Ireland she visited.

*

Emily Anderson was seventy years old when her *Letters of Beethoven*, in three volumes, was finally published on 19 October 1961[72] to universal acclaim. Described by one reviewer as 'the long-awaited answer to an enormous challenge',[73] the publication was widely advertised, and a full set, in slip case, cost the not inconsiderable sum of £10 10s.[74] The three volumes contained more than 1,570 letters, 230 of which had never before been published in any other edition; many more of them had not appeared in English, and so required translation, and thirty-three had previously missing passages restored. The fruits of Anderson's meticulous research were contained in *c.* 100 pages of appendices. Unsurprisingly, given her obsessive attention to detail, many of the reviews praised that fact that, for a work of its size, spread over three volumes, the text was 'amazingly free of factual or typographical errors'.[75] But it was the substance of the *Letters* that really stunned the world of music scholarship. Anderson's editing and translation was described as 'meticulous', with the music critic of *The Times* observing:

> She has been 15 years on the task. Rarely can a more detailed, honest and thorough job have been done for the correspondence of any genius [. . .] this is indeed a noble work: it shall stand alongside Rolland's *Jean Christophe*.[76]

Praise for the work was universal, with *The New York Times* acknowledging:

> Along with the endless search for new letters [. . .] came the task of interpreting the composer's scrawl,

which is sometimes so nearly illegible that former editors had had to leave a given word or passage blank. Almost all of these puzzles have been solved by Miss Anderson: it is safe to call the one or two that remain insoluble.[77]

A review in *The Musical Times* observed that 'this edition is by far the fullest, as well as the most scholarly, that has appeared in any language'.[78]

Unquestionably, Anderson's was a massive work of scholarship in translating, editing, introducing and annotating the letters. Everything, but everything, is included, and it was Anderson's forensic palaeographic approach to music history that really set her apart from all other translators of Beethoven's letters. A propensity for thoroughness and exactness had always been a feature of her personality, a characteristic honed by her cryptographic work. However, it is clear that Anderson worked in the way she did not merely because it was her way, but because it was the fairest and most responsible manner in which she could be faithful to Beethoven and the details and motivations of his life. She observed:

> [I]n fairness to the composer, his handwriting must be mastered in order to find out what he actually wrote; and this can only be done by an intensive study of its characteristics followed by a careful transcription of the autographs.

A further complication of her interpretation of the letters was Beethoven's use of punctuation, the rules of which she noted he 'flouted with as great effrontery as he did those of orthography [. . .] his persistent use of dashes which either do duty for a full stop or merely serve as a kind of pause for thought'.

The Times was greatly impressed with Anderson's editing skills, noting that it was 'almost self-effacing inasmuch as it is devoted to elucidating the problems inherent in the text'.[79] This was a critical point, because in examining the letters of Beethoven, Anderson not only became expert in distinguishing the composer's normal handwriting, but also the trembling hand that affected his writing when he was afflicted or emotionally shaken. She also became expert in identifying the handwriting of the various associates who added notations to his letters, or to whom he dictated letters in later life, which he then signed with his own hand. Here, then, was a translator and editor for whom years of diligent, determined study of the great musical genius had resulted in an ability to 'read' Beethoven in a way that no other editor had done before. An assessment of the *Letters* following her death observed:

> Just as nothing available in the composer's handwriting was too insignificant to escape her net, none of his puns, orthographical eccentricities or casual references seemed too elusive for her attention, and new problems revealed by the letters received the scrupulous consideration that she brought to all her work.[80]

The word 'exhaustive' is frequently used in reviews of the *Letters* to describe Anderson's scholarly study of the source materials. A review in the *Guardian* noted:

> All of the known letters of Beethoven (about 1,600 of them), and a number of other documents written or signed by him, are given, with detailed annotation

and indications of the whereabouts (if known) of the autographs – which wherever possible Miss Anderson has examined and re-transcribed for her new translation.[81]

The same review reflected on 'the wretched quarter of a century of life that Beethoven endured between the writing of the Heiligenstadt Testament[82] in 1802 and his death in 1827', and observed that 'his was the most grievous early death in the history of music, for his tenth symphony, and eighteenth quartet, are more real losses to us than all the unwritten works of Mozart, Schubert, Purcell and Bizet together. To read these letters is to become aware how much of the joy in our lives we owe to Beethoven's being not only the greatest musical genius in history but a hero, too.'[83]

For Anderson, *The Letters of Beethoven* was her great work. Her *Letters of Mozart and his Family* was a remarkable achievement, in which she took great pride, but in all her correspondence related to the Beethoven letters, there is a sense that Beethoven was something of a hero for Anderson, and it is easy to understand why. His prodigious work ethic, his resilience, his ability to overcome adversity, his determination to be himself, no matter what anyone else thought, were all characteristics Anderson shared with the great composer. Beethoven also managed to be reclusive and shy, while at the same time viewing himself as somehow above conventional morality and norms. 'I don't want to know anything about your system of ethics,' he wrote to a friend, 'strength is the morality of the man who stands out from the rest, and it is mine.'[84] Like Beethoven, Anderson was inherently shy, but had always lived her life as she wished to live it, without compromise. She had never married nor sustained any long-term personal relationships, and throughout her life had resolutely ploughed her own furrow – and, in the process, had broken new ground. For Anderson, the work was all that mattered, and completing that work to the highest possible standard. It is hardly surprising, then, that she brought not just scholarly precision but personal insight into her translations of his letters. In a letter to her friend Dagmar following the publication of the *Letters*, Anderson wrote: 'for years we have attempted to climb the Mount Everest of Beethoven'.[85] Now, finally, Emily Anderson had reached the summit, and that towering achievement, and the approbation it generated worldwide, would sustain her for the remainder of her life.

18

Hiding in Plain Sight

The publicity surrounding the publication of *The Letters of Beethoven* appeared to confirm that Emily Anderson had succeeded in once again presenting herself as a retired civil servant who had worked at the Foreign Office and, in her spare time, indulged her passion for musicology. The fact that she had, throughout all of her professional career, been leading a double life appeared not to have occurred to those journalists and music experts who reviewed her latest musicological work. Anderson's natural inclination had always been to shun personal publicity, and let the scholarship reflected in both her Mozart and Beethoven *Letters* speak for itself. Yet her secret career as the most senior female codebreaker in the British intelligence service was, in reality, hiding in plain sight. Her wartime secondment to the War Office was known about, and this, coupled with the fact that her OBE had been awarded 'For services to the forces and in connection with Military operations'[1] should have caused many to wonder why a linguist had found herself in Cairo at a critical time in the war, and what she had been doing to warrant such a significant award. No suspicions were raised, however, and no awkward questions asked – but with her last great work now published, and her health failing, Anderson was tempted to lift the veil, ever so slightly, on her codebreaking career. In typical fashion, she did so in a way that she knew would only be perceptible to those, like herself, who had the skills to decipher her secret signals – and the discretion to keep such knowledge to themselves.

In late November 1961, Emily Anderson arrived at Broadcasting House, Portland Place, London, to record an appearance on one of the BBC's foremost classical music programmes.[2] She was to be interviewed about *The Letters of Beethoven* by the distinguished broadcaster, editor and impresario Denis Stevens.[3,4] In its advance publicity, the *Radio Times* noted: 'Only three or four people in the world can read Beethoven's handwriting with ease, and Miss Anderson spent fifteen years collecting and translating this edition of Beethoven's correspondence.'[5]

For Beethoven fans, this would be an opportunity to hear from someone with a very rare skill in interpreting the almost illegible correspondence of the great composer, and who had dedicated a significant portion of her life to the task of transcribing it into English. For Emily Anderson, this radio interview, the only one she ever gave, was one of the high points of her life. It was also the only occasion when Anderson afforded the wider world a tantalising glimpse into her closely guarded double life. The now-seventy-one-year-old woman, seated in the unfamiliar surroundings of a recording studio, showed no nerves whatsoever, and her responses to Stevens' questions were delivered in a clear, calm voice, in a distinctly upper-class accent betraying nothing of her Irish origins.

Denis Stevens began the interview by stating: 'Miss Anderson's English version reads with such splendid fluency that when I talked with her I made a point of asking how she became so skilled in the art of translation?'

In posing this innocent question, Stevens could not have known that he would, inadvertently, be tapping in to the origins of Britain's greatest female codebreaker. In her response, this notoriously guarded woman revealed more than she had ever done before about her personal life, and what had led to her tackling the letters of the complex genius that was Beethoven. Anderson began by saying:

> I was brought up in the west of Ireland, by a father who was a scientist, and a very keen linguist at the same time. And he had learned German at Cambridge, and he made up his mind that his children should know modern languages because he found learning German to be, as a young man [. . .] so very difficult, which it is of course, that we had German governesses. And then of course he used to take us, my sister and me, to Germany, when I was about 14 and she was 16. We detested it, but we were put into German families and they spoke German.

As a consequence of the fluency she had acquired during her time in Germany, Anderson declared that the problems of translation were 'quite easy', in comparison with the task of reading the actual script of the letters, which was 'very difficult':

> It's an extraordinarily difficult handwriting. It's the gothic script, altered to a certain extent by Beethoven himself because sometimes he used a Latin script, you see.

Stevens posited the view that Beethoven's handwriting was 'perhaps the most difficult in the world to read?', and Anderson agreed:

> I think so. I never came across a handwriting where one has first to make out every single letter of the alphabet, the form it takes in his handwriting, and then its combination with other letters, particularly consonants. I may say without boasting that only two other people in the world, that is to say at Bonn,[6] can read Beethoven's handwriting with ease. I can do so now, but after years of working on it, and frequently I have to take a magnifying glass and go over and over again a particular word which defeats me. But it's strange, you throw the autograph aside, and make up your mind, that it can't be that, you go back to it, again and again and again, and it suddenly comes like a flash what the word is. It's rather like dealing with papyri I should think . . . you have to fit them together . . .

It is likely at this point that Stevens, who had served with the RAF as a codebreaker during the war,[7] began to recognise in Anderson's description the classic methodology of codebreaking in which he had been trained. He interjected with '[there are] about three or four people in the whole world who can decipher it?', and Anderson agreed, adding:

> But I started off on my own. I first used letters that had already been published, either in reviews or in small collections, German collections, and then gradually became expert at reading the handwriting.

Stevens understood completely, observing: 'Comparing the printed version with the original?' and Anderson replied, 'Yes, I started in that way, I used the version as a crib.'

If Stevens had been in any doubt up to that point, the use of the word 'crib' by Anderson would have been enough to convince him that Miss Emily Anderson's work in the Foreign Office is unlikely to have had much to do with translating the speeches of diplomats, or compiling itineraries for state visits. Just as the standard of her work confirmed that Anderson was no ordinary amateur musicologist, it must have been clear to Stevens that neither had she been an ordinary civil servant. Anyone taught to break codes – as Stevens had been – would have known that breaking into a code by guessing at least part of the plaintext (i.e. the original message), and using that guess to deduce the encryption pattern, is called a known-plaintext attack. He would also have known that the character sequence that you believe you know is called a 'crib', i.e. a word or phrase known (or assumed) to appear in the plaintext of the message before it is encrypted. If the codebreaker knows that word or phrase, they can identify it in the encrypted message and begin to see a pattern emerging.

What Anderson was saying, in effect, was that in reading the notoriously illegible handwriting of Beethoven, she had employed the skills of the codebreaker. Looking for patterns and repetitions in the same material, over and over again, had enabled her to recognise letters, words or phrases – even down to the curl on the end of a particular letter – which became her 'crib', and after years of practice, she could 'crack' the code of Beethoven's inaccessible handwriting, and decipher it. It was a remarkable example of a specific skill set being used to striking advantage in two totally separate spheres of application, both of which had yielded quite exceptional results. Anderson explained that she had begun work on the Beethoven letters before the outbreak of the Second World War, 'but unfortunately the war came, and nothing could be done at all; well, you know what war conditions were, until 1946'. For obvious reasons, Anderson did not acknowledge the fact that while the war had interrupted her work on the Beethoven letters, she had not completely abandoned it during the war, to the extent that she had continued to work on the letters at Bletchley, Cairo and Berkeley Street whenever she could manage it. Nor, as Stevens no doubt suspected, had she been employed as a civil servant with the Foreign Office during the time her work on the letters had been completed.

The Emily Anderson who presented herself that day at Broadcasting House was clearly a woman of immense talent. She was an accomplished linguist and musicologist, and a woman with the tenacity and skill to decipher the almost illegible handwriting of Beethoven, a feat that few before or after her were able to master. Yet if the radio interview at the BBC had finally shone something of a light on the unique talents of Miss Anderson, a persistent air of mystery continued to hang about a woman who took pride in her musicological achievements but was resolutely unwilling to reveal anything of her professional life as a codebreaker. The fact that this aspect of her life remained unknown and unacknowledged, except by the very few in the British intelligence service, was a testament to just how well she had managed to strike a delicate balancing act between her private and professional lives. Emily Anderson, the musicologist, could occasionally stand in the light, while operating, professionally, completely in the shadows.

As Anderson left Broadcasting House that November morning, she must have felt highly satisfied that her work on Beethoven – work she had laboured on for over twenty years, work she had carried with her from Bletchley to Cairo at the height of the war, and brought back with her to Berkeley Street in 1943 – had been given the recognition it deserved. She must also have known that, in her interview for the BBC, she had, for the first and only time, subtly revealed that what she considered her 'real work' had been made possible by the skills learned and honed during her career as a secret codebreaker for nearly forty years. That was a secret she determined to take with her to the grave.

19

Acclaim, Illness and Death

Anderson was understandably thrilled with the critical reaction to *The Letters of Beethoven*. She wrote an uncharacteristically exuberant letter to thank her friend Dagmar for a bouquet of carnations that had been delivered to her home. She informed Dagmar that 'right now I am sitting answering letters of congratulation!!', and included in the letter a review of the *Letters* by Frank Howes,[1] of which she observed: 'It is too flattering I think.'[2] Anderson's former Bletchley Park colleague Stuart Milner-Barry recalls that there was a lunch held in Anderson's honour in November 1961 to celebrate the publication of her Beethoven *Letters*. The identities of all those who attended the lunch are not known, but certainly Milner-Barry did,[3] as did Erich Hertzmann, Cecil B. Oldman and his wife,[4] and, given their long friendship and professional association, it is almost certain that Harold Macmillan himself attended.[5] *The Letters of Beethoven* was listed as one of Macmillan's 'Books of the Year' in 1961.[6]

Following the publication of the Beethoven *Letters*, it had been Anderson's intention to immediately turn her attention to producing a revised edition of the *Letters of Mozart and his Family*. But before she did so, for reasons that are unclear, Anderson undertook another translation task. She may have been commissioned to do so, or it may have been her own decision, but in any event, Anderson's last published work was a translation of *Hebel's Bible Stories* into English. In March 1962, she received copies of the book from her publisher[7] and declared: 'I am charmed with the illustrations and layout and hope indeed that it will go well.'[8] It was an interesting choice of project for Anderson, but, in a sense, she was coming full circle. Her first published work had been a translation of Croce's *Goethe*, and it was widely known that one of Hebel's greatest admirers was Goethe. The great German writer had emphatically declared that translating Hebel's work was something that could not, and should not, be done, stating: 'Such a great poet should be only read in the original! One just needs to learn this language!'[9] Anderson clearly disagreed, and was sufficiently confident in her powers of translation that she took on the task, and succeeded to the degree that her edition of the *Bible Stories* was widely acclaimed. Her reasons for doing so, however, could conceivably go back to her childhood. Hebel had been a pioneering supporter of a Swiss-German dialect that had defeated even Goethe. Anderson had been taught by a Swiss-German governess, Elisa Curtet, and it is entirely possible that, as a child, she had been given *Hebel's Bible Stories*, in Swiss-German, and therefore felt able to translate the stories as they had been taught to her by her native-speaking governess. For Anderson, it constituted yet another linguistic challenge to be nipped away at, and had the advantage of allowing her to revisit the Bible stories that had formed a major part of her religious instruction as a child in an avowedly Presbyterian household.

With the *Bible Stories* published, Anderson lost no time in turning to her next task, a second, slightly enlarged edition of *The Letters of Mozart and his Family*. It was a task she would not live to complete. By the time of her sudden death, however, she had:

> [. . .] finished a preliminary revision of the Mozart letters, in the course of which she had noted many passages which required checking for re-translation and footnotes which needed to be amended or amplified. She had also marked various points in her text at which corrections and suggestions, sent to her over the years by Mozart scholars, were to be incorporated.[10]

This appears to have been a very happy time in Anderson's life; ongoing health issues aside, she was infinitely more relaxed when it came to the revisions to the Mozart *Letters*, and her correspondence at the time reflects a more active social life, which featured attendance at lectures, concerts and musical soirées in the homes of friends. Her friends Gerald Gover, a voice coach, conductor and accompanist with Sadler's Wells Opera, and his wife Rose-Inlander Gover, an acclaimed concert pianist and teacher, lived around the corner from Anderson at 30 Arkwright Road, and regularly held musical soirées in their home, which Anderson attended. She is pictured in the front row of one such concert in the late 1950s. With more time on her hands, Anderson also reached out to some of her oldest friends and collaborators, including the by-now also retired musicologist and literary scholar Cuthbert Girdlestone,[11] whom she invited to visit her in her flat, and play music with her, when he was next in London. Girdlestone replied that he would be happy to do so and would 'bring my flute – though I should prefer to hear you play Mozart to me on the piano'.[12]

A date and venue for Anderson's long-awaited lecture to the Royal Musical Association – Tuesday, 20 March 1962, at the Royal Academy of Music – was finalised in August 1961. Anderson had indicated that it was her intention to incorporate a live performance element to elucidate the paper's points, and to this end she was fortunate in being able to call on a number of her friends who were opera singers or musicians, informing Fortune: 'I may be able to get live illustrations free of charge.'[13] Thanks to her contacts, the 'live illustrations' materialised, and the lecture would feature excerpts from the operas *Fidelio* and *Vestas Feuer*, performed by Pauline Brockless (soprano), Adrian de Peyer (tenor) and Gordon Honey (baritone), with Gerald Gover arranging the performance of *Vestas Feuer* and directing it from the piano. Anderson informed Fortune that while Gover himself agreed to perform without a fee, he felt that that they 'couldn't offer less than 10 guineas to each singer, particularly as the work they are performing is operatic. I hope this is not excessive?'[14]

The integration of a performance element into an RMA lecture was something that had never been done before; the RMA were anxious regarding the question of paying the singers, and stalled on making a commitment to do so. Anderson was unwilling to allow a question of costs to undermine her plans and she wrote, privately, to Fortune, informing him:

> [I]f the Council feels the fee is excessive and cannot be paid out of the fund of the RMA, I am quite prepared to pay the difference between what the RMA can

afford and the fee demanded. But you will understand that I should not like this to be known.[15]

The question of who would pay the singers rumbled on for some months, with Anderson eventually deciding to deal with the situation in her own way. She informed Fortune:

I wish to pay the 30 gns myself [. . .] for I am anxious that the performance of this unknown fragmentary work of Beethoven's should be as good as possible. I have not discussed, nor do I propose to discuss, this procedure on my part with my friend Gerald Gover, who is arranging the performance (which will necessitate two or three rehearsals at least) without any payment to him. But it would make all this very much easier for me if you would now write to each of the three singers [. . .] saying that 'the Council of the Royal Musical Association will be very glad to have your services on March 20th at 5.45 pm for 6pm and agree to the fee of 10gns which will be paid to you immediately afterwards' [. . .] What I desire to avoid <u>at all costs</u> is that anyone should hear that my singers are receiving 10 gns each (from the Associations funds) and should inform other singers who, I understand, are to receive smaller fees. In short, I should be very sorry if I were to be the cause of any difficulty arising in the case of the other singers. But this might not to happen if you will kindly write to each of my singers on the lines I suggest. I will send you a cheque for £31. 10.0[16] at the end of February 1962.[17]

It was classic Anderson – managing everything deftly from the sidelines while herself remaining invisible. Ultimately, the RMA baulked at the idea of setting a potentially costly precedent, and it was agreed that the engagement and payment of the singers would be undertaken by Anderson, and that the RMA 'shall not be involved in any way in the music illustrating [the] paper'. Anderson was her usual pragmatic self, writing to Fortune: '[I]t doesn't matter where the money comes from. The main thing is that they should be paid; and I am quite prepared to pay the piper.'[18]

In early 1962, Anderson worked steadily on her paper, and by March informed Fortune that:

> Mr. Gover, who was a pupil at the Royal Academy, knows the people there quite well. He and the singers have been rehearsing at his house and in my flat. He will certainly get in touch with the Secretary of the Royal Academy if he considers it necessary to have a rehearsal in the hall as well. All that I require is a lectern and a carafe of cold water with a glass, in case my throat begins to feel dry. I am bringing about 15 guests (not including the performers) – not too many I hope.[19]

As Anderson was well known and well liked within music circles in London, and the recent success of her *Letters of Beethoven* had brought her international acclaim, her lecture at the Royal Academy proved immensely popular, with standing room only in the lecture hall. Anderson spoke for forty-five minutes and the performance lasted a further fifteen minutes, with a sherry reception following. A copy of Anderson's lecture was published in the *Proceedings of the Royal Musical Association* in 1963.[20] Entitled 'Beethoven's Operatic plans', the lecture focused on 'Beethoven's plans for operas which were never completed.'[21] Anderson was characteristically forthright in her introduction to the lecture, noting that having been asked to deliver a lecture on Beethoven to the Association, she was surprised to discover that, since its foundation in 1874, 'only six papers had been read on subjects closely relating to Beethoven . . . Six papers in eighty-eight years!' She noted that the last paper delivered had been in 1927, thirty-five years previously, and remarked:

> I need hardly add that such an apparent lack of inter-
> est in the life and work of this composer prompted me
> to make some amends, however small, for an indignity
> amounting almost to *lèse-majesté*.[22]

In a sense, Anderson had, in her last public lecture, returned to ground she had already partially covered in her first published work, the translation of Benedetto Croce's *Goethe*, as one aspect of the lecture referred to an ultimately unsuccessful attempt by Beethoven to write an opera based on Goethe's *Faust*. The lecture, enhanced by the performances of world-class opera singers, was a sensation. Cecil Oldman, who attended the event with his wife, provided an account of Anderson's RMA lecture to their mutual friend Erich Hertzmann: '[. . .] you have probably heard long before now that it was a great success. What she said was interesting to specialist and layman alike and she spoke clearly and forcefully.'[23]

It had been a rare occasion when Anderson was cast in the spotlight, speaking on a topic on which she was an acknowledged expert, to an audience of music enthusiasts, musicians and musicologists, and she had triumphed. The fact that she could enjoy the post-lecture reception, relaxed in the company of colleagues and friends from the world of music who fully recognised the quality and value of her scholarship, must have been an incredibly gratifying experience, and she relished it. Sadly, however, the effort that Anderson had put into the lecture impacted on her already precarious health, as her friend Oldman recalled:

> Unfortunately, the strain of the occasion, and of the celebrations which followed it, took its toll and a few days later came the sudden and alarming collapse. I went to see her several times while she was in hospital, but since she has been back I have so far only spoken to her over the telephone. She sounds a little tired, which was only to be expected, but, typically, she is already working quite hard on the revised edition of her translation of the Mozart letters and is now as wrapped up again in W. A. M. as she was for so long in L. v. B.*

It appears from Oldman's account that degenerative heart disease had been the cause of Anderson's collapse, requiring her hospitalisation. But Oldman's account is also revealing of the extent to which Emily Anderson realised that, when it came to her health, time was rapidly running out. Knowing her as he did, Oldman's lack of surprise at her determination to push on regardless in order to get the revised Mozart *Letters* finished is entirely understandable.

There was certainly a good deal of competition in the race to produce works on the major composers. Musicology, still a minority interest when the Second World War ended, grew to become a major academic industry, and as a result academic rivalry also reared its head as competition in the Mozart market became more intense. One

---

* Wolfgang Amadeus Mozart and Ludwig von Beethoven.

such incident is recorded in a letter to Anderson written by Professor Otto Erich Deutsch in July 1962, just four months after her collapse following the RMA lecture. Deutsch had been a long-time collaborator of Anderson's, and she had written to him regarding her revised edition of the Mozart letters, seeking information on the ownership of certain letters that had changed hands since 1937. Deutsch refused to help, in pretty bald terms, because:

> [. . .] our relationship concerning the Mozart letters has altered considerably since 1960. We are now, I am sorry to say, competitors in that field, not collaborators any more. Bauer[24] and I feel compelled to deny you any such information which might help you to improve your text and commentary for the second edition.

Though not explicitly stated, Deutsch appears to have been annoyed that, in 1959, Macmillan, having indicated that they would publish his and Bauer's book in an English edition, had then changed their minds in 1961 when Anderson indicated that she would produce a revised edition of the Mozart *Letters* herself. Anderson must have been stung by this rather petty response from someone with whom she had always willingly shared information. She may also, however, have allowed herself a wry smile that Deutsch's principal gripe appears to have been that he and Dr Bauer felt it would not have been fair to share the fruits of research that had been sponsored via 'large payments from the Internationale Stiftung Mozarteum in fees and postage for the immense correspondence of Dr Bauer and in paying the bills for microfilms and enlargements'.[25] Anderson, in comparison, had never received a penny from anyone, or any institution, in undertaking either her

Mozart or Beethoven research, and had even gone so far as to provide stamped addressed envelopes to those – including Deutsch and Bauer – with whom she had corresponded. But Anderson had neither the time nor the energy to pander to such petty rivalries. As had been the case when the issue of a collaboration on the Beethoven letters had arisen in the early 1950s, Anderson decided to rise above the petty squabbles of rival academics, and do what she had always done: forge ahead with her own work, on her own terms.

In doing so, Anderson must have been buoyed by news she received just prior to her lecture for the RMA. In February 1962, she received word that she had been recommended for the awarding of the Order of Merit, First Class – the highest honour the government of the Federal Republic of Germany could bestow – in respect of her work on the Beethoven *Letters*. The recommendation[26] that Anderson receive the award originated from the Foreign Office of the Federal Republic of Germany, and was signed by the Foreign Office Minister, Gerhard Schröder.[27] By 2 March, the document confirming the conferring of the Order of Merit, First Class on Anderson was signed by the President, Heinrich Lübke, the Chancellor, Dr Konrad Adenauer, and Schröder. The recommendation stated that the award was for 'the best and most comprehensive collection of Beethoven's letters [. . .] the result of fifteen years of extensive research', and described the work as being of 'outstanding merit'. A copy of the recommendation survives in the Bundesarchiv (German Federal Archives), and Anderson herself would have received a copy. Anderson is unique in having been awarded one of the highest honours that the British government can bestow, the OBE, for her cryptologic work in Cairo during the Second World War, and subsequently being awarded one of the highest honours the government of the Federal Republic of Germany could bestow, for her work on Beethoven.

In so honouring Anderson, the question remains: did the Germans know the precise nature of Anderson's work during the war, or did they accept the narrative that she worked 'in a department of the British Foreign Office'? There is no evidence to suggest that they did know that Anderson had been breaking German and Italian codes in both the First and Second World Wars, and the interwar period. They were no doubt aware of her OBE, the citation for which made it clear that the award had been 'For services to the forces and in connection with Military operations'. They may have assumed that, as a linguist, Anderson's services were likely to do with translation or interpretation services. What is significant is that, when her former Bletchley colleague, Hugh Alexander, competed in a chess tournament in Hamburg in 1954, the German newspaper *Der Spiegel* published an article that noted: 'Alexander is an employee of the English Foreign Office and works there as an expert for the deciphering of foreign secret codes.'[28] No such association was ever attributed to Anderson. Her friend Dagmar, however, does recall an incident that occurred at a party attended by Anderson when she visited Bonn in the final year of her life. A young girl, the granddaughter of renowned autograph collector Louis Koch, excitedly asked Anderson about the sort of 'secret work' she did back in England. Emily reacted in a way Dagmar had never seen her behave before: she was furious and immediately stormed off. This story would indicate that at least some of her German friends and colleagues had some inkling that Anderson might have been involved in secret work during the war, but not the precise nature of it. Dagmar and Friedrich, who knew her best, were instinctively aware that it was best not to ask her about her professional life, and so they never did so. They were astonished to learn the precise nature of her work when they first met this author in the course of interviews conducted for this book.

There were certainly no awkward questions when Anderson visited Bonn in October 1962 to be conferred with her Bundesverdienstkreuz (Order of Merit). Anderson was invited to stay with Dagmar and Friedrich in the *schloss* they had purchased in 1959, on the outskirts of Bonn. The couple by then had a child about a year old, and Dagmar recalls that Anderson arrived with a present for their child, 'a beautiful fine wool scarf, from India, woven, turquoise, and she said "to wrap your baby in"'.[29]

The conferring ceremony itself took place in what was then the office and official Residence of the Federal President, Villa Hammerschmidt, on the banks of the Rhine in Bonn.[30] Anderson attended the conferring ceremony unaccompanied, and while she did not make too much of a fuss about the event itself – Dagmar believes she was 'not so dependent on things like that' – she nonetheless considered it a great honour, and was very pleased to receive it. The remainder of her time in Bonn was spent with Dagmar and Friedrich, and in socialising with other friends. The visit was purely social, and Friedrich recalls that there was 'no work on Beethoven during her visit', as the three volumes had by that stage been published.

Unlike his wife, who had known Anderson for a number

of years and worked closely with her on the Beethoven *Letters*, Friedrich met Anderson only once, for two days, on the occasion that she visited them in October 1962, 'only weeks before her untimely death'. Anderson, however, made quite an impression on the young Physics lecturer, and he described her as being 'the most intelligent person he ever met'. Friedrich recalls Anderson being 'full of questions' and 'drawing him into a conversation' the moment he came in the door from work. The conversation flowed, on a variety of topics, with Friedrich perceptively observing of Anderson: 'she wasn't stiff at all, but I think she could be if she wanted to'. Dagmar and Friedrich both identified a strong sense of self-control in Anderson, but as Friedrich acknowledged, 'working for the secret service, always having to be in control of yourself, must have shaped her personality. It becomes second nature, otherwise you cannot stay in that mood all the time, as you are required to do.'

Subsequently, and to Dagmar's delight, Friedrich accompanied Anderson on the violin while she played Mozart on the grand piano in the music room of their home. Friedrich recalls that she played 'very well . . . I think she must have been practising very regularly. We had a good time together.' Dagmar recalls that her friend 'never talked about her sisters, about her brother, only about her father', and, as we have seen, took great delight in recounting the story of her father keeping the cigar on his desk when he had given up smoking, as an act of 'self-tormentation'.

The poignancy of Anderson's departure from Bonn is vividly recorded by Dagmar. As the couple were leaving Anderson at the airport for her return flight, all the talk was of a planned trip to the Wagner opera festival at Bay-reuth[31] the following year. Anderson told Dagmar that 'a good friend of hers in the British Museum [. . .] loved Wagner, and she made a proposal that [the four of us] would go together to Bayreuth. And we agreed, we intended to go.' Anderson was eagerly anticipating the visit to the festival, but she was also anxious to let her friends know how very much she had enjoyed her stay with them in Bonn. Her joy at having received the Order of Merit for her work on the Beethoven *Letters*, coupled with her pleasure at having spent time in the company of good friends, prompted Anderson to tell Dagmar just before she boarded her flight: 'If that plane falls out of the sky, I will die happy'. The couple parted from Anderson with promises of a wonderful reunion at Bayreuth. They were never to see her again.

The friend Anderson was planning to visit Bayreuth with was almost certainly Alex Hyatt King, and it was he, in collaboration with another of Anderson's good friends, Monica Carolan, who would later complete work on Anderson's revised edition of the *Letters of Mozart and his Family* following her death.

Anderson's last letter to the Beethoven-Haus in Bonn is dated 5 October 1962. Some weeks later, on 25 October 1962, Anderson wrote an inscription on a copy of her *Letters of Beethoven*, dedicating it:

For His Excellency
The German Ambassador,
yours sincerely,
Emily Anderson.[32]

It was one of the last things she ever wrote. She died the following day, 26 October 1962.

*

The success of Anderson's lecture to the RMA in March 1962 appears to have prompted another invitation to deliver a similar lecture, possibly on the theme of Mozart. Dagmar recalls that, on the evening of her death, less than two weeks after her return from Bonn, Anderson had been visiting a friend[33] to rehearse a paper she was about to deliver to 'some Royal institution' (most likely the RMA) and left the friend's house to return to her home in good spirits. Sometime later, the friend[34] became aware of a commotion outside in the street, heard the sound of an ambulance arriving, and on investigating discovered that Anderson had collapsed suddenly in the street not far from her friend's house. She was taken to New End Hospital, Hampstead, where she later died. The death certificate records the cause of death as 'rupture of atheromatous thoracic aortic aneurysm'.[35] This would appear to confirm that Anderson's ongoing ill-health, and the 'serious operation' she had undergone some time before, had related to problems with her heart, which doctors had attempted to treat with surgery, but which ultimately led to her death. The death certificate listed Anderson's profession as a 'spinster and writer'.

Reaction to Anderson's sudden death, among friends and colleagues alike, was one of profound shock and sadness. Professor Schmidt-Görg, Director of the Beethoven-Haus archive, was informed of Anderson's death by her second cousin, Mrs Patricia Crowden (*née* Anderson) of Chiswick, London, who appears to have been Anderson's only relative in the UK (apart from her estranged brother, Alexander) and upon whom the task of informing Anderson's vast coterie of friends and colleagues of her passing fell.[36] A wreath of white carnations was ordered for delivery to Anderson's home at Ellerdale Court by Schmidt-Görg on behalf of the Beethoven-Haus,[37] and a bouquet of white carnations was also sent by Dagmar. Sadly, and to the great distress of both parties, the flowers never arrived, the florist with whom the order was placed[38] having gone out of business. Schmidt-Görg wrote to Mrs Crowden expressing their sincere regard for Miss Anderson and their 'great dismay' that the flowers had not arrived, and assuring her that they would 'always remember her, with whom we have worked and collaborated for many years'.[39] Dagmar recalls that, in the days that followed, she received a personal note from Emily, posted just before her untimely death, thanking her for hosting her during her recent visit to Bonn. The note included a limerick she had written for the couple.

Mrs Crowden replied to Schmidt-Görg in January 1963, and apologised for her delay in replying, which, tellingly, she attributed to the fact that:

> I have had a lot of correspondence in connection with my cousin, Miss Emily Anderson's death. Her sudden death was a great shock to me and to her many friends. She was certainly a wonderful woman, and somehow managed to complete her great work on Beethoven in spite of much ill health.[40]

Once word of Anderson's sudden passing began to circulate among her friends and former colleagues, it was Cecil Oldman who broke the news to Hertzmann, and

Hertzmann's reply is deeply revealing of the affection both men had for her.

Your letter with the sad news was a great shock to us. We had neither heard nor read about it [. . .] Since Emily lived such a quiet, sheltered life and knew so well to take care of herself, her collapse is hard to believe. We feel a great sorrow and miss her chatty letters, and London will not be the same for us. Even though she could be at times trying or almost obstreperous, underneath her seemingly austere facade was a very kind and warm-hearted person. Fortunately she lived long enough to finish the Beethoven Letters, to see their publication and to have the pleasure of receiving the deserved honours from all parts of the world. The only consolation her friends must feel is the fact that she was spared from a prolonged illness and a bed-ridden existence, which would have caused her great anguish. During the past few years she was even irritated when asked how she was feeling because she did not want to be reminded of the ebbing of her physical resources. In her fight of mind over matter she proved her mettle in character and fortitude. And character she had: she would not lower her high standard of principle even if it meant self-denial. Her work on Mozart and Beethoven is proof of her indefatigable zeal and her integrity as a scholar. It is for me, at least, amazing that she could develop what started out as a hobby to reach such high degree of scholarship. Though there are some shortcomings in both publications and though she could not have done the job without the help from you and other scholars, the accomplishment is great. The world, her friends and colleagues, are poorer without her. You probably miss her very much – at least her telephone calls since you may not have seen her lately. It is regrettable that you could not be present at the funeral services, but it is more important that you live carefully [. . .] [41]

Oldman missed Anderson's funeral as he himself was ill, and only a few months later, in March 1963, Hertzmann died of a heart attack.[42] Hertzmann's reference to the fact that Anderson did not want to be reminded 'of the ebbing of her physical resources' appears to confirm that Anderson had been experiencing heart trouble for some time, a fact confirmed by the cause of death, which indicates that a contributing factor to the ruptured aneurysm that ultimately killed her was a build-up of cholesterol or 'plaque' in the artery.[43] It is also revealing that both men were of the view that becoming a bed-ridden invalid would have been the worst possible thing for Anderson to endure, given her constant need to be busy and productive.

The genuine affection and respect that Hertzmann (and, by inference, Oldman) had for Anderson is striking, as is the honest recognition that she was not always the easiest person to deal with. Nonetheless, it was her remarkable scholarship and strength of character that both men appear to have admired, along with her kindness and decency as a person. The letter is revealing in another important respect. Hertzmann's comment that Anderson 'lived such a quiet, sheltered life' would indicate that, like the majority of her friends, he and Oldman knew nothing of her professional career and codebreaking work, and assumed, as did most people, that she was a diligent yet unremarkable civil servant, who was only distinguished by the fact that she turned what he terms her 'hobby' into something that stimulated her, and provided some degree of excitement in an otherwise rather conventional life. In that respect, at least, Anderson, remarkably, appears to have succeeded in never having let the mask slip.

As we have seen, Anderson's funeral service took place on 1 November 1962 at Hampstead parish church. The church was packed with the cream of London's classical music world, seated alongside the great and the good of the British intelligence service. It is an indication of just how highly they valued her Beethoven scholarship that the embassy of the Federal Republic of Germany was represented at her funeral by one of its most senior Embassy staff, Herr Dr Jurgen Trumpf, second secretary.[44] There was, however, one person, her closest living relative, who was not in attendance at Anderson's funeral. According to his grandson, Anderson's one surviving sibling, Alexander (now Arthur Andrews), did not attend the service.[45]

Unsurprisingly, the music performed at her funeral reflected Anderson's own musical tastes, and included Brahms' *Ye now are Sorrowful* and Mozart's *Ave Verum Corpus*. After the service, her remains were removed to Golders Green, where another short service was conducted by Rev. Barney, and her body subsequently cremated.[46]

A number of obituaries followed in the press and in scholarly music journals to which Anderson had contributed. Unsurprisingly, the narrative that Miss Anderson had 'entered the Foreign Office in which she remained – apart from three years' war service from 1940–1943 during which she was seconded to the War Office and engaged in Intelligence work in the Middle East which led to her being given an O.B.E. – until her retirement in 1951' was repeated in all the obituaries, with no hint given of her actual occupation with GC&CS and later GCHQ. Her obituaries all focused on her linguistic skills and musicological career, with *The Times* noting:

> Languages were her pleasure as well as her profession and together with music and travel (her other pleasures) lay behind the patient achievements of scholarship which brought her a celebrity in the world of music which she managed entirely to disregard.[47]

Her Mozart and Beethoven *Letters* were widely praised, with a number of obituaries acknowledging that 'the volume of work involved in either translation or in presentation is such that its combination from the hands of a single scholar occupied at the same time with a busy professional career is amazing'.[48]

Although obituaries in *The Times* are always written anonymously, Anderson's was clearly written by someone who knew her exceptionally well – quite possibly her long-time friend Alexander Hyatt King.

> Whatever celebrity attached to her achievements, Emily Anderson refused to acknowledge its existence. It might well prove difficult to disentangle a genuine modesty from an equally genuine disdain in her rejection of anything that seemed likely to divert attention from her work to her personality. Brusque and by no means unformidable if she felt that an unwelcome publicity was pursuing her, impatient of merely personal considerations, she relaxed into warmth and cheerfully alert wisdom when she felt secure upon her

own ground. It was as if she refused to live on the trivial level at which music and scholarship could be put aside to make room for gossip and chatter to pass the time of day.[49]

Anderson's will was a profound statement as to who and what truly mattered to her, yet reflected the clinical precision she had always shown in life. There were no relatives or friends named as her executors, the sole executor being her bank, Coutts & Co. of 440 Strand, London, WC2.[50] The beneficiaries of her will reflected, as might have been expected, her lifelong love of music. It is, however, significant that the first, and largest, single bequest was to the Royal United Kingdom Beneficent Association, amounting to £1,685, which was provided 'to help persons of reduced means in the Republic of Ireland'. For a woman who had left Ireland in 1919, rarely ever returned thereafter, and never spoke of her Irish origins to close friends or colleagues, it is telling, and somewhat poignant, to see her country of birth foremost in her thoughts when she was settling her affairs. It is interesting to ponder what prompted her to make such a bequest. A nostalgia for her birthplace, perhaps, and possibly a nod to her Presbyterian faith, which had at its core a charitable imperative to help others less fortunate? We will never know for sure.

To the wife of her late cousin, Mrs Dorothy Binns of Dalkey, Co. Dublin, she left £500.[51] To her friend Monica Carolan, the woman who, with Alexander Hyatt King, would complete the work on the revised edition of the *Letters of Mozart and his Family* following Anderson's death, she left her 'china tea service and all my glass'. To her longtime friend and collaborator Hyatt King, she left 'all my pictures and etchings and all my printed music (bound and sheet)'. This was a very generous, and valuable, bequest, as Anderson had amassed quite a collection of printed music over the years, much of it rare, via her extensive contacts in the antiquarian market. She had also lived among artists for years in Hampstead, including Ben Nicholson and Mark Gertler, from whom she acquired pieces. To Mrs Madge Massey Cooper, she left 'my green leather-bound Shakespeare (in twelve volumes) in leather box, and a sum of £200'. Massey Cooper had studied Arts at Royal Holloway and Bedford College[52] and, at the time of Anderson's death, she was sharing a house with Monica Carolan at Windmill Hill, Hampstead.[53] To her second cousin, Mrs Patricia Crowden (*née* Anderson), she left 'my antique corner cupboard and my jewellery and a sum of £200'.[54] To her friend Heinrich Eisemann, the book and manuscript dealer, she left, appropriately, her 'leather-bound facsimile edition of Beethoven's Waldstein pianoforte Sonata and my leather-bound first edition (three volumes) of Dr *Charles Burney's Travels* 1773'.

Mrs Valerie Emery's friendship with Anderson straddled both aspects of her life – she was the daughter of Sir Edward 'Jumbo' Travis, who succeeded Commander Denniston as head of GC&CS at Bletchley Park (Valerie herself had worked as a codebreaker at Bletchley), and the wife of Walter Emery, the acclaimed organist and arranger. Together, the couple founded the Travis and Emery Music Bookshop, which still exists. Unsurprisingly, therefore, Anderson left Mrs Emery her prized 'facsimile editions of Mozart's musical compositions'. To Dr Hede Pollak, Anderson left a memento of her time in Cairo: 'my Egyptian brass card tray and cigarette box' and a sum of

£200.[55] Hedwig (Hede) Pollak was born in Vienna, Austria, in 1898. Dr Pollak's PhD was in Modern Languages, and she worked as a Librarian in Vienna. Pollak was Jewish, and in 1939 she fled Austria and moved to the UK as a refugee to avoid Nazi persecution.[56] There, she found refuge with, and became the secretary to, Dr Moses Gaster of Maida Vale, a prominent Jewish scholar and collector of manuscripts.[57] It is unclear how Anderson and Dr Pollak knew each other, but it may have been the case that they had originally met before the war in the course of Anderson's work on the Mozart *Letters* in various archives in Vienna.

To Mrs Barbara Sidwell, she left perhaps her most prized possession: 'my Bechstein boudoir grand piano', as well as 'my copy of Grove's Dictionary of Music (nine volumes) Fifth Edition'.[58] To a Miss Bessie Whiteman, she left 'my bow-fronted chest of drawers, my spare room wardrobe, my clothes and my house and table linen and a sum of £200'. Bessie Whiteman, otherwise known as Elizabeth Martha Whiteman or Betsy Martha Whiteman, is something of a mystery woman in the life of Anderson. She lived near Anderson, in the garden flat of 94 Heath Street, and does not appear to have ever married. Born in Hampstead, the daughter of upholsterer George Whiteman, she appears to have lived all of her life in the Hampstead area, but no other information regarding her occupation or any other aspect of her life has come to light. The fact that Anderson left Whiteman her clothes – something that arguably one would only be inclined to do to a close personal friend – is, however, rather striking.

As to everything else, Anderson left instructions that Mr John Pashby of Sotheby's was to be consulted by Coutts regarding 'the disposal of the remainder of my books and to take expert advice about the disposal of the remainder of my furniture'. Pashby was the Music Manuscripts expert at Sotheby's, and on many occasions he had called on Anderson's advice to verify both the provenance and authenticity of Mozart and Beethoven manuscripts. She was now calling on him to return the favour, and secure the best price for the remainder of her antique furniture and book collection, the proceeds of which would be used to endow a trust fund established by Anderson under the terms of her will. All income of her residuary estate accrued after her death (including the sale of her remaining furniture and other effects, royalties from book sales, and income from investments which Coutts were empowered to undertake on Anderson's behalf) were to be added to the trust fund, and used to provide a lasting legacy for two causes close to Anderson's heart. As we have seen, two thirds of the trust fund income was to be used to support the careers of emerging young musicians in the form of an annual prize – 'The Emily Anderson Prize for Violin-playing', to be administered by the Royal Philharmonic Society. The final third was to be used to support established musicians in need, i.e. the Musicians, Benevolent Fund.

Anderson's bequests to two extended family members – the wife of a first cousin in Ireland, and a second cousin in the UK – and the fact that nothing was left to her brother Alexander or his family is striking. The fact that they are not mentioned in Anderson's will appears to indicate that the rift that had occurred in the Anderson family many years previously ran very deep. Probate was granted on 15 January 1963 to Coutts and Company,

Anderson's bank, with her effects listed as amounting to £11,783-9s.[59]

Anderson's will had seen to it that there would be no discernible remains of her life at her rented flat at Ellerdale Road, where she had lived since 1939. Her flat was cleared of its contents, and by the following year it was occupied by new tenants,[60] the art historian Michael Baxandall and his wife, Katherina.[61] No tangible evidence of Anderson's life remained, apart from two landmark collections of the translated letters of Mozart and Beethoven, and a remarkable, but as yet hidden, legacy as Britain's greatest female codebreaker.

20

Conclusion and Legacy

A number of unanswered questions about Emily Anderson remain, the most significant of which is why so little has been known about her until now. There are reasons for this, some general and some specific to her, yet questions still remain.

The business of codebreaking is, by its very nature, so secret that even its own heroes could disappear. Anderson may, ostensibly, have disappeared, but in reality she was hiding in plain sight. There was a strong element of gender blindness in the earliest memoirs to emerge about Bletchley, all of which were written by men. Those who write the history define the history, and the simple fact was that until relatively recently women were largely ignored in the history of codebreaking because they did what they were asked to do: they kept their heads down and their mouths shut for the sixty years required of them under the Official Secrets Act. It was a long time to keep silent.

The nature of the work was one thing; the ability and mental powers it took to do it was entirely another. Patricia Bartley's son observed that, for his mother, the woman who broke Floradora, it was not just maintaining secrecy surrounding the work she found a strain, but that 'The sacrifice of any recognition for her brain cost her very dearly.'

The longevity and secrecy surrounding Emily Anderson's career is to a large degree attributable to the fact that she was not just willing to maintain a secrecy surrounding her codebreaking career, but that it suited her purposes to do so. Drawing a discreet veil over her professional life enabled her to live a public life and engage in her 'real work', as she saw it, work for which the abilities of her keen brain could be recognised: her musicological work. Professionally, she wanted to be invisible because it made her other work possible.

Her aversion to being photographed, doubtless a feature of her desire to blend into the background, accounts for the fact that images of Anderson are extremely rare. It is significant that of the three photographs of her as an adult that have so far come to light, two were taken in places where she was confident the images would be in safe hands – the group photograph of MI1(b) staff on the roof of Cork Street in 1919, and the image of her in Cairo posing with Colonel Jacob and another unidentified officer. The third, and clearest, image of her was taken at the behest of Macmillan Publishing for use in promotional material when *The Letters of Beethoven* volumes were published. By that stage, Anderson had been retired for almost ten years, her professional life and its responsibilities were well behind her, and as a retired Foreign Office official and acclaimed musicologist, for once she could smile happily and confidently for the camera.

One of the most perceptive statements written about Anderson following her death was that she was 'one of those rare scholars who was completely at home in the world of action'.[1] This was certainly the case, and Anderson was the type of woman for whom the First World War provided an opportunity to stretch herself and prove her worth. Crucially, in Anderson's case, it also offered her another way of life, and living, which was far removed from the provincial university she was destined to return to. For Anderson, it could be argued that her career in codebreaking was a job, not a vocation. Certainly, during the First World War, she was imbued with a patriotic commitment to 'do her duty', as she saw it, a resolution consolidated by the fact that her brother was a prisoner of war. But once that duty was done, and the war ended, there is every indication that she planned to return to her pre-war academic life. The fact that she did not do so was not born of a desire to continue to play her part in providing the intelligence necessary to continue to keep Britain safe, but rather was a pragmatic and strategic response to an offer made to her by Denniston to join the new GC&CS. The terms and conditions were good, it was a respectable and responsible post, she would strike a blow for women's rights by being appointed the first female Junior Assistant in the civil service, and perhaps, most importantly, it allowed her to live an independent life in London, one of the most vibrant cities in the world, far away from prying eyes in Galway.

The longevity of Anderson's career may be attributed in no small measure to her undoubted abilities. However, from a technical perspective, it was also only possible because she never married. Civil service rules stipulated that female candidates to GC&CS 'must be unmarried or widows' and, once appointed, female staff were 'required to resign their appointments upon marriage'.[2] This would never be a problem for Anderson, as there never appears to have been any prospect of her marrying. From the earliest stages of her career, there was a sense that she was a trailblazer, although she herself never acknowledged that a trail needed to be blazed. She believed that women were the equals of men, and as long as they worked hard and were capable, they would and should be recognised in just the same way as men. Although the fact that this wasn't necessarily true was glaringly obvious to most people around her, it was something Anderson was never prepared to admit, either to herself or others, and through the sheer force of her personality, it never curtailed her career in the way it did the careers of other women of her seniority.

When it came to Anderson's sexuality, we cannot definitively know the precise nature of it, nor is it necessary that we should. But if Anderson was a gay woman, and there is compelling evidence that this was the case, then she was fortunate to be working for GC&CS, and later GCHQ, which

> [. . .] more than in virtually any other government department, GCHQ's institutional interests protected staff with scarce talents, which shielded some gay people directly, and reinforced the emphasis on individual rights to privacy and tolerance of eccentric behaviour that generally restrained investigations.[3]

Anderson worked for and with a wide variety of men and women throughout her career, of doubtless every sexual persuasion, but from her own perspective, and that of her colleagues, the only thing that mattered was the ability to do the job – nothing else of a private nature was relevant. Anderson's personal relationships with other women – for only one of which, her relationship with Dorothy Brooks, does compelling evidence exist – were not just tolerated but, it could be argued, were necessary. For women of her generation, relationships with other women were far more common, and more complex. They were women in their twenties during the First World War, and an entire generation of the young men they could have gone on to marry were lost for ever to the war. The basic need for the love and companionship of another human being was still there, but as the pool of marriageable men was severely reduced, for many women that need was satisfied – in either an emotional or physical way (or both) – by some variety of same-sex relationship. Anderson may, of course, have been inherently and irrevocably lesbian in her sexual preferences, but if she was, then other than her relationship with Brooks, and the fact that she shared her flat with another woman in the 1950s, there is no evidence to suggest it. Ultimately, her sexual orientation is entirely irrelevant. It never impacted on her work or her career, and for her superiors, it never appears to have been an issue.

It was frequently said of Anderson, by friends and colleagues alike, that hers was not always an easy personality to deal with, but being a woman in her profession at that time, she probably found such an attitude necessary. Like many of her female colleagues, Anderson often had to be twice as good as the men around her in order to prove her worth. The perception by some that Anderson was a difficult employee and exacting boss was not unique to her in the context of other women cryptologists. Her female contemporaries, the Americans Elizebeth Smith Friedman and Agnes Meyer Driscoll, were rightly considered, with Anderson, as 'among the best cryptanalysts in the world' during the interwar period.[4] Yet Smith Friedman was described as 'impatient, and at best strongly opinionated, with a disdain for stupidity',[5] while Meyer Driscoll was 'considered a character by some, a mystery by others, and a genius to the few who had known her';[6] she was a woman who 'affected an air of intense detachment' yet frequently 'cursed as fluently as any sailor'.[7] Both women, brilliant and vastly more capable than most of their male counterparts, suffered sexism, barriers to promotion, and male colleagues taking credit for their work in the course of their careers. Anderson was less prone to such gendered bias in the British intelligence service, due in part to the more enlightened system that pertained in GC&CS under Denniston, who valued talent over everything else, and in part to the fact that Anderson simply would not have stood for it. She still had to contend with the jealousies and patronising comments of those vastly inferior to her in abilities, but she was also entirely cognisant of her own abilities as a cryptanalyst, and in her constant ability to evolve and innovate her cryptanalytic skills over the decades she rendered herself irreplaceable to her superiors – and both she, and they, knew it. Anderson always believed, as Meyer Driscoll[8] observed, that 'any man-made code could be broken by a woman', and she never tired of rising to that challenge. Her many achievements must therefore be considered in the context of the barriers and obstacles that might have been placed in her way – had she not stubbornly decided to ignore them. What she, and the other women around her, achieved was therefore truly inspiring.

Many things about Emily Anderson were impressive, but most impressive of all was the quite remarkable degree of mental resilience she possessed. The mental powers required to do the job she did, often under brutal time pressures, were demanding in their own right, and broke many of her colleagues, who succumbed to mental breakdowns. Yet Anderson herself never succumbed, never allowing her formidable brain to relax for a second, unless it was to listen to music. The distractions of her musicology career to a large degree enabled her to cope better with the pressures of her professional life, with the competing egos, interdepartmental disputes and personality clashes which characterised so much of the world of codebreaking in both the First and Second World Wars. With few exceptions, Anderson's music friends and colleagues inhabited entirely different worlds to her codebreaking ones. In moving from one world to the other, she could entirely shed one skin and take on a different one. Her evenings were spent in her various flats, laboriously working though impenetrable letters of Mozart or Beethoven, and holding all the information gleaned in a lifetime's work in her head or on the index cards she kept in her home office; she was able to retrieve details stored away to make sense of something to a quite remarkable degree. It is for this reason that her footnotes, which provide context for the translations of the letters themselves, are a work of astonishing scholarship in their own right, and a resource that continues to be mined by musicologists and musicians to this day.

But it is worth considering whether Anderson was, in a sense, living a life through the men whose letters she translated. Was this woman, who spent so much of her non-working life alone in her flat, working through the correspondence of two of the world's greatest composers, in a sense vicariously experiencing the dramas of their families, their love affairs, their triumphs and challenges?

Did they become her companions, and, to an extent, her family? All of this is entirely academic, of course, and doubtless would have been brushed aside as emotive nonsense by Anderson. What is incontrovertible, however, is that the work gave her enormous pleasure, and she repaid the pleasure music gave her with her services to it. From the suburban comfort of her various Hampstead flats, she produced musicological works of international significance and the highest scholarly calibre. In her two collections of *Letters*, she employed her professional background in cryptanalysis to remarkable effect, teasing out the coded allusions of Mozart, and deciphering the almost illegible handwriting of Beethoven.

Emily Anderson was utterly self-controlled, with an iron discipline in her quest for perfection in both her professional and scholarly work. She had a keen sense of purpose, a determination to see the task through, to leave no stone unturned, to be *right*, to the degree that she felt it her duty to correct anyone who got it wrong, regardless of their status or qualifications. Similarly, the nature of Anderson's codebreaking work was such that the intelligence thereby gleaned saved countless lives during wartime, but it was also indirectly responsible for taking countless more. Yet Anderson never wavered in doing what she knew to be her duty. The admiralty's Room 40 chief, Sir Alfred Ewing, in his controversial lecture of 1927, observed that war 'caused us to embrace without a qualm the stealthy occupation of the eavesdropper, usually so ignoble'.[9] Anderson had no qualms when it came to her responsibilities at the highest echelons of the professional 'eavesdropper' agency in British intelligence. If the work needed to be done, she would do it, and she would do it better than anyone else. And then she would go home. The American cryptanalyst Frank Rowlett, when asked what his contribution had been to a difficult codebreaking challenge, replied: 'I was the one who believed it could be done.'[10] Emily Anderson was another who always believed it could be done, and set about doing it with a tenacity and focus she was able to sustain for over three decades. Even in retirement, she was prodigiously busy, that razor-sharp intelligence and characteristic perseverance being put to good effect in her musicological work right up until the end, as she raged against the inevitable ebbing of her powers.

Anderson was driven, to the point that, as we have seen her friend Hertzmann remark, 'she would not lower her high standard of principle even if it meant self-denial.'[11] Yet there are numerous testimonials to the fact that, in relaxed circumstances, she could be charming, witty and sociable, and there is no denying the fact that her generosity was remarkable. She quite literally gave away everything she ever possessed, to the extent that there was no physical trace left of her in any of the places she had lived. In particular, she ensured in her will that her single women friends were given not just mementos of her, but also practical funds with which to support themselves.

Yet still, questions remain. Why did she never buy a flat or house, when she could have easily afforded to do so? Was it from a desire to be able to move without too much fuss if she was receiving unwelcome attention from overly inquisitive neighbours? Or was it simply down to the fact that she wanted to spend whatever capital she had on her international travel in pursuit of her musicological studies rather than invest it in property? We will never know for sure. Why did she allow the family rift with her brother to continue, when a train journey to Liverpool, or the sending of one of her well-written letters, with a stamped addressed envelope enclosed, could have brought her back into contact with her only surviving sibling, and only nephew? It is strange that she did not do so, but perhaps the fault lay on both sides, and Anderson may have had her reasons.

What happened to the two honours that appeared on her coffin – her OBE and her Order of Merit – and the Bronze Medal she received from the Mozarteum, whose whereabouts are unknown? Although admittedly her will, written in 1959, preceded the awarding of the Order of Merit, her OBE and Mozarteum Foundation Medal had by then been awarded, yet she made no provision for them. They disappeared after her funeral, and it is conceivable that they may have been placed in her coffin following the funeral service and subsequently incinerated when she was cremated. The only item of Anderson's personal possessions whose whereabouts is known is her beloved pianoforte, which remains in the care of Timothy Sidwell.

For a woman who shied away from any attention, did the awarding of the OBE even matter to her? It undoubtedly did. That much is clear from her letter to the Secretary of the Royal Musical Association in 1955, when it had been omitted from her name in the listing of members of the Association.[12] Similarly, in her will, signed by her on 3 June 1959, she styles herself 'I, Emily Anderson OBE . . .'. She was justifiably proud of her work on the Mozart and Beethoven *Letters*, so it is likely that she was equally proud of her Bronze Medal from the Mozarteum, and her Order of Merit, First Class.

Another source of pride for Anderson was something

she did not live to see herself, but which became a lasting legacy. The first 'Emily Anderson Prize for Violin Playing' took place in June 1967 in the Wigmore Hall, London. The competition was open to violinists of any nationality aged between eighteen and thirty, and the not-inconsiderable prize on offer was £500.[13] The prize continues to be offered, with a prize fund today of £2,500, and a succession of talented early career violinists have benefited over the years from the bequest. In Anderson's home city the concert hall at the University, where Anderson studied and became the first Professor of German, was renamed the Emily Anderson Concert Hall in 2017, and an annual 'Emily Anderson Memorial Concert'[14] is held in her honour.

Anderson's one surviving brother-in-law, Dr Francis Lydon, husband of her younger sister Helen, remarried in 1946, and had two daughters. He died in 1966.[15] The following year, the last of the Anderson siblings, Emily's brother Alexander, aka Arthur Andrews, also died, in October 1967. Like his sister, his fluency in the German language appears never to have deserted him, and his grandson recalls him reciting passages from Goethe aloud in his old age. He never reconciled with any members of his extended family, but, poignantly, did not forget his native city. Following Emily's death, Arthur Andrews took his wife Lilian to Ireland to visit Galway. He was suffering at the time from the brain tumour that would eventually kill him, but photographs survive of a happy, smiling man on a beach on the picturesque shores of Galway Bay. The couple spent a few days exploring Galway, and may even have visited the UCG Quadrangle where Alexander Anderson and his sisters had grown up. Had they done so, it is unlikely that anyone would have recognised Arthur Andrews as the war-hero son of the former college president, who had left Galway in 1919, and stayed away for over forty years.

As for Emily Anderson, hers was a life full of high-stakes drama lived at the uppermost tier of British Signals Intelligence, juxtaposed with periods of intense private work and concentrated scholarly effort. A life of secrets and sonatas, of codes and codas, but ultimately a life that was lived entirely on her own terms. Following the cremation of her remains on 1 November 1962, per her instructions, there was to be no funeral urn, no burial plot, no interment, no monument. Her ashes were scattered on the Crocus Lawn at Golders Green on 27 December 1962 by crematorium staff, with no one else in attendance.[16] As had been her wish, all trace of this intensely private woman disappeared. All that remained was what she herself perceived as her greatest legacy: her scholarly works on the letters of Mozart and Beethoven. That, and her reputation as the greatest British female codebreaker, known only to the very few at the heart of British intelligence.

Until now.

Notes

Introduction

1 Author's interview with Mrs Elizabeth Oliver, 4 June 2020. I am deeply indebted to Timothy Sidwell for providing the initial contact details, and am especially grateful to Mrs Oliver for her invaluable reminiscences regarding her one-time neighbour.

2 *Irish Independent*, 16 November 1961.

1. Family, Early Life and Education

1 Civil Register, April/May/June 1981, vol. 4, p. 229.

2 Alexander Anderson was born 12 May 1858.

3 He was Goldsmith Exhibitioner for 1882, and graduated Sixth Wrangler in 1884. A 'Wrangler' is a student who gains first-class honours in the third year of the University's undergraduate degree (Tripos) examination in mathematics. The highest-scoring student is the Senior Wrangler. As Sixth Wrangler, Anderson gained the sixth-highest marks in the university in his examinations.

4 Joseph Larmor was born in 1857 in Magheragall, County Antrim. Educated at the Royal Belfast Academical Institution, he studied mathematics and experimental science at Queen's College, Belfast (BA 1874; MA 1875). He attended St John's College, Cambridge, where in 1880 he was Senior Wrangler.

5 Thompson, D. W., 'Joseph Larmor', *Year Book of the Royal Society of Edinburgh* (1941–42), p. 13.

6 In 1883, Larmor was appointed to the Chair of Natural Philosophy at Queen's College, Galway. He taught Physics for two years before accepting a lectureship in Mathematics at Cambridge in 1885.

7 Alexander Anderson was elected a Fellow of the Royal University of Ireland in 1886, and a Fellow of Sidney Sussex College, Cambridge, in 1891. He was awarded an honorary LLD by Glasgow University in 1901.

8 William N. Binns later became engineer to the Galway Harbour Board.

9 In 1903, Larmor was appointed Lucasian Professor of Mathematics at Cambridge, a post he retained until his retirement in 1932.

10 Civil Register of Marriages Index 1888, vol. 2, p. 509.

11 The younger Alexander Anderson was born 30 September 1895, according to the 1939 England and Wales Register.

12 National Archives of Ireland, 1901 and 1911 Census, household schedules for House 8.1 in Townparks (Galway West Urban, Galway).

13 Cunningham, J., *'A Town Tormented by the Sea': Galway 1790–1914* (Geography Publication, 2004), p. 183.

14 Ibid., p. 270.

15 Galway Petty Sessions Dog Licence Register 1911, CSPS2/1143, no. 356.

16 Clancy, M., ' "It was our joy to keep the flag flying": A Study of the Women's Suffrage Campaign in County Galway', *UCG Women's Studies Centre Review*, 3 (1995), p. 99.

17 Clancy, M., 'On the "Western Outpost": Local Government and Women's Suffrage in County Galway, 1898–1918', *Galway: History and Society* (Geography Publications, 1996) p. 573.

18 *Connacht Tribune*, 25 November 1911.

19 The 1911 census records him as aged fifteen, and a pupil at Mountjoy School in Mountjoy Square, Dublin.

20 'Woodman spare that tree', written by George Pope Morris in 1830, was later set to music by Henry Russell in 1837 and became a popular parlour song in the late 1880s.

21 *Philosophical Magazine*, series vi, 39 (1920), pp. 626–28.

22 Anderson's paper is referenced in Hawking, S. W., and Israel, W. (eds), *300 Years of Gravitation* (Cambridge University Press, 1987).

23 *Connacht Sentinel*, 8 September 1936.

24 Donovan O'Sullivan, M., and O'Halloran, J., 'The Centenary of Galway College', *Journal of the Galway Archaeological and Historical Society*, vol. 51 (1999), p. 37.

25 Ibid.

26 Ibid. The *Athenaeum* was a literary magazine published in London from 1828 to 1921. In 1921, it was incorporated into its competitor, the *Nation*, becoming *The Nation and Athenaeum*, before in 1931 merging with the *New Statesman*, to form the *New Statesman and Nation*.

27 Donovan O'Sullivan graduated with a BA in 1908, and an MA in 1909. She was Professor of History from 1914 to 1957.

28 Donovan O'Sullivan, M., and O'Halloran, J., 'The Centenary of Galway College', p. 29.

29 Ibid., p. 30.

30 This was located in a building adjacent to what is now the Taibhdhearc Theatre in Middle Street, Galway.

31 Donovan O'Sullivan, M., and O'Halloran, J., 'The Centenary of Galway College', p. 33.

32 An obituary of Elsie Rochford (*née* Anderson) published in 1957 observed that 'she had the gift of languages in a remarkable degree, and was a fluent speaker in German, French, Russian, Flemish, Irish, English and Greek. She could converse on the literature of all these countries with amazing skill.' (*Westmeath Independent*, 2 November 1957)

33 The census was taken on 2 April 1911.

34 Elizabeth (Elsie) Anderson graduated, *in absentia*, with first-class honours in French and German in November 1912, so it is likely her absence may be explained by her being abroad furthering her studies (*Connacht Tribune*, 9 November 1912).

35 The Browne Scholarship is awarded annually to the student with the highest degree of proficiency in both the French and German languages.

36 *The National University of Ireland Minutes of Senate*, vol. II, 27 October 1911–13 December 1912, p. 292.

2. Berlin and Marburg

1 The oldest of Berlin's four universities, the University of Berlin (Universitätzu Berlin) had been established by Frederick William III on the initiative of Wilhelm von Humboldt and others in 1809, and opened in 1810. From then until its closure in 1945, it was named Friedrich Wilhelm University

(Friedrich-Wilhelms-Universität). During the Cold War, the university found itself in East Berlin and was split in two when the Free University of Berlin opened in West Berlin. The university was renamed Humboldt University of Berlin (Humboldt-Universitätzu Berlin) in 1949, in honour of Alexander and Wilhelm von Humboldt.

2 Evans, S., 'Berlin 1914: A city of ambition and self-doubt', *BBC Magazine*, 8 January 2014.

3 *Freeman's Journal*, 3 September 1912. EA was listed on a ship's manifest of passengers leaving the port of Kingstown, Co. Dublin, on a Royal Mail steamer bound for England.

4 For women, this consisted of a dirndl, a dress comprising a bodice, a skirt, a shirt (worn underneath the bodice) and an apron (worn at the front, on top of the skirt). Men wore lederhosen, i.e. leather trousers traditionally made out of tanned deer leather.

5 De Mallac, G., 'Pasternak and Marburg', *The Russian Review*, vol. 38, no. 4 (October 1979), p. 423.

6 Ibid., p. 424.

7 Harvard student Eliot had been appointed Sheldon Travelling Fellow in Philosophy for the academic year 1914–15, and was due to take up a place at Merton College, Oxford, in Autumn 1914. He took the opportunity, while in Europe, to attend a philosophy summer-school at the University of Marburg.

8 Eliot spent a difficult few days criss-crossing Germany, making his way to Frankfurt on a train crowded with soldiers, then onwards to Cologne, followed by a twelve-hour journey by train to the Netherlands border. He reached Rotterdam, took another train to Vlissingen, a seaport, and boarded a ship to England (Miller Jr, James E., *T. S. Eliot: The Making of an American Poet, 1888–1922* (Pennsylvania State University Press, 2005), pp. 195–96).

9 P. J. Webb had been appointed to the position in May 1911 (*Connacht Tribune*, 20 May 1911).

10 *Connacht Tribune*, 20 May 1911.

11 He was conferred, *in absentia*, with a BSc (Honoria Causa) in 1918, and is listed in the college calendar as 'Lieutenant, Connaught Rangers, attached to R. F. C. (Prisoner of War)'.

12 Courtney, T., BMH WS 447.

13 Alexander Anderson was given the regimental number H/26770. He was described as being 5'9" in height, weighed 134 lbs, and had

a pale complexion, with blue eyes and brown hair (WO, TNA, Letter No. AG2b, dated 17/10/14).

14 *Connacht Tribune*, 25 December 1915.

15 In 1911 and 1912, students from Queen's College, Barbados, were awarded prizes by the Royal Drawing Society (*The Times*, 24 August 1911, and *The Times*, 15 August 1912).

3. Barbados and the 1916 Rising

1 Miss James served as Principal from 1898 to 1916 (*A History of Queen's College 1883–1993*, Department of Archives, St James, Barbados).

2 Minutes books, Queen's College, Barbados, 1915–1917, Queen's College Archive. I am indebted to Stephen O'Malley, a family relative living in Barbados, who kindly agreed to access the Queen's College Archive on my behalf.

3 Ibid.

4 Ibid.

5 A reference in 1916 refers to 'Miss Anderson taking morning duty'. Staff minutes books, Queen's College, Barbados, 1915–1916, Queen's College Archive.

6 Ibid.

7 Carter, Dr Dan C., *A Short History of the Ministry of Education of Barbados* (Barbados, 2013), p. 54.

8 There were divisions among Galway's citizens about the visit. Galway County Council had a nationalist majority and had voted to boycott the King's visit. After heated debates, Galway Urban Council, which represented the city, voted 8–4 to take part in the official welcome. Its Chairman, Martin McDonogh, was however adamant that in presenting an address of welcome 'there will be nothing subservient about it' (*Galway Express*, 1 July 1903).

9 The hanging, in August 1916, of Roger Casement for his attempt to land weapons destined for the rebels from a German submarine at Banna Strand, Co. Kerry, brought the number to sixteen.

10 From 1880 to 1886, Valentine Steinberger had been at the Modern Languages School at Belfast Royal Academy.

11 *Galway Express*, 19 September 1914.

12 Steinberger had been born on 7 January 1853, according to his Certificate of Naturalization to an Alien, issued by the Home

Office, 5 June 1913 (Home Office No. 190325, Certificate No. 23561).

13 Anonymous obituary of Professor Steinberger, attributed to 'Simplicissimus', and published in the UCG College Annual of 1917.

14 The anonymous obituary was likely written by Cornelius O'Leary, who travelled on the HMS *Gloucester* with Professor Steinberger.

15 *Connacht Tribune*, 27 May 1916.

16 The Battle of the Somme officially ended on 18 November 1916.

17 Raleigh, Sir. W. A., *The War in the Air: Being the Story of the Part Played in the Great War by the Royal Air Force* (Oxford University Press, 1922), p. 314.

18 Prisoner of War: Circumstances of Capture, Register No. 3835/5, TNA.

19 Bapaume is located in the Hauts-de-France region of northern France.

20 Prisoner of War: Circumstances of Capture, statement dated 23 February 1919, Register No. 3835/5, TNA.

21 Libby, F., *Horses Don't Fly* (Arcade Publishing, 2000), pp. 136–37.

22 Raleigh, Sir. W. A., *The War in the Air*, p. 314.

23 In 1905, he inherited the barony of Lucas and the lordship of Dingwall from his maternal uncle, the 7th Earl Cowper, and in 1907 took his seat in the House of Lords. Lucas served as private secretary to Richard Haldane, Secretary of State for War, from 1907 to 1908.

24 Raleigh, Sir. W. A., *The War in the Air*, p. 314.

25 Raleigh confirmed that 'of the four officers in the two aeroplanes shot down with him, one was killed and two were wounded. Two of them had fallen, with their machine, on to an enemy kite balloon on the ground, and set it on fire.' (Raleigh, Sir. W. A., *The War in the Air*, p. 315)

26 Prisoner of War: Circumstances of Capture, Register No. 3835/5, TNA.

27 Alexander Anderson's account of what had happened was written on 19 December 1918 from the president's residence, University College, Galway.

28 31 March 1919, from the War Office. Report of Standing Committee of Enquiry into the Circumstances of Capture of Lt. A.

Anderson, dated 31 March 1919. The report is contained in the same register as all of the other material related to his war record, i.e. Register No. 3835/5, TNA.

4. Academic Career

1 This comprised EA's time as an assistant to Professor Steinberger following her return to Germany at the outbreak of the war, and her two years' experience at Queen's College, Barbados.
2 *The National University of Ireland Minutes of Senate* – vol. V, 3 December 1915–16 July 1917, p. 327.
3 *Irish Times*, 9 June 1917.
4 A first-class honours MA graduate in Modern Languages from University College, Dublin, Hanna Sheehy was introduced to Francis Skeffington by the writer James Joyce, who attended university with Skeffington. Sheehy was a leading suffragist and feminist, and upon their marriage, husband and wife took the surname Sheehy Skeffington as a symbol of their respect for one another.
5 Ward, Margaret, *Hanna Sheehy Skeffington: A Life* (Attic Press, 1997), p. 176.
6 UCG College Calendar, 1917–18.
7 O'Neill, R., 'On Modern Languages', in Foley, Tadhg (ed.), *From Queen's College to National University: Essays on the Academic History of QCG/UCG/NUIG, Galway* (Four Courts Press, 1999), p. 375.
8 Ó Briain retained the position of Professor of Romance Languages at UCG from 1917 until his retirement in 1958.
9 Donovan O'Sullivan, M., and O'Halloran, J., 'The Centenary of Galway College', p. 38.
10 UCG College Annual, 1917–1918, Special Collections, Hardiman Library, NUI Galway.
11 Ó Briain had been born William O'Brien, but his espousal of all things Gaelic extended to his name, and he used the Irish form of his name for most of his adult life.

5. 'Passed Under the Microscope'

1 Letter from Richard Hippisley to Alastair Denniston, 11 September 1952, DENN 2/1, CCAC.

2 Toye, F., *For What We Have Received* (A. A. Knopf, 1948), quoted in papers of Clarke, W. F., CLKE3, CCAC.

3 This is particularly the case in respect to the section in which EA worked, MI1(b). Major Hay, who commanded the section, was not chosen as the Director of the post-war combined military and naval intelligence services, known as the Government Code & Cypher School (the naval officer, Commander Denniston, was). In a fit of pique, Hay destroyed the majority of the records of MI1(b).

4 Savory resigned his chair in 1940 when elected as an Ulster Unionist MP for Queen's University, Belfast (as decreed by the Government of Ireland Act 1920, Queen's University of Belfast was a university constituency of the Parliament of Northern Ireland from 1921 until 1969, when it was abolished – it returned four MPs). He was appointed as special investigator into the Katyn massacre of Polish officers in 1940.

5 Donovan O'Sullivan, M., and O'Halloran, J., 'The Centenary of Galway College', p. 38.

6 Bruce, James, ' "A Shadowy Entity": M.I.1 (b) and British Communications Intelligence, 1915–1922', *Intelligence and National Security*, vol. 32, no. 3 (2017), p. 315.

7 Letter from EA to Fr John Hynes, 18 March 1919, UCG Governing Body Minutes (Correspondence), March–May 1919.

8 Obituary of Alda Milner-Barry in the 1938 College Annual of St Christopher's College, Blackheath, London.

9 The dates would indicate that Alda Milner-Barry deputised for EA during the 1918–19 academic year.

10 Sir Philip Stuart Milner-Barry, born in 1907, was thirteen years younger than his sister Alda. An international chess player, Milner-Barry became head of Hut 6, the section responsible for deciphering messages that had been encrypted using the German Enigma machine.

11 History of M. I. 1(b); 'Lists'; M. I. 1(b) tea fund for November/ December 1917, HW 3/185, TNA.

12 The Hotel Stuart was located at 161–165 Cromwell Road.

13 Fr Hynes was also the Professor of Archaeology. As Monsignor Hynes, he subsequently served as President of University College, Galway, from 1934 until 1945.

14 Letter from EA to Fr Hynes, 22 July 1918, UCG Governing Body Minutes (Correspondence), 1918–1920, Special Collections, University of Galway.

15 The term 'Hush WAAC' was not the official term used to describe the women codebreakers or the division in which they worked – the division was officially known as I(e)C. Remarkably, considering the highly secret nature of their work, in December 1917 one of the division's senior male officers revealed their existence, informing a newspaper correspondent 'that he had a group of "Hush WAACs" doing "very confidential work"'. The word 'Hush' was used to signify that the work was 'very Hush Hush' (Beach, J., 'The Hush WAACs – The secret ladies of St Omer', https://www.gchq.gov.uk/information/hush-waacs).

16 Another Irishwoman recruited to the Hush WAACs was Catherine Hayes Osborne, born in Milford, Co. Donegal. A doctor's daughter, she was fifty-one when she joined the first group of Hush WAACs sent to France in September 1917. She served with the Hush WAACs for the duration of the war, but little is known about her subsequent life. Like EA, she was also a Presbyterian. She died at her home in Milford, Co. Donegal, on 24 November 1948 (*Belfast Newsletter*, 26 November 1948).

17 Hannam was mentioned in despatches for her work in France, and later served with EA in MI1(b) and later GC&CS, from 1918 to 1920.

18 Watkins was mentioned in despatches for her work in France and served with EA in MI1(b) from 1918 to 1919.

19 Peel was a languages lecturer at the University of Manchester. She was originally recruited as a German language censor in the War Office in June 1917, and in September 1917 was transferred to Military Intelligence GHQ and assigned to I(e)C and sent to France (*The Welwyn Times*, 3 February 1938).

20 Chevalier was a lecturer at Cheltenham Ladies' College.

21 Watkins, G. E. G., 'Memories of a Hushwaac in France', 1998-01-110-1, National Army Museum, p. 1.

22 Devonshire House was the London home of the Dukes of Devonshire. In 1914, part of the house was taken over by the British Red Cross Society and it became the VAD (Voluntary Aid Detachment) headquarters throughout the war.

23 Watkins, G. E. G., 'Memories of a Hushwaac in France', pp. 1–2.

6. 'A Shadowy Entity'

1 Extract from Florence Hayllar's 'The Shade of M. I. 1(b) to its Chief', which features in the Cork Street Book (see p. 57). Hayllar's contribution concluded with the lines: 'And, by the gracious Art of Memory/Lend yet a Form, a shadow Entity/to that which once we were – M. I. 1(b)' (MS 2788/2/10, Hay Papers, University of Aberdeen, Special Collections and Archives).

2 Denniston, A. E. G., 'The Government Code and Cypher School Between the Wars', *Intelligence and National Security*, vol. 1, issue 1 (1986), p. 49.

3 Transcript of a talk given by Mavis Batey on the 'History of WWI SIGINT' in 2012, GBR/0014/BTEY 3/4, CCAC.

4 Ibid.

5 Room 40 is often referred to in official correspondence as Room 40 OB (Old Building).

6 He drafted it in his own hand.

7 Denniston, A. G., 'History of Room 40 and Codebreaking, 1944', GBR/0014/DENN 1, CCAC.

8 MI1 stood for Military Intelligence, Section 1, and it incorporated a number of subsections. Apart from MI1(b), which dealt with Interception and Cryptanalysis, other divisions of MI1 dealt with Distribution of Reports and Intelligence Records (MI1(a)), the Secret Service (MI1(c)), Communications Security (MI1(d)), Wireless Telegraphy (MI1(e)), Personnel and Finance (MI1(f)) and Security, Deception and Counter Intelligence (MI1(g)).

9 The 1920 history of MI1(b) by Major Brooke-Hunt, cited in 'Note on the division of responsibility between the War Office and the GC&CS', MI1(b), 21 July 1932, HW 62/19, TNA.

10 Ibid.

11 James Bruce's ' "A Shadowy Entity" ', pp. 313–32, has significantly redressed this imbalance.

12 William Clarke, 'A History of MI1(b)', HW7/35, TNA.

13 Ibid. This changed during the Second World War, when code-breaking became a more mathematical task.

14 Obituary in *The Times*, 2 April 1942. Hayllar died on 1 April 1942.

15 Hayllar joined MI1(b) on 2 July 2017.

16 Letter dated 11 June 1907, DDX 1137/3/13, TNA. After the war, Claribel Spurling served as editor of *Notes and Queries* for many years.

17 Spurling was born in 1875 in Oxford, where her father was a tutor at Kebel College. He subsequently became Canon of Chester Cathedral.

18 Captain Francis Spurling of the Rifle Brigade, 7th Battalion, was killed on 6 December 1917, and is buried in Poperinge, West Flanders.

19 John Fraser helped to break codes from Greece, Spain, Uruguay, Argentina, Turkey, Switzerland, Sweden, Norway, Brazil and the Netherlands, and also helped break codes used by the Vatican. He was recruited in February 1916 (CV, HW 3/35, TNA).

20 The epitaph relates to the Second World War and appears on the Cenotaph, commemorating the fallen of the Battle of Kohimain, April 1944.

21 There is evidence in EA's personal correspondence indicating that insomnia troubled her for the remainder of her life.

22 There are several pointed references in the Cork Street Book to Hay's love of fresh air.

23 William 'Nobby' Clarke identified this person as the actor Gerald Lawrence (CLKE 3, CCAC).

24 MS 2788/2/4, Hay, M., chapter vi, 'Notes on Cryptography', Hay Papers, Special Collections, University of Aberdeen.

25 MS 2788/2/4, Hay, M., p. 3.

26 Ibid.

27 The multi-linguist John Fraser succeeded where others had failed in cracking the Greek code. Fraser had a light-bulb moment when he realised that the reason they couldn't break the code was because the messages were not written in Greek but in French, the language of European diplomacy. Fraser sent a telegram to Denniston that simply read: 'The Pillars of Hercules Have Fallen!'

28 Bruce, James, ' "A Shadow Entity" ', p. 326.

29 McKay, S., 'The greatest hackers of the First World War', *The Spectator*, 14 January 2017.

30 Long hair was considered feminine, short hair was not, and popular women's magazines, such as the *Ladies' Home Journal*, printed editorials asking 'To Bob or Not to Bob?'. The actress Mary Pickford, although opting not to cut her famous curls and risk upsetting her fan base, nonetheless acknowledged that the woman who chose to cut her hair 'looks smarter with a bob, and smartness rather than beauty seems to be the goal of every woman these days'

(Mary Pickford, 'Why I Have Not Bobbed Mine', *Pictorial Review*, April 1927, p. 9).

31 *Hamlet*, Act 1, Sc. 5.

7. War's End

1 Fraser, Lionel, *All to the Good* (Heineman, 1963), p. 61.

2 Ibid.

3 Fraser recalled that he had felt frustrated by the lack of a proper celebration, 'so I mounted a bus and went on to the open roof' (Fraser, Lionel, *All to the Good*, p. 61).

4 Brownrigg, Rear Admiral Sir Douglas, *Indiscretions of the Naval Censor* (George H. Doran & Co., 1920), p. 277.

5 Bruce, James, ' "A Shadowy Entity" ', p. 323.

6 Ibid.

7 Ibid, p. 324. The Government Code & Cypher School came into being on 1 November 1919, under the leadership of Commander Alastair Denniston.

8 Maxwell Edmonds (1875–1958), a graduate of Jesus College, Cambridge, was a classicist, poet and dramatist.

9 Ronsard (1524–1585), known to his contemporaries as the 'prince of poets', was destined for a career in diplomacy before a sudden onset of deafness in 1540 necessitated a shift in focus to literary pursuits.

10 I am indebted to Professor Phyllis Gaffney, formerly of the School of Languages and Literature at University College, Dublin, for this translation.

11 Bruce, James, ' "A Shadowy Entity" ', p. 323.

12 Beesley, Patrick, *Room 40: British Naval Intelligence 1914–1918* (Hamish Hamilton, 1982), p. 303.

8. 'Double Jobbing'

1 Fara, Patricia, *A Lab of One's Own: Science and Suffrage in the First World War* (Oxford University Press, 2018).

2 Bruce, James, ' "A Shadowy Entity" ', p. 326.

3 Freeman, P., 'MI1(b) and the origins of British diplomatic cryptanalysis', *Intelligence and National Security*, vol. 22, no. 2, p. 222.

4 The name was suggested by Countenay Forbes, a former ambassador to Peru and Head of the Foreign Office Communications

Department. The name implied that codes and ciphers were two different things, whereas the term 'codebreaking' is now used for both. 'School' was chosen to underline to the public the defensive role of the new organisation in studying and advising on 'the security of codes and ciphers by all government departments and to assist in their provision' (HW 3/32).

5 Transcript of a talk given by Mavis Batey on the the History of WWI SIGINT in 2012, GBR/0014/BTEY 3/4, CCAC.

6 HW3/35 TNA – the document is a listing of the staff of MI1(b), their specialisms and experience, drawn up by Major Hay.

7 The inference was that should Hay provide work for this lady, Major G– would use his influence to ensure that Hay was included in the New Year's Honours List.

8 Draft memoirs of Malcolm Hay of Seaton, Special Collections, University of Aberdeen.

9 Gwen Watkins, who had served as a Hush WAAC in France, was identified as one of those 'indispensable to the running of this office as at present constituted' and she too indicted her willingness to remain.

10 Claribel Spurling, considerably older than her female colleagues, declined the invitation to join the new organisation, and in 1920 returned to the world of education when she took up the position of Warden at the Ellis Lloyd Jones Hall, a hostel associated with Manchester University College. A passionate advocate for women in education, she attended the International Federation of University Women in Paris in 1921, and in December 1926 resigned from her Wardenship in Manchester and moved to London to take up the position of first Warden of Crosby Hall, the new International Hall of Residence opened by the British Federation of University Women (now the British Federation of Women Graduates). She died on 8 December 1940.

11 George Bailey Samson (1883–1965), later Sir George, was a Japanese expert, who opted to return to his career in the diplomatic service. Sansom's career straddled both World Wars, the diplomatic service and academia.

12 Hotel Madrid, located at 147 Cromwell Road, South Kensington, was close to where EA had stayed when she first came to London in 1918, the Hotel Stuart at Cromwell Road. Hotel Madrid was described in an advertisement as: 'A batchelor [sic] and family hotel.

Excellent cuisine, gas fires, constant hot water,' The rent was three guineas (*The Times*, 18 September 1920).

13 Prisoner of War: Circumstances of Capture, Flight Lieutenant Alexander Anderson, 19 December 1918, Register No. 3835/5, TNA.

14 I am grateful to Stephen Andrews for this memory of his grandfather.

15 Letter from the Air Ministry to the War Office, 14 March 1921, on Alexander Anderson's personnel file, TNA, File Register No. 3835/5.

16 Papers Relating to the Foreign Relations of the United States, The Paris Peace Conference, 1919, vol. XIII, section IV – Inter-Allied Commissions of Control (Art. 203 to 210), Article 203 https:// history.state.gov/historicaldocuments/frus1919Parisv13 acessed 31/1/2019.

17 The Commission was dissolved on 30 September 1924.

18 The Black and Tans were in the main ex-soldiers recruited as constables into the Royal Irish Constabulary (RIC) as reinforcements during the Irish War of Independence. Notoriously ill-disciplined, they were deployed in regions where the IRA was most active and fighting was heaviest. They were responsible for numerous atrocities against both combatants and civilians, including murders and the deliberate burning of a number of towns.

19 Letter from EA to Fr John Hynes, 2 February 1919, UCG Governing Body (Correspondence), 1919–20, Special Collections, University of Galway.

20 Letter from EA to Fr John Hynes, 8 December 1919, UCG Governing Body (Correspondence), Special Collections, University of Galway.

21 The successful candidate in the Browne scholarship examination, Miss Curran, subsequently applied for the vacant Professorship of German when Anderson resigned, but Miss Cooke, a protégée of Anderson's, was appointed.

22 Letter from EA to Professor Anderson, 8 December 1919, UCG Governing Body Minutes (Correspondence), Special Collections, University of Galway.

23 Letter from EA to Fr John Hynes, 8 December 1919, UCG Governing Body Minutes (Correspondence), Special Collections, University of Galway.

24 The Forum Club, a club for women, was located at 6 Grosvenor Place, Hyde Park Corner, London, SW1.

25 Letter from EA to Professor Anderson, 24 June 1920, UCG Governing Body Minutes (Correspondence), Special Collections, University of Galway.

26 Memo from the Foreign Office, dated 20 November 1920, HW 3/35, TNA.

27 UCG College Annual, 1920–1921, Special Collections, University of Galway.

9. 'Miss Anderson of the Foreign Office'

1 GC&CS was, in essence, the codebreaking arm of the Foreign Office.

2 Ashton-Gwatkin, Frank Trelawny Arthur, *The British Foreign Service: A Discussion of the Development and Function of the British Foreign Service* (Syracuse University Press, 1950), pp. 34–35.

3 Ferris, John, *Behind the Enigma: The Authorised History of GCHQ, Britain's Secret Cyber-Intelligence Agency* (Bloomsbury Publishing, 2020), p. 89.

4 It is unclear why EA, whose preferred language was German, was assigned to the Italian Diplomatic Section. There may have already been sufficient German and French speakers, and a deficit of Italian speakers, and with her decent command of Italian, EA was possibly willing to put in the extra effort to hone her proficiency in that language.

5 Ferris, John, 'Whitehall's Black: British Cryptology and the Government Code and Cypher School, 1919–29', *Intelligence and National Security*, vol. 2, issue 1 (1987), p. 55.

6 The Hapsburg civil service had a motto: '*Warum einfach wenn es auch kompliziert geht?*', which translates as: 'Why simple if it can also be made complicated?', Papers of Sir Philip Stuart Milner-Barry, (MNBY 7, CCAC).

7 Papers of William F. Clarke, 'History of Room 40 and the Government Code and Cypher School', CLKE 3, CCAC.

8 He died, in Oxford, in May 1945.

9 Hay, M., *Memoirs*, held in Special Collections, University of Aberdeen Library.

10 The most infamous breach was the lecture given in Edinburgh in 1927 by Sir Alfred Ewing, former Director of Naval Intelligence

and Room 40 chief, which contained the first semi-official disclosure of the work done by Room 40.

11 Denniston, A. G., 'The Government Code and Cypher School Between the Wars', *Intelligence and National Security*, vol. 1, issue 1 (1986), p. 49.

12 The women were to be paid increments of £20, up to a maximum of the scale of £400 p.a.

13 Report of the Chief Clerk of the Foreign Office, 7 July 1922.

14 Female civil servants did not achieve total equality of pay and conditions until 1962 (Hede, A., 'Women Managers in the Civil Service: The Long Road Towards Equity in Britain', *International Review of Administrative Sciences*, vol. 61, no. 4 (1995), pp. 587–600).

15 The transfer of control of GC&CS from the Admiralty to the Foreign Office saw Hugh Sinclair placed in overall charge, with Alastair Denniston as (Deputy) Director of GG&CS.

16 Memo dated 20 November 1920, HW 3/35, TNA.

17 Treasury correspondence re: pay, 29 March 1921, T162/656, TNA.

18 Memo from Hugh Sinclair to Alastair Denniston, T162/656, TNA.

19 Ibid.

20 Letter from Hugh Sinclair to the Under Secretary of State for Foreign Affairs, dated 8 June 1922, TNA.

21 It was noted in a memo that: 'Having regard to the fact that Miss Anderson really up to the present has been receiving a rate of pay somewhat in excess of that appropriate for a woman officer, that her increment should be £15.' The handwritten amendment to the memo from EA's boss, Hugh Sinclair, stated that, in view of EA's value to GC&CS, he would authorise 'a jump of £40' instead, effective the following month (Memo from Treasury Chamber to the Under Secretary of State, Foreign Affairs, 26 May 1922, T162/656, TNA).

22 8 June 1922, T162/656, TNA.

23 Insomnia impacted many of those working in intelligence as a result of having to stay up on watch. Group Captain M. G. Christie, working for the Foreign Office in Berlin, reported in 1928: '[. . .] insomnia as bad as ever'. Christie left Berlin on the grounds of ill-health, in January 1930 (CHRS 1/1 CCAC, 17 November 1928).

24 Ferris, John, *Behind the Enigma*, p. 78.

25 Undated memo from Hugh Sinclair to GC&CS staff, HW 3/83, TNA.

26 During the Second World War, it had a brass plaque identifying it as the offices of the 'Minimax Fire Extinguisher Company'. Remarkably, Sir Stewart Menzies, Chief of SIS, had access to a tunnel that connected 54 Broadway to his private residence in Queen Anne's Gate.

27 Philby, K., *My Silent War: The Autobiography of a Spy* (Modern Library, reprint edition, 2002; first published 1968), p. 64.

28 Wilfred Bodsworth joined GC&CS on 1 June 1927, and his experience working on Italian with Anderson stood him in good stead when it came to Enigma. Dilly Knox had initially attacked the Italian Enigma traffic, having discovered the use of new wheel wirings with his 'buttoning-up' method. Italian traffic was received by two intercept stations situated at Fort Bridgewoods, outside Chatham, and at Flowerdown, the Admiralty station at Littleton near Winchester. The breakthrough came in April 1937, when twenty Italian naval messages were enciphered on the same Enigma setting. This blunder, breaking the most basic of all cryptographic rules, allowed Knox to find the wiring of all the three wheels on wiring D. It was soon discovered that the Spanish Enigma used the same wheel wirings so that they could communicate with the Italian machines. Bodsworth, a Spanish expert, and a member of Knox's team of codebreakers, took over the Spanish traffic (Soler Fuensanta, José Ramón, López-Brea Espiau, Francisco Javier, and Weierud, Frode, 'Spanish Enigma: A History of the Enigma in Spain', *Cryptologia*, vol. 34, issue 4 (October 2010), p. 15).

29 Memo by Bodsworth, Wilfred, 'Naval Section, 1927–1939', HW 3/1, TNA, p. 10.

30 Ibid.

31 Ibid.

32 Bodsworth's apprenticeship under EA lasted three years, and it was only in his third year that she let him translate messages for distribution (Ibid.)

33 Ibid.

34 Ibid.

35 Ferris, John, *Behind the Enigma*, p. 114.

36 Joshua Edward Synge Cooper (1901–1981), known to all as Josh, was the eldest son of an Anglo-Irish family. He joined GC&CS as a Junior Assistant in October 1925. With a First in Russian from King's College, London, he was assigned to Ernst Fetterle to work

on Soviet diplomatic ciphers. Less than a year later, he was promoted and established on the Air Ministry staff. From late 1929 to 1930, he was in the Naval Section working on Russian naval codes, and was sent to Sarafand for a fifteen-month investigation of Black Sea Fleet communications. In 1936, he was seconded back to GC&CS, and in 1939, he moved to Bletchley Park, where he was Head of the Air Section. He was awarded a Companion of the Most Distinguished Order of St Michael and St George in 1943 and a Companion of the Order of the Bath in 1958.

37 Cooper, J., 'Personal Notes on GC&CS 1925–1939', HW 3/83, p. 2, TNA.

38 Sir Samuel Hoare was a senior Conservative politician who served as Secretary of State for Air during most of the 1920s.

39 Cooper, J., 'Personal Notes on GC&CS 1925–1939', p. 4.

40 This is confirmed in a letter sent to EA in Cairo, in which he referred to 'the subject on which you were engaged about 1933' and expressed the hope that the Hungarian books built by herself and Knox 'are in some safe place' (see also p. 187).

41 This scheme was established to regularise the employment statuses of the variety of people the civil service had acquired by various entry routes that no longer fitted peacetime recruiting regulations. The Reconstruction Scheme operated from 1919 until 1924, and the situation was complicated by the fact that there was a drive to employ ex-servicemen and post-war financial stringency was in operation. Appointing Anderson to an established civil-service post in such circumstances would have been problematic, so this was an administrative sleight of hand that regularised Anderson's position and gave her pension rights. I am indebted to James Bruce for these insights.

42 *Connacht Tribune*, 10 March 1923.

43 Ibid.

44 Memo by Bodsworth, Wilfred, 'Naval Section, 1927–1939', HW 3/1, TNA, p. 10

45 Bodsworth, Wilfred, 'Naval Section 1927–1939', Paper 91, HW 3/1/6, TNA.

46 Bettina Brentano von Arnim, an admirer of Beethoven, had corresponded with her friend Goethe and advised him of Beethoven's desire to meet him. Through her intervention, the two met during the summer of 1812 (Knittel, K. M., 'The Construction

of Beethoven', in Samson, Jim, (ed.), *The Cambridge History of Nineteenth-Century Music* (Cambridge University Press, 2001), https://doi. org/10. 1017/CHOL9780521590174. 006, p. 119).

47 Unger, M. (ed.), *Introduction to Beethoven, Egmont, Overture for Orchestra Op. 84*, Edition Eulenburg no. 604 (Ernst Eulenburg Ltd, 2019).

48 Although Ainslie had been the first translator of Croce into English, his skill as a translator was compromised by the fact that his approach was more literary than philosophical. His translations of Croce's were consequently unfavourably reviewed (Paton, H. J., 'Review of D. Ainslie', *Philosophy of the Practical, Mind*, New Series, vol. 23, no. 91 (July 1914), p. 432).

49 It must be noted that 1927 was also the year when Neville Chamberlain read out deciphered Soviet telegrams in Parliament.

50 Ewing was at that time Principal of the University of Edinburgh, a position he accepted in 1916 and held until his retirement in 1929.

51 Letter from Arthur Balfour to W. Addis Miller, Secretary of the Edinburgh Philosophical Institution, 1 December 1927, reproduced in Jones, R. V., 'Alfred Ewing and "Room 40"', *Notes and Records of the Royal Society of London*, vol. 34, no. 1 (1979), pp. 67–68.

52 The Zimmermann telegram was a secret diplomatic communication issued from the German Foreign Office in January 1917 that proposed a military alliance between Germany and Mexico if the United States entered the First World War against Germany. With Germany's aid, Mexico would recover Texas, Arizona, and New Mexico. The telegram was intercepted by Room 40, and decoded by Nigel de Grey. Revelation of its contents enraged Americans, especially after German Foreign Secretary Arthur Zimmermann publicly admitted that the telegram was genuine. It helped to generate support for the American declaration of war on Germany in April 1917. The decryption of the Zimmermann telegram was the most significant intelligence triumph for Britain during the First World War, and one of the earliest occasions on which a piece of signal intelligence influenced world events.

53 Ewing left Room 40 to become Principal of the University of Edinburgh by the time the Zimmermann telegram had been decoded, but, ignoring Churchill's stipulation that the Room 40 chief would 'do no other work', insisted in his lecture that he was

still 'definitely in [. . .] charge' of Room 40 until, as he put it, 'I hauled down my flag' on 31 May 1917 at the request of the Admiralty (Jeffries-Jones, R., 'The Sensitivity of SIGINT: Sir Alfred Ewing's lecture on Room 40 in 1927', *Journal of Intelligence History*, vol.17, issue 1 (2018), p. 18).

54 The lecture did not appear in print until 1979, when it was reproduced in Jones, R. V., 'Alfred Ewing and "Room 40"', pp. 65–90.

55 Admiralty circular, 16 December 1927, quoted in Freeman, P., 'The Zimmermann Telegram Revisited', vol. 30, issue 2 (2006), p. 110, n. 23.

56 Ibid.

57 In 1925, an American lawyer, Amos Peaslee, accessed over 10,000 highly secret decrypts from Room 40 via dubious means, but with the unintentional complicity of Admiral Hall. He took several hundred out of Britain to be used as evidence in a German court case for compensation initiated by some American businesses who had incurred losses during wartime. Within weeks, the German Army and German Foreign Office embarked on programmes to improve their cryptography. A subsequent NSA report expressed the view that: 'The steckered Enigma, and greatly increased production and use of one time pad, were the direct results of these programs.'(NSA, DOCID 3978516, p. 1).

58 In the US, all of the significant progress made in establishing a cryptologic bureau during the First World War was undone in 1929 when Secretary of State Henry Stimson closed it down when he came into office on the prosaic grounds that 'gentlemen don't read each other's mail'.

10. Life in London and Family Matters

1 Prior to its conversion into a Ladies' Club, during the First World War the building had been seconded by the government and housed Princess Christian's Hospital for Officers.

2 One of The Forum Club's founders, and its first chairman, was Alice Williams, first honorary secretary and treasurer of the National Federation of Women's Institutes.

3 EA's letters are addressed from 9 Grosvenor Place.

4 The Forum Club continued to operate at Grosvenor Place until 1952, when the lease on the building expired and the club moved to a new premises at Belgrave Square.

5 A letter from the Air Ministry, Kingsway, London, 14 March 1921, stated that Flying Officer A. Anderson 'is being retained on his temporary commission while serving with the Inter-Allied Aeronautical Commission of Control, Germany' (WO 339/2735).

6 The King and Queen were attending the funeral of the Empress Eugenie at Farnborough that morning, which necessitated the Duke of York deputising for them (*The Times*, 21 July 1920).

7 I am grateful to Alexander Anderson's grandson, Stephen Andrews, who filled in this aspect of his grandfather's life for me.

8 Ibid.

9 Redman had been born on 26 March 1891, making her four years older than her husband. At the time the 1939 register was compiled, the couple were living at 40 Elm Vale and Arthur Andrews (previously known as Alexander Anderson) was working at Liverpool Power Plant, giving his occupation as 'Control Room Engineer (Elec. Eng.)'. (District NISU, 455/7).

10 Civil Registration Marriage Index, July/Aug/Sept 1925, vol. 8b, p. 502.

11 Arthur Henry Andrews was born 25 October 1927 in Liverpool. He died in January 1973 (England & Wales Civil Registration Death Index, 1973).

12 Ballykinlar, in Co. Down, was an internment camp in which thousands of Irish men who actively opposed British rule in Ireland were detained by the British Army during the Irish War of Independence.

13 *Sunday Independent*, 15 May 1921.

14 Ibid.

15 *Evening Herald*, 19 November 1923.

16 The wedding took place on 26 December 1925.

17 *Connacht Sentinel*, 18 May 1937. Dr Anderson subsequently saw to it that her son took her name also, and so his surname was Anderson Lydon.

18 *Irish Independent*, 22 May 1937.

19 The UK medical register for 1927 shows Dr Anderson as living at Brooklands, Yeadon, Leeds. She may have been working at St James's University Hospital, affectionately known as 'Jimmy's',

which was one of the largest teaching hospitals in the UK (UK Medical Register, 1927, p. 27).

20 *Connacht Sentinel*, 18 May 1937. The 1930 UK Medical Register shows the couple living in two places as they continued their respective medical training, Dr Anderson in London and Dr Lydon in Sheffield.

21 Francis Lydon's grandfather, also John Lydon, had been an inveterate poacher of the Galway Salmon Fishery until, in 1852, the new owners of the Fishery, Edmund and Thomas Ashworth from Bolton in Lancashire, decided that it would be wiser to pay him to work as a bailiff on the fishery rather than pay the cost of ongoing prosecutions against him for poaching. John Lydon was appointed as a bailiff in the late 1850s, and thereafter became a much respected professional angler and fishing-tackle manufacturer in Galway.

22 *Irish Independent*, 6 July 1966.

23 Rents started at two guineas per week (*The Times*, 18 January 1930).

24 *The Times*, 17 June 1938. The electoral registers confirm that, when it was advertised to let in June 1938, this could only have been EA's flat, as the other tenants remain the same, apart from one new family, who presumably now occupied EA's former flat, in the 1939 register.

25 Letter from Treasury Chambers to the Under Secretary of State at the Foreign Office, 8 June 1922, T162/656, TNA.

26 I am grateful to EA's friend and colleague, Dr Dagmar von Busch-Weise, who visited EA at her Ellerdale Road flat, for this insight.

27 My thanks to C. Bechstein Pianoforte manufaktur GmbH for information on the manufacture of the piano based on its serial number.

28 Built in 1901, Bechstein Hall was a showroom and concert venue that operated until 1916. The outbreak of war in 1914 had generated anti-German sentiment to the degree that even the playing of a Bechstein piano was considered an unpatriotic act. In 1916, the entire business – including studios, offices, warehouses, 137 pianos and the Hall itself – was sold to Debenhams for £56,500. The Hall alone had cost £100,000 to build.

29 *The Times*, 9 April 1931.

30 Interview with EA on BBC radio's Third Programme on 2 December 1961, British Library.

31 *Westmeath Independent*, 2 November 1957.

32 *Limerick Leader*, 11 October 1926.

33 Ibid.

34 There were 500 Germans employed on the scheme, ranging from engineers to skilled metal workers, as well as administrative staff (Bielenberg, Andy, *The Shannon Scheme and the Electrification of the Irish Free State* (Lilliput Press, 2002), p. 69).

35 McLaughlin was subsequently appointed as the first Managing Director of the Electricity Supply Board, the first semi-state body established in Ireland, in 1927.

36 Rishworth was seconded from his post in UCG for the duration of the construction period.

11. Mozart and the Interwar Years

1 Ferris, John, *Behind the Enigma*, p. 89.

2 Born Agnes Meyer in 1889 (she married lawyer Michael Driscoll in 1924), Driscoll was an American cryptanalyst who joined the US Navy in June 1918, and served almost continuously as the Navy's most senior cryptanalyst until her retirement in 1949. Driscoll broke a multitude of Japanese naval systems, as well as becoming a developer of early machine systems. A gifted mathematician, scientist and linguist, like Anderson she was also a talented and passionate musician, and her first job out of college was as director of music at a military academy. She died in 1971, and is buried in Arlington National Cemetery.

3 Acknowledged as America's first female cryptanalyst, Friedman was born Elizebeth Smith in 1892. Her husband, William Friedman, was the US's top cryptanalyst, but Mrs Friedman was an exceptional cryptanalyst in her own right. She died in 1980.

4 Like many codebreakers, Oliver Strachey was also a first-class bridge and chess player, and was described as 'a crossword wizard, both in compilation and in solution' (Obituary, *The Times*, 16 May 1960).

5 Ibid.

6 James Turner was a highly regarded bookbuilder, fluent in fifteen languages, ranging from Arabic to Japanese.

7 Notes by Turner re: management of GC&CS, HW 3/1, TNA.

8 Letter from Marshal of the RAF Sir Cyril Newell to Group Captain M. G. Christie from the Air Ministry, Adastral House, 21 December 1928, CHRS 1/1, CCAC.

9 Many of those with whom EA collaborated and consulted on the Mozart letters in Europe were Jews. Through them, EA would have been aware of the evolving situation in Germany and Austria once Hitler came to power. A number of her closest associates (including Stefan Zweig and Heinrich Eisemànn) fled and moved to London in advance of the outbreak of war, where they continued their association with EA.

10 Anderson, E., *The Letters of Mozart and his Family* (Macmillan & Co, Ltd, third edition, 1997; first published 1938), p. xii.

11 Harold Macmillan was leader of the Conservative Party, and served as Prime Minister, from January 1957 to October 1963.

12 At the time *The Letters of Mozart and his Family* was published, Macmillan was MP for Stockton-on-Tees, and he served the constituency until 1945. He remained a backbencher until 1942, sometimes rebelling against the party line – in 1936, he resigned the Whip over sanctions on Abyssinia – before returning to the party fold in 1937. In 1940, he received his first appointment, as Parliamentary Secretary for the Ministry of Supply under Lord Beaverbrook. He resumed working for the family publishing firm from 1945 to 1951, when the party was in opposition.

13 Anderson, E., 'An Unpublished Letter of Mozart', *Music and Letters*, vol. 18, no. 2 (April 1937), pp. 128–33 (this quote p. 128).

14 Ibid., p. 128.

15 Of the more than 900 letters translated in the three volumes, *c.* 300 were written by Wolfgang, and *c.* 600 by his father Leopold. EA discovered a dozen new letters, which had not been included in any previous collection, and corrected six dozen letters that had been incorrectly translated or attributed in other collections. She also included an extra dozen letters from Mozart's widow to the publisher Johann André, which had not been published before (Fox Strangways, A. H., 'Review of *The Letters of Mozart and his Family*', *Observer*, 18 December 1938).

16 Harrison, C. T., 'Review of *The Letters of Mozart and his Family*', *Virginia Quarterly Review*, Spring 1939, vol. 12, no. 2.

17 Beethoven's correspondence was even more challenging; his later letters in particular were so messy and in such poor handwriting that they were unintelligible to all but a handful of people. Anderson was one of the few who could decipher his writing.

18 Anderson, E., *The Letters of Mozart and his Family*, vols I–III (Macmillan & Co Ltd, 1938), p. xxi.

19 Alfred Einstein came from the same small town (Buchau am Federsee near Ulm) as the scientist Albert Einstein. They attended the same school in Munich and, during the 1920s they were neighbours in Berlin, and were plagued with mail getting misdirected to the wrong 'A. Einstein'. Alfred Einstein fled Germany in the mid-1930s and moved to the US to escape Nazi persecution. He held teaching posts at universities including Smith College, Columbia University and Princeton University. Prior to leaving Germany, Einstein had been working on the third edition of the Köchel catalogue (K^3). Leeson notes that, shortly before the start of the Second World War, 'the decision to print K^3 under Einstein's editorship rose through the Nazi hierarchy as each bureaucrat pushed the decision upward. Finally it reached the desk of Joseph Goebbels, the Nazi Minister of Propaganda. K^3 was printed only after his personal approval.' (Leeson, D., 'Thanks, old timer!!', Music Associates of America. Available at: http://www. musicassociatesofamerica.com/madamina/1993/thanksoldtimer. html, accessed 21/4/2021.)

20 Cecil Bernard Oldman was an English bibliographer who joined the Department of Printed Books at the British Museum in 1920 and was appointed Principal Keeper of Printed Books in 1948. He remained in that position until 1959. He published a number of articles and books on Mozart, and was generous in sharing his own collection of Mozart letters with EA.

21 Born in Frankfurt in 1890, Heinrich Eisemann came to England after Hitler's rise to power. He became prominent in the field of collectors of rare and valuable manuscripts, and was widely known for his purchases at Sotheby's and Christie's. He became a good personal friend of EA's, and was one of the beneficiaries of her will.

22 Born in Vienna in 1881, Stefan Zweig was a novelist, playwright, journalist, biographer and manuscript collector. In the 1920s and 1930s, he was one of the most widely translated and most popular writers in the world. As a Jew, fearful of the rise of Hitler, he moved to London in 1934, and then to Bath in 1939. Zweig was a passionate collector of manuscripts, and there are important Zweig collections at the State University of New York at Fredonia and at

the National Library of Israel. The most significant Stefan Zweig Collection is held at the British Library.

23 Letter from EA to Henry George Farmer, 6 April 1934, British Library. The meeting with Schiedermair was to take place on 21 May 1934.

24 Years later, during the Second World War, Ludwig Schiedermair served as a member of the Reichsleiter Rosenberg Taskforce (Einsatzstab Reichsleiter Rosenberg or ERR), a Nazi Party organisation dedicated to appropriating cultural property during the war. Much of the looted material was recovered by the Allies after the war, and returned to its rightful owners, but a substantial part has been lost or remains with the Allied powers.

25 The number was Hampstead 2463, and it was included on her headed notepaper.

26 1935 Electoral Register.

27 *The Times*, 9 June 1936.

28 The hospital was operated by a Miss Geraldine Edge (Marylebone and St John's Wood Directory, 1935, p. 40).

29 Hirschsprung's Disease is a condition that affects the large intestine (colon) and causes problems with passing stools. The condition is present at birth as a result of missing nerve cells in the muscles of the baby's colon. In mild cases, the condition might not be detected until later in childhood. Surgery to bypass or remove the diseased part of the colon is the usual treatment.

30 L. E. Barrington-Ward practiced as a paediatric surgeon at the Hospital for Sick Children, Great Ormond Street, London, and as a general surgeon at the Royal Northern Hospital, London. He had an international reputation and his book *The Abdominal Surgery of Children* (1928) became a standard medical text. In the year Hukis Anderson Lydon died, Barrington-Ward had been appointed Surgeon to the Household of HRH The Duke of York, who, as Prince Albert, had been his patient eighteen years previously. When the Duke ascended the throne as King George VI, Barrington-Ward became surgeon to the Royal Household. Subsequently, in 1952, following his retirement, he was appointed by Queen Elizabeth II as Extra-Surgeon to the Queen's Household (as he was retired, he could not be Surgeon to the Queen's Household, but his services were retained in a consultative capacity).

31 *The Times*, 6 June 1936.

32 Register of Deaths, District No. 4, Dublin, October 1934, p. 377.

33 *Evening Press*, 9 September 1936.

34 Ibid.

35 Professor Anderson's funeral service took place at Adelaide Road Presbyterian church, and he was afterwards buried in Dean's Grange Cemetery (*Connacht Sentinel*, 8 September 1936).

36 This amount would be worth in excess of £539,000 or €620,000 in 2022.

37 *Irish Independent*, 31 October 1936. There is, however, some discrepancy as to the exact value of Professor Anderson's estate, as the probate record in the National Archives of Ireland record an amount of £5,885 (CS/HC/PO/4/89/60, NAI).

38 Author's interview with Dagmar von Busch-Weise and Friedrich von Busch, 26 June 2019.

39 *The Times*, 17 May 1937.

40 General Register Office for England and Wales, Death Certificate.

41 London Electoral Register, 1935, p. 44.

42 England & Scotland Select Cemetery Registers, Hendon Cemetery and Crematorium, 1935–1936.

43 Dr Lydon placed a poignant memorial notice in *The Times* of 4 June 1937, which read 'In ever-loving memory, Mummy and Hukis. – Daddy.'

44 Treloyhan Manor, overlooking St Ives Bay, still operates as an hotel. Built in 1892 by Sir Edward Hain, a Cornish shipping magnate, it remained in the Hain family until 1928, when the estate was sold and the mansion was converted into a hotel, which opened on 1 July 1930.

45 In the letter, EA thanks Farmer for offering to lend printer's blocks for images of Constanze Weber and Josef and Aloysia Lange for use in the book (Letter from EA to Henry George Farmer, 7 July 1937, MS Farmer 270/14, University of Glasgow).

46 Da Costa Greene had much in common with EA, as both lived secret lives. As J. P. Morgan's personal librarian, and later Director of the Morgan Library, she controlled an acquisitions budget of millions of dollars, toured the salons of Europe, had affairs with a Norwegian count and an Italian duke, dined with opera stars and royalty, and charmed all she met with her wit and intelligence. She later admitted that she had lived 'behind the curtain of my mind'. Those who met her attributed her dusky complexion to her

purported Portuguese origins, but da Costa Greene (born Belle
Marion Greener) was Black, born to a family of free people of
colour. Greene had changed her name and invented a Portuguese
grandmother in order to enter white society.

47 A letter from EA to Greene, 22 September 1937, refers to the fact
that Anderson had 'about three years ago' received 'photostats of
two Mozart letters in the Pierpont Morgan library' for her *Letters of
Mozart* book.

48 Letter from EA to Belle da Costa Greene, 22 September 1937, the
Morgan Library and Museum. I am deeply indebted to Robinson
McLellan and Mara Isabel Molestina of the Morgan Library and
Museum, who performed the same task for me as their predecessor,
Belle da Costa Greene, had done for Anderson, in searching the
Library's archive on my behalf for notes 48 and 50–53.

49 Elizabeth Linley was a renowned beauty and talented opera singer
who later married the Irish playwright Richard Brinsley Sheridan;
her brother Thomas Linley was a talented musician and composer,
and a contemporary and friend of Mozart's. He was often called
'the English Mozart'. He died in a tragic drowning accident aged
just twenty-two. Mozart observed that Linley was a true genius, and
that had he lived, 'he would have been one of the greatest
ornaments of the musical world' (Kelly, Michael, *Reminiscences of
Michael Kelly of the King's Theatre, and Theatre Royal Drury Lane, Including
a Period of Nearly Half a Century; with Original Anecdotes of Many
Distinguished Persons, Political, Literary, and Musical*, vols I–II (Henry
Colburn, 1826), p. 222).

50 Letter from Belle da Costa Greene to EA, 5 October 1937, the
Morgan Library and Museum.

51 Letter from Belle da Costa Greene to EA, 13 June 1938, the
Morgan Library and Museum.

52 Letter from Belle da Costa Greene to EA, 5 October 1937, the
Morgan Library and Museum.

53 Letter from EA to Belle da Costa Greene, 25 October 1937, the
Morgan Library and Museum.

54 One of those whom EA credits in the introduction to *The Letters of
Mozart and his Family* is Robert Nigel Carew-Hunt. Born in 1890,
Carew-Hunt would later attain recognition for his biography of
Calvin, and his book *The Theory and Practice of Communism*. Carew-Hunt

had served with Anderson in MI1(b), and would serve with her again in the Diplomatic Section at Bletchley from 1939 to 1940.

55 Ernst Boucke was born in 1908, and was twenty-seven when he wrote a letter to EA dated 2 October 1935. He was also an artist, who in additional to his transcription work for her, made ends meet by completing paintings to order for clients (Letter from Ernst Boucke to EA, 12 October 1935, British Library).

56 Letter from Ernst Boucke to EA, 2 October 1935, MS 62678, British Library. The London Leopold Letters refers to letters written by Mozart's father, Leopold Mozart, between April 1764 and July 1765, when the Mozart family had relocated from Paris to London, where they hoped that the sibling prodigies Maria Anna, then aged twelve, and her brother, the eight-year-old Wolfgang, would create a sensation in London's musical society.

57 HW 3/83, TNA.

58 Stone, Jean, *Mavis Batey: Bletchley Codebreaker – Garden Historian – Conservationist – Writer* (Matador Publishing, 2020), p. 20.

59 *The Times*, 19 July 1938.

60 *The Times*, 8 November 1938.

61 Charles T. Harrison, 'Review of *Letters of Mozart and his Family*', *The Virginia Quarterly Review*, Spring 1939, vol. 15, no. 2.

62 Ibid.

63 *The Times*, 11 August 1960.

64 *Daily Telegraph*, 6 August 1938.

65 *Irish Independent*, 16 August 1938.

66 *Connacht Tribune*, 20 August 1938.

67 *The Times*, 20 August, 1938.

68 The Bäsle letters (from the German word *Bäsle*, a diminutive form meaning 'little cousin') were written by Mozart to his cousin (and probable lover) Maria Anna Thekla Mozart in 1777–78.

69 Bernard E. Wilson, 'Review of *The Letters of Mozart and his Family* (second edition), Hyatt King & Carolan (eds.)', in *Notes*, Second Series, vol. 23, no. 3 (March 1967), p. 513.

70 *The Spectator*, 12 August, 1966.

71 The second edition, published in 1966, was prepared and revised by EA's long-time friends and collaborators Alexander Hyatt King and Monica Carolan, and the third edition, published in 1985, was revised by Stanley Sadie and Fiona Smart.

12. The Gathering Storm: Prelude to War

1 Bletchley Park was purchased for £6,000. Financial records regarding the purchase are scant, but it is likely that Sinclair purchased Bletchley Park in his name but using SIS petty cash. Sinclair died in November 1939, three months after GC&CS had moved to its war station in August. His sister later 'sold' Bletchley Park to the Ministry of Works for a nominal sum in 1945 or 1946.

2 Cooper, J., 'Personal Notes on GC&CS 1925–1939', HW 3/83, TNA.

3 Cooper, J., 'Personal Notes on GC&CS 1925–1939', p. 3.

4 Memo from Alastair Denniston to Admiral Sir Hugh Sinclair, 21 October 1938, HW 3/1, TNA.

5 McKay, S., 'Hack of the Century', *The Spectator*, 14 January 2017.

6 Cooper, J., 'Personal Notes on GC&CS 1925–1939', HW 3/83, TNA.

7 Extract from the speech given by Sir Alfred Ewing in December 1927, quoted in Jones, R. V., 'Alfred Ewing and "Room 40"', p. 88.

8 David Kenyon, Bletchley Park research historian, quoted in 'Bletchley discloses real intention of 1938 "shooting party"', *Guardian*, 18 September 2018.

9 Papers of Mavis Batey on the Establishment of Bletchley Park, GBR/0014/BTEY 3/4, CCAC.

10 Ibid.

11 The Italians were at that time using book codes (groups of numbers that represent words or phrases) as opposed to ciphers, but this would change as war commenced.

12 Ferris, John, *Behind the Enigma*, p. 90.

13 Papers of Mavis Batey, materials relating to interpretation and display panels for the exhibition 'From Bletchley With Love' at Bletchley Park, 2010, GBR/0014/BTEY 3/5.

14 De Grey, N., 'The Diplomatic Sections' in 'Summary of Sigint operations 1939–1945', HW 14/145, TNA.

15 Ibid.

16 Ibid.

17 EA is listed at the Ellerdale Road address in the 1939 electoral register.

18 From 1924 to 1925, she lived at 13 Lyndhurst Gardens; from 1926 to 1938 she lived at 38 Arkwright Road, before finally moving to Ellerdale Road in 1939.

19 EA's former flat at 38 Arkwright Road was taken over by Margaret J. Hosford, a 'Piano Teacher & Professional Accompanist'.

20 The opening of this co-educational school was performed by Millicent Garret Fawcett, leader of the suffrage movement, on 24 June 1898.

21 Winterbotham, F. W., *Secret and Personal* (HarperCollins, 1969), p. 15.

22 Winterbotham was a former RFC fighter pilot in the First World War, who later became an RAF intelligence officer and a senior member of MI6, involved in the distribution of Ultra intelligence.

23 Winterbotham, F. W., *Secret and Personal*, p. 15.

24 Admiral Hugh Sinclair, also known as 'C', director of GC&CS and SIS.

25 Report written by Commander Denniston, 2 December 1944, HW 3/32, TNA.

26 Bodsworth became Head of first Italian, and later German Naval sub-sections at Bletchley. Cooper became Head of the Air Section at Bletchley. He was Chief Cryptographer for Service Sections from March 1942, and was appointed Deputy Director (Air Section) in March 1944.

13. Bletchley Park

1 Welchman, G., *The Hut Six Story: Breaking the Enigma Codes* (Allen Lane, 1982), p. 7.

2 Papers of A.G. Denniston, 'History of the Government Code and Cypher School, GBR/0014/DENN 1/4, CCAC.

3 Beesley, Patrick, *Room 40: British Naval Intelligence 1914–1918*, p. 303.

4 Stone, Jean, *Mavis Batey*, p. 20.

5 Bletchley was the tenth in a line of properties acquired by MI6 to house its staff, and consequently the Roman numeral for 10, 'X', was used to identify it.

6 Denniston, A. G., 'The Government Code and Cypher School between the Wars', *The History of SIGINT in its Documents*, no. 1, series published by GCHQ, p. 27.

7 She was listed among the established Senior Assistants at GC&CS (Undated document, HW 3/82, TNA).

8 In 1942, petrol for private use was withdrawn completely, and was only available for work deemed essential, so a special permit was needed to obtain it. By that stage, however, EA had moved to Cairo.

9 Mavis Batey recalled that Commander Denniston had informed her that 'Bletchley Park was to be referred to as Box 101' (Stone, Jean, *Mavis Batey*, p. 20).

10 Cooper, J., cited in Smith, Michael, *The Secrets of Station X: How Bletchley Park Helped Win the War* (Biteback, 2011), p. 22.

11 Memo 11 July 1939, HW 3/37 TNA.

12 Ibid.

13 Testimony of Patricia Brown, writing in the *Guardian*, 25 September 2010.

14 Mair Russell-Jones (*née* Thomas), a codebreaker in Hut Six, was at Bletchley the day in September 1941 that Churchill visited. She recalled: 'He thanked us for our hard work and the way our skills were contributing to the war effort and the victory we were pursuing. With a smile on his face he then used a metaphor which would become very famous. He said that we were his geese that laid his golden eggs and never cackled. He clearly prized our secrecy over anything else.'(Russell-Jones, Mair and Gethin, *My Secret Life in Hut Six: One Woman's Experiences at Bletchley Park* (Lion Hudson, 2014), p. 191).

15 Walter Schellenberg had risen through the ranks of the SS, becoming one of the highest-ranking men in the Sicherheitsdienst (SD), the intelligence agency of the SS and the Nazi Party. He eventually became Head of Foreign Intelligence for Nazi Germany following the abolition of the Abwehr in 1944.

16 Papers of Mavis Batey, Correspondence regarding her research into intelligence history. GBR/0014/BTEY 3/7, CCAC.

17 Memo dated 11 July 1939, HW 3/37, TNA.

18 Undated Memo to GC&CS staff regarding approaches to be made to civilian property owners regarding the use of accommodation for billeting purposes. HW 64/45, TNA.

19 Billeting List headed 'Second Wave', dated 12/7/39, HW 3/1, TNA.

20 Marjorie Hayward (then aged forty-four) listed her occupation on the 1939 Register as 'shorthand typist', so she may have also been working at Bletchley Park at that stage. She died, unmarried, in 1981.

21 The Manor House is now a Grade II-listed building, and operates as a school.

22 She is listed as a resident of the Manor House on the 1939 Register, which was compiled on 29 September 1939. EA had already moved to her Ellerdale Road flat by that date.

23 Chapter III, entitled 'A Newcomer to Swanbourne' by M. J. Hayward, in an unpublished *History of Swanbourne* compiled by Mr Ken Reading. I am most grateful to Mr Ken Harris and the Swanbourne History Society for this and other information provided about the village of Swanbourne.

24 Ibid.

25 The 1939 Register was designed to capture the details of every member of the civilian population on a specific date and used as the basis for the issuing of identity and ration cards.

26 The Americans took a broader approach. All American recruits were given an IQ test, and those who scored the highest were proposed for cryptologic work. This resulted in extraordinarily high brainpower being recruited to US codebreaking units.

27 Cooper, J., 'Personal Notes on GC&CS 1925–1939'.

28 Dilly Knox famously forgot to invite his brothers to his wedding.

29 Batey, Mavis, *Dilly: The Man Who Broke Enigmas* (Dialogue, 2009), p. 5.

30 Patricia Bartley (later Brown) was recruited by EA, who was billeted with her family in Swanbourne. She subsequently served at Bletchley Park from October 1939–*c.* 1942, becoming Head of the German Diplomatic Section, at a salary of £3/5/-per week (Document dated 5 March 1941, HW 14/147, TNA).

31 *Guardian*, 25 September 2010.

32 Formerly known as Bletchley Grammar school, in 1939, just prior to the outbreak of hostilities, Elmer's School was requisitioned by the government, and became part of Station X at Bletchley Park.

33 Nigel de Grey's 'History of Bletchley Park', HW 3/95, TNA.

34 Patricia Bartley formally joined the staff of Bletchley Park on 23 October 1939, so EA, who recruited her, must have been in residence at The Cottage prior to that date (HW 64/45, TNA).

35 Patricia Brown (*née* Bartley) died, aged 103, on 26 February 2021.

36 Born in Belfast in 1882, Sir Charles Bartley, a barrister, had served as a judge in the Calcutta High Court, and as secretary to the government of Bengal.

37 EA's hair colour is variously described by friends and those who knew her as being 'red', 'auburn' or 'Titian'. EA's great nephew, Stephen Andrews, also has red hair.

38 Author's interview with Patricia Brown (*née* Bartley), 12 May 2019. Patricia also recalled that EA was what she called a 'Doness', i.e. a

female professor of German, and that therefore she was, in Patricia's words, 'made for the job'.

39 Bartley was born in Dakar. A spirited, clever girl, she was sent to boarding schools in England aged ten, and hated them so much that she ran away from a succession of them. When her father retired from the Calcutta High Court, the reunited family moved to Swanbourne, where he took over responsibility for her education. She went up to Oxford in 1936, aged nineteen. By the age of twenty-four, she was Head of the German Diplomatic Section, with twelve people working for her, and had an office next to the Director's in the main house at Bletchley Park.

40 Sir Charles Bartley retired in the 1930s, at which point the entire family moved to Swanbourne.

41 Patricia recalled that, shortly after moving in to the billet, EA had identified herself as a former Professor of German, and had conversed with her in German to ascertain her fluency in the language.

42 The phrase itself is resonant of EA's letter to her friend Fr Hynes in July 1918, signalling her intention to move to London as 'people with a thorough knowledge of Modern Languages are very badly wanted for Military Intelligence work in France and I was asked to apply'.

43 *Guardian*, 25 September 2010.

44 Ibid.

45 Author's interview with Patricia Bartley Brown, 12 May 2019.

46 Barbara Abernethy became Barbara Eachus when she met, and married, one of the Americans who came to Bletchley to collaborate with Denniston and their fellow codebreakers.

47 German cryptanalysis comprised the Chiffrierabteilung of the Armed Frces High Command, Pers Z of the Foreign Office, and Göring's Forschungsamt. The army, the navy and the air force each had its own unit and, for a time, the SD (Sicher-heitsdienst, the SS's intelligence arm), had its own cryptologic agency. As a result, the available manpower was thinly spread and the codebreaking effort diffused.

48 *Westmeath Independent*, 30 December 1939.

49 The BBC Symphony Orchestra and the BBC singers were evacuated to Bedford, a few miles from Bletchley, and their rehearsals were accessible to staff working at the Park. String quartets regularly gave recitals at Bletchley Park, and at one point the staff gave a performance of Purcell's *Dido and Aeneas*, with some external help from, among others, members of the BBC Symphony Orchestra.

50 Winterbotham, F. W., *The Ultra Secret* (Harper & Row, 1974), p. 15.

51 Obituary of Gordon Welchman, *Newburyport Daily News*, 9 October 1985.

52 McKay, Sinclair, *The Secret Lives of Codebreakers: The Men and Women Who Cracked the Enigma Code at Bletchley Park* (Aurum Press Ltd, 2010), p. 19.

53 Cairncross, John, *The Enigma Spy: An Autobiography: The Story of the Man who Changed World War Two* (Century, 1997), p. 65.

54 Myra Hess was a concert pianist who became an unlikely hero during the Second World War in Britain as she defiantly organised a series of morale-boosting classical music concerts at the National Gallery in London. With the prospect of bombing raids ever present, Hess herself gave the first concert on 10 October 1939, and a queue of 1,000 formed to hear her. Thereafter she persuaded the best musicians of the day to perform, and in spite of the constant dangers, no concert was ever cancelled. She often performed in a fur coat as wartime restrictions made heating the building impossible. Born in 1890 to orthodox Jewish parents in Hampstead, she has been described as 'classical music's Dame Vera Lynn'. She was appointed CBE in 1936. (See also p. 226)

55 McKay, Sinclair, *The Secret Lives of Codebreakers*, p. 246.

56 The invasion of all three countries took place on the same day, 10 May 1940.

57 Memo from Denniston to Bletchley Staff, HW 14/5, TNA.

58 Memo from Josh Cooper to Group Captain Blandy, dated 2 October 1940, HW 14/7, TNA.

59 Bartley was instrumental in cracking Floradora, the German diplomatic code. As discussed on page 218, one of her subordinates, P. W. Filby, tried to take credit for the crucial breakthrough, which Bartley had made. A furious Bartley went directly to Denniston, informing him that she would not stand for anyone taking credit for her work. During my first interview with Patricia, she initially struggled to remember details regarding her work at Bletchley. Her son, Andrew Brown, advised: 'Ask her about Filby, and watch her spit feathers.' I did as he suggested, and the result was instantaneous. The resulting interview revealed details never before recorded regarding her role in breaking Floradora at a crucial stage in the war.

60 In his memoirs, Clarke noted that 'The full correspondence on this matter will be found in my files labelled The White Conspiracy'

Papers of William F. Clarke, 'History of Room 40 and the Government Code and Cypher School', GBR/0014/CLKE 3, CCAC.

61 Ibid.

62 Mavis Batey, cited in Black, S., and Colgan, S., *Saving Bletchley Park: How #Social Media Saved the Home of the Second World War Code Breakers* (Unbound Publishing, 2016), chapter 11, p. 6.

63 Letter from Frank Birch to Denniston, dated May 1940, HW 14/5, TNA.

64 Russell-Jones, Mair and Gethin, *My Secret Life in Hut Six*, p. 252.

65 Gwen Watkins, quoted in 'How we won the war', *Guardian*, 18 January 1999.

66 Rozanne Colchester (*née* Medhurst) was a Foreign Office civilian attached to the Italian Air Section at Bletchley from 1942 to 1945.

67 On 7 April 1939, the Italians entered South Albania, and by 22 May, an Italo–German alliance had been signed in Berlin.

68 Cooper, J., 'Personal Notes on GC&CS 1925–1939', p. 4.

14. Cairo and Combined Bureau Middle East

1 Egypt remained neutral during the Second World War, but as a result of British pressure, did break diplomatic relations with Germany in September 1939. Egypt remained officially neutral until the final year of the war.

2 Sarafand al-Amar was a Palestinian Arab village situated five kilometres north-west of Ramla on the coastal plain of Palestine. In the British Mandate period (1920–1948), the British Army established their largest military base in the Middle East near Sarafand al-Amar. The area was depopulated during the 1948 Arab–Israeli War.

3 Telegram dated 25 May 1940, HW 14/5, TNA.

4 MI8, or Military Intelligence, Section 8, was a British military intelligence division responsible for signals intelligence. Originally established in 1914, during the Second World War, MI8 was responsible for the extensive War Office 'Y' Service and, briefly, for the Radio Security Service.

5 CR6 was the Italian cipher that Anderson was then working on at Bletchley.

6 Telegram dated 26 May 1940, HW 14/5, TNA.

7 CBME Q306, HW 51/37, TNA.

8 Letter from EA to Denniston, dated May 1940, HW 14/8, TNA.

9 CBME also had an outstation located in Nairobi.

10 Italy declared war on France and Great Britain on 10 June 1940. On 22 June 1940, after a sustained attack, the French signed an armistice, surrendering to the Germans.

11 Axelrod, Alan, *The Real History of World War II: A New Look at the Past* (Sterling Publishing, 2008), p. 180.

12 Smith, Michael, and Erskine, Ralph (ed.), *The Bletchley Park Code Breakers: How Ultra Shortened the War and Led to the Birth of the Computer* (Biteback, 2011; first published 2001), p. 39.

13 Papers of William F. Clarke, 'History of Room 40 and the Government Code and Cypher School', GBR/0014/CLKE 3, CCAC.

14 Letter from Alastair Denniston to T. J. Wilson, Foreign Office, 20 July 1940, HW 14/6, TNA. In another letter, Denniston confirmed that Anderson was on the maximum of the scale for Senior Assistants, at a salary of £738–12– £905-3 per annum. Dorothy Brooks, as a temporary assistant, was paid far less: –£3–10 +5/- bonus per week, but even this was a £2 per week increase on her salary prior to the move to Cairo (HW 3/83, TNA).

15 Letter from Alastair Denniston to T. J. Wilson, Foreign Office, 20 July 1940, HW 14/6, TNA. Denniston confirmed that EA was a 'Senior Assistant' and Brooks a 'Temporary Linguist Officer'.

16 Marie Rose Egan was Head of the Air Section at Heliopolis from March 1939.

17 Confirmation of reservation of First Class Passage for EA and Brooks on the RAF Freight Ship *Windsor Castle*, 20 July 1940, addressed to Undersecretary of State at the Foreign Office from the Director of Sea Transport, Ministry of Shipping, FO 366/1110, TNA.

18 Located in Heliopolis, a suburb in north-eastern Cairo, Almaza airport was established as a civilian aerodrome in 1910, but was subsequently taken over by the British military, and designated RAF Heliopolis and later RAF Almaza.

19 CBME Q306, HW 51/37, TNA.

20 I am deeply grateful to Peter Carr, Dorothy's son, for sharing her passport – and a whole host of recollections and documents associated with his mother – with me.

21 Brooks' passport was issued to facilitate her move to Cairo, as it states: 'Holder of this passport is in the service of the Crown.'

Diplomatic visas from the embassies of Greece, Egypt and France in London, dated from June 1940,were also included in the passport.

22 Denniston's replies to EA are addressed to her at the British Embassy in Cairo. The reference to EA's letters being 'on their way around the school' probably explains why they were mislaid.

23 The Government Code and Cypher School (GC&CS), the name by which the cryptologic section at Bletchley was then known.

24 The letter is addressed to EA 'c/o H. M. Embassy, Cairo' and dated 4 December 1940 (HW 14/9, TNA).

25 Brooks' passport contains a transit visa, dated 6 August 1940, issued by the Consulat Generale de Belgique in Cape Town, allowing her to travel through the Belgian Congo.

26 My thanks to Maureen Newcombe for recounting this and other stories from her late aunt to me.

27 Letter from Alastair Denniston to EA, 4 December 1940, HW 14/9, TNA.

28 Letter from Alastair Denniston to Freddie Jacob, 4 December 1940, HW 14/9, TNA.

29 The Naval Memoirs of Admiral J. H. Godfrey, vol. VII, p. 182, GDFY 1/10, CCAC.

30 'Raymond Hare: Our Man in Cairo during WWII', Association for Diplomatic Studies and Training (available at https://adst. org/2017/07/raymond-hare-man-cairo-wwii/, accessed 31/5/2022).

31 The letter related to EA's salary and allowances.

32 Lieutenant Commander Titterton had served in Naval Section and had previously worked on Russian naval material.

33 Letter from G.A. Titterton to Denniston, dated 15 September 1940. HW 14/7, TNA.

34 Dr Rene Najera, an expert in the history of vaccines, suggests that the most likely candidates at that time in Egypt were smallpox or typhoid.

35 Memo, 15 September 1940, HW 51/86, TNA.

36 Letter EA to Alastair Denniston, 9 November 1940. HW14/8 TNA.

37 Note from Freddie Jacob to Alastair Denniston, 9 November 1940 HW 14/8.

38 *The Times*, 24 July 1936.

39 I am deeply grateful to Dorothy Brooks' niece, Maureen Newcombe, for this information.

Notes

40 The Distinguished Service Cross is awarded 'in recognition of an act or acts of exemplary gallantry during active operations against the enemy at sea'. Lieutenant Commander Brooks' first DSC was awarded in November 1942 for his actions during Operation Pedestal at Malta, and his second in May 1944 for an attack on the German battleship *Tirpitz* in April 1944. (See: Royal Naval Reserve Volunteer Officers, 1939–1945, https://www.unithistories.com/officers/RNVR_officersB3.Html).

41 Fit out of the building had been delayed due to a shortage of blackout material.

42 Undated, letter from Freddie Jacobs to Alastair Denniston, HW 14/8.

43 G. A. Titterton referred, in a letter to Alastair Denniston, to the 'palatial building' with 'marble floors and marble staircase!', 15 September 1940, HW 14/7, TNA.

44 RAF Section occupied the ground floor, the Army Section the first floor (CBME Q306, HW 51/37, TNA).

45 Letter from EA to Alastair Denniston, HW 51/14.

46 HW 51/14, TNA, p. 13.

47 BMEC comprised troops from the United Kingdom, South Africa, British India, Uganda Protectorate, Kenya, Somalia and West Africa, Northern and Southern Rhodesia, Sudan and Nyasaland, who were joined by the Allied Force Publique of Belgian Congo, Imperial Ethiopian Arbegnoch (resistance forces) and a small unit of Free French.

48 Italian East Africa comprised Eritrea, Somalia, and parts of Ethiopia.

49 EA and Dorothy Brooks.

50 Letter from EA to Alastair Denniston, 9 November 1940, HW 14/8, TNA.

51 Ibid.

52 Ibid.

53 Letter from Freddie Jacob to Alastair Denniston, 19 November 1940, HW 14/8, TNA.

54 Letter from EA to Alastair Denniston, 9 November 1940, HW 14/8, TNA.

55 Ibid.

56 Letter from EA to Alastair Denniston, 16 October 1940, HW 14/7, TNA.

57 Egan had been sent to Cairo in March 1939, specifically to work on Italian Air Force cipher traffic from East Africa. Originally based at the RAF base at Heliopolis, after the Italians entered the war, the section combined forces with EA's newly arrived Military Section to form CBME under Colonel Jacob (HW 3/83).

58 Ferris, John, *Behind the Enigma*, p. 440.

59 Egan's treatment by the civil service was shameful. Promoted to a position that would normally have been held by a Senior Assistant (such as EA), although she did the work the Treasury denied her that status, or allowances equal to male peers, on grounds of 'administrative inconsistency'. In 1943, when CBME's sections against Italy were broken up, Egan entered a retraining programme in Japanese, and joined that section as a subordinate cryptanalyst on a team. She was eventually awarded the MBE in January 1946 for work 'in a Department of the Foreign Office'.

60 HW 51/14, TNA.

61 Ferris, John, *Behind the Enigma*, p. 244.

62 Memo from General Cunningham, dated 6 June 1941, 'East Africa Force, Report on Operation from 1st November 1940, to 5th April 1941, HW 51/14, TNA.

63 In 1937, the Duke of Aosta became Viceroy and Governor-General of Italian East Africa. He was also Commander-in-Chief of all Italian military forces in Eritrea, Ethiopia and Somaliland.

64 Letter from Director of Intelligence to Colonel Freddie Jacob, 23 November 1940 (HW 14/8, TNA).

65 Memo from General Cunningham, dated 6/6/41, 'East Africa Force, Report on Operation from 1st November 1940, to 5th April 1941, HW 51/14.

66 Ibid., p. 42.

67 Ibid.

68 Letter from Alastair Denniston to EA, 4 December 1940 14/9, TNA.

69 I am deeply indebted to Peter Carr, son of Dorothy Carr (*née* Brooks), who shared this recording with me.

70 Letter from Denniston to EA, dated 4 December 1940, HW 14/9, TNA.

71 Letter from Alastair Denniston to EA, 4 December 1940, HW 14/9, TNA.

72 Telegram from Freddie Jacob to Denniston, 12 December 1940, HW 14/9, TNA. This is a reference to the strongroom at Bletchley Park.

73 Hungarian has thirty-five distinct cases and relies on idioms more than other languages. It also has fourteen different vowels, twice as many as English, making it a notoriously difficult language to decipher.

74 Telegram dated 13 December 1940, HW 51/22, TNA.

75 The Duke of Aosta was an Anglophile who had attended Eton and Oxford University and won a medal for valour in the First World War fighting on the Allied side.

76 Gondar and Amba Alagi are cities in Northern Ethiopia.

77 The Battle of Amba Alagi (4–19 May 1941) ended with the garrison of about 5,000 men marching down the hill to hand in their arms. The British and Indian detachments conceded full military honours to the Italian troops in recognition of the valour of the Italian soldiers and presented arms as they passed. Their commander surrendered the following day. He was moved to Kenya, where he died in captivity in March 1942 of tuberculosis and was buried with full honours at the military cemetery in Nairobi.

78 'The Duke of Aosta Surrenders (1941)', British Pathé, YouTube (available at: https://www.youtube.com/watch?v=3hUV0H2RTBI).

79 Draft letter from Freddie Jacob to Alastair Denniston, 15 October 1941, HW 51/85, TNA.

80 'The Cottage' was located in the stable yard next to The Mansion (i.e. the main house) at Bletchley. Established by Dilly Knox as a research section, his team of codebreakers (known as 'Dilly's Fillies') worked on codes and ciphers that had not yet been broken by the codebreakers in Hut 6.

81 Admiral Andrew Browne Cunningham, 1st Viscount Cunningham of Hyndhope, was the older brother of General Sir Alan Cunningham.

82 Mavis Batey obituary, *Telegraph*, 13 November 2013.

83 Cape Matapan is located off the coast of Greece.

84 Batey, M., *Dilly: The Man Who Broke Enigmas* (Biteback Publishing, 2017), p. 130.

85 Ibid.

86 From July 1941, when he was replaced as Commander-in-Chief in the Middle East by General Auchinleck, Wavell served as Commander-in-Chief, India, from July 1941 until June 1943, and subsequently served as Viceroy of India until his retirement in February 1947.

87 The 4th Indian Infantry Division was formed in 1939 in Egypt, and was involved with Operation Compass in December of 1940. It was deployed to the British Sudan, where it joined with the Indian 5th Infantry Division, and tasked with preventing the numerically superior Italian forces from taking the sea supply routes to Egypt as well as the Suez Canal and Egypt itself. The Sudan campaign ended in March with the defeat of forty-two Italian battalions by nineteen British and Indian battalions.

88 Schofield, Victoria, *Wavell: Soldier and Statesman* (Pen & Sword Military, 2010), chapter 10.

89 Undated memo from Air Marshal Tedder, Air Officer Commanding in Chief, RAF Middle East to Denniston, HW 51/14, TNA.

90 Memo by General Cunningham, 6 June 1941, 'East Africa Force, Report on Operation from 1st November 1940, to 5th April 1941', Alan Cunningham Papers 8303104-12-1, National Army Museum Templer Study Centre.

91 Matters came to a head in October 1941 when the cryptanalysts Turing, Welchman, Alexander and Milner-Barry wrote to Winston Churchill, over the head of Alastair Denniston, to alert him that a shortage of staff at Bletchley was preventing the timely deciphering of messages, to the detriment of the war effort. Churchill issued an 'Action this Day' memo in support of the cryptanalysts' demand for more staff to be allocated, and Denniston's fate as operational head of Bletchley was sealed.

92 Draft letter from Freddie Jacob to Alastair Denniston, 15 October 1942, HW 51/85, TNA.

93 Author's interview with Patricia Brown (*née* Bartley), 5 September 2018.

94 Obituary of Patricia Bartley Brown, *Guardian*, 2 May 2021.

95 Author's interview with Patricia Bartley Brown, 5 September 2018.

96 Letter from Anthony Eden to Patricia Bartley and her staff in German Diplomatic Section, 8 October 1942, marked 'Personal and Most Secret', FO 1093 309, TNA.

97 Bartley also received letters of commendation from the Cabinet Secretary Sir Edward Bridges and MI5.

98 Memo from Foreign Secretary Anthony Eden to Colonel Stewart Menzies, Director SIS ('C'), 8 October 1942, FO 1093/309, TNA.

99 El-Alamein was a battle of two halves. The first Battle of El-Alamein (1–27 July 1942) ended in a stalemate; the second (23

October–11 November 1942) was decisive, and marked the beginning of the end for the Axis in North Africa.

100 5IS was No. 5 Intelligence School. It's Commander Officer was Major George Wallace, who described cryptographers as 'charming lunatics'.

101 The Auxiliary Territorial Service (ATS) was the women's branch of the British Army during the Second World War. Formed in September 1938, initially as a women's voluntary service, it existed until 1 February 1949, when it was merged into the Women's Royal Army Corps.

102 Letter from 5IS to Jacob, dated July 1942, HW 51/1, TNA.

103 Memo dated 24 August 1942, HW 51/68, TNA.

104 Letter from Air Command to Jacob, dated 24 August 1942, HW 51/22, TNA.

105 Correspondence of Michael Egan, nephew of Marie Rose Egan, with Professor John Ferris.

106 He was in Cairo 8–10 August 1942.

107 While in Cairo, Winston Churchill replaced Eighth Army General Auchinleck with Lieutenant General Montgomery.

108 Churchill, Winston S., *The Second World War*, vols I–VI (Cassell, 1948–1953).

109 See Alexander Cadogan, Alanbrooke and Jacob papers at CCAC.

110 Winston Churchill's personal papers, CCAC.

111 Denniston, R., 'Diplomatic Eavesdropping, 1922–1944: A New Source Discovered', *Intelligence and National Security*, vol. 10, issue 3 (1995).

112 Hinsley, F. H., *British Intelligence in the Second World War* (Stationery Office Books, 1979), p. 215.

113 Letter from Wing Commander Mapplebeck to Freddie Jacob, 26 August 1941, HW 51/22, TNA.

114 Telegram from Alastair Denniston to Freddie Jacob, undated, HW 51/82, TNA.

115 Memo from Freddie Jacob to Alastair Denniston, 16 March 1943, HW 51/82, TNA.

116 Signals, sent on various unspecified dates in April 1943, HW 51/82, TNA.

117 Letter of Passage, dated 30 April 1943, from British Embassy, Cairo, in respect of Emily Anderson and Dorothy Brooks. HW 51/82, TNA.

118 Author's interview with Mrs Maureen Newcombe, niece of Dorothy Brooks, 22 October 2021.

119 Officer File WO 339/29735, TNA.

120 There was no provision made for his Italian wife or children in Carr's will, which benefited Dorothy and their son Peter only.

121 She arrived on 14 August and left, via the Suez Canal, on 21 August 1941.

122 Thomas Bowring Carr's son, Peter, confirms that his father was awarded the equivalent to a knighthood – the Commendatore del l' Ordine della Corona d'Italia – by King Umberto II in 1946 for services to Italy. Umberto II was the last King of Italy, and reigned for just thirty-four days, from 9 May 1946 to 12 June 1946, so it must have been during this period that Thomas Bowring Carr received this honour. Peter Carr has the medal his father received on that occasion.

123 The couple were married in the house in which Dorothy was then living in Genoa, Italy, after she had moved to the city to be close to her fiancé, who was also living in Genoa at the time.

124 Memo from Jacob to Denniston, dated 26 April 1943, HW 51/82, TNA.

125 Telegram dated 29 April 1943, HW 51/82, TNA.

126 Letter of Passage, dated 30 April 1943, from British Embassy, Cairo, in respect of Emily Anderson and Dorothy Brooks. HW 51/82, TNA.

127 Letter of Passage, dated 30 April 1943, from British Embassy, Cairo, in respect of Marie Rose Egan. HW 51/82, TNA.

128 Group Captain Frederick W. Winterbotham was an RAF pilot and a top-ranking member of MI6. He had served as a fighter pilot in the First World War and was shot down and captured on 13 July 1917, in Passchendaele. He spent the rest of the war in a prisoner-of-war camp in Germany.

129 Winterbotham, F. W., *Secret and Personal*, p. 169.

15. Berkeley Street

1 Robert Cecil, one of Menzies' (aka 'C') senior staff, quoted in Denniston, Robin, *Thirty Secret Years: A. G. Denniston's Secret Work in Signals Intelligence 1914–1944* (Polperro Heritage Press, 2007), p. 82.

2 Denniston remains the only head of GC&CS/GCHQ never to have been awarded a knighthood.

3 Bletchley Park, which concentrated on military intercepts, was designated Government Communications Headquarters (GCHQ) (Croft, J., 'A note on diplomatic intercepts in England during World War II', *Journal of Intelligence History*, 13:1, (2014), p. 91).

4 The building was opposite the Mayfair Hotel, and adjacent to the Berkeley Hotel.

5 Croft, J., 'A note on diplomatic intercepts in England during World War II'.

6 Ibid, p. 93.

7 Records of the Japanese School note Egan attending Course IV, which ran from 5 July to 20 December 1943, Papers of Oswald Tuck, Bedford School Report 1942-1945, GBR/0014/TUCK 5/5, CCAC.

8 Ferris, John, *Behind the Enigma*, p. 213.

9 'Scaling Up', *Bletchley Park Podcast*, episode 136 (available at: https://audioboom. com/posts/8070925-e136-scaling-up, accessed 5/5/22)

10 Papers of Mavis Batey, quoting Barbara Abernethy, secretary to Denniston, GBR/0014/BTEY 3/4, CCAC.

11 William Friedman (1891–1969) was a US Army cryptographer who ran the research division of the army's Signal Intelligence Service (SIS) in the 1930s, and parts of its follow-on services into the 1950s. In 1949, he became head of the cryptographic division of the newly formed Armed Forces Security Agency (AFSA) and, in 1952, became chief cryptologist for the National Security Agency (NSA), when it was formed to take over from AFSA.

12 Telford Taylor (1908–1998) was a lawyer, and was Counsel for the Prosecution at the Nuremberg Trials after the Second World War. Taylor joined Army Intelligence as a major in 1942 and led the American group at Bletchley that was responsible for analysing information obtained from intercepted German communications using Ultra encryption. In 1943, he returned to England, where, with McCormack and Friedman, he helped negotiate the 1943 BRUSA Agreement, which facilitated cooperation between the US War Department and GC&CS.

13 Colonel McCormack's trip to London, May–June 1943, National Archives and Records Administration, College Park, Maryland, Historic Cryptographic Collection, RG 457, nos. 3443, 3600, p. 1.

14 McCormack's Report, p. 1. At Alford House, an additional fifty staff were employed in Commercial Section.

15 Ibid, p. 62.

16 Ibid, p. 63.

17 Ibid, p. 23.

18 Colonel McCormack's trip to London, May–June 1943, National Archives and Records Administration, College Park, Maryland, Historic Cryptographic Collection, RG 457, nos. 3443, 3600.

19 Ferris, John, *Behind the Enigma*, p. 336.

20 These are held in the HW 12 series (Croft, J., 'A note on diplomatic intercepts in England during World War II', p. 92).

21 Ibid.

22 Croft, J., 'Reminiscences of GCHQ and GCB 1942–45', *Intelligence and National Security*, 1998, 13:4, p. 137.

23 Regene Lewis later married a Russian-born Israeli and became Jean Nissan.

24 Hollerith machines were punch-card-operated index machines. Developed in the 1900s, they were used for storing information from earlier decrypts of encoded German messages, significantly speeding up the decryption process.

25 De Grey, N. 'The Diplomatic Sections', HW 14/145, TNA.

26 Papers of Mavis Batey, Materials relating to interpretation and display panels for the exhibition 'From Bletchley With Love' at Bletchley Park, 2010. GBR/0014/BTEY 3/5, CCAC.

27 Filby, P. W., 'Bletchley Park and Berkeley Street', *Intelligence and National Security*, vol. 3, issue 2 (1988), p. 272.

28 NSA Archive, 06-78, DOCID: 4236153.

29 He notes in the interview that EA was a cryptanalyst 'in the old standard codebook and additive method', ibid.

30 Filby, P. W., 'Bletchley park and Berkeley street', p. 277.

31 In a report on the German Diplomatic Section from January to March 1944, Filby refers to the 'Shanghai Letter', and notes: 'This has defeated us. Miss Andersen (sic) made a little progress in December.' (Filby, P. W., Report on German Section, January–March 1944, 29 January 1944, HW 53/44, TNA).

32 Patricia Bartley recalled: 'I collapsed. You weren't supposed to talk about it. I had a sort of breakdown, I got ill, and the doctor said she must have a much lighter burden.' Bartley went on sick leave in Spring 1942, and was out for a year.

33 De Grey, N. 'The Diplomatic Sections', HW 14/145, TNA.

34 McCormack's report, p. 58.

35 Ferris, John, *Behind the Enigma*, p. 442

36 *The Times*, 17 July 1943.

37 *Second Supplement to the London Gazette*, 13 July 1943, (available at: https://www.thegazette.co.uk/London/issue/36093/ supplement/3213/data. pdf, accessed 6/6/2022).

38 *The Times*, 17 July 1943.

39 Note by Alastair Denniston, 24 January 1944, HW 53/45, TNA.

40 Ferris, John, *Behind the Enigma*, p. 445.

41 Gordon Welchman was a Mathematics graduate and Dean of Sidney Sussex College, Cambridge, when he was recruited as one of four early recruits to Bletchley Park, the others being Alan Turing, Hugh Alexander and Stuart Milner-Barry.

42 Croxson, P. W., 'The Creation of Combined Bureau Middle East (CBME)', Friends of the Intelligence Corps Museum, (available at: https://friendsintelligencemuseum.org/2017/04/13/the-creation-of-combined-bureau-middle-east-cbme/, accessed 20/02/2020).

43 Ferris, John, *Behind the Enigma*, p. 440.

44 Known as the 'flying bomb', the V-1 was an early cruise missile. The V stood for '*Vergeltungswaffe*', i.e. 'Vengeance weapon', as the V-1 had been developed as a response to heavy Allied bombing of German cities towards the end of the war.

45 The V-2 was the world's first long-range guided missile, and unlike the V-1, was silent on approach to its target.

46 The date of the attack was Sunday, 18 June 1944. Following a direct hit by a V-1 rocket, the Royal Military Chapel (the Guards Chapel) at St James Park was completely destroyed.

47 Interview with Nancy Winbolt, GCHQ, (available at: https://www. gchq.gov.uk/information/nancy-winbolt).

48 Ibid.

49 Filby, P. W., *Bletchley Park and Berkeley Street*, p. 279.

50 Filby, P. W., quoted in Smith, Michael, *Station X: The Codebreakers of Bletchley Park* (Boxtree, 1998), p. 13.

51 Brown, Andrew, 'At 96, my mother is one of the oldest surviving Bletchley Park codebreakers', *Guardian*, 28 March 2014.

52 P. W. Filby had served under Tiltman in Hut 5 at Bletchley.

53 Denniston, Robin, *Thirty Secret Years,* p. 80.

54 Letter from P. W. Filby to Ronald Lewin, 11 April 1979, Lewin CCAC.

55 Interview with Nancy Winbolt, gchq.gov.uk

56 The publication of F. W. Winterbotham's *The Ultra Secret* (Harper & Row) in 1974 meant that, finally, a public discussion of Bletchley's work became possible. It was not until July 2009 that the British government announced that Bletchley personnel would be recognised with a special commemorative badge.

57 Thirsk, James, *Bletchley Park: An Inmate's Story* (Hadlow, 2008), p. 128

58 Ferris, John, *Behind the Enigma*, p. 339.

59 This came about as a result of interviews conducted by this author with Patricia Brown (*née* Bartley) in 2019.

60 Brown, Patricia, review of McKay's *The Secret Life of Bletchley Park*, *Guardian*, 25 September 2010.

61 Ferris, John, *Behind the Enigma*, p. 439.

62 The chief of the Secret Intelligence Service is known as 'C', a practice that originated with the first chief, Sir Mansfield Smith-Cumming, appointed in 1909. He developed the practice of signing letters with a 'C' in green ink. Since then the chief has always been known as 'C'. The practice of signing documents in green ink continues down to the present 'C'.

63 Robert Cecil, one of Menzies' (aka 'C''s) senior staff, quoted in Robertson, K. G. (ed.), *British and American Approaches to Intelligence* (Palgrave Macmillan, 1987), p. 125.

64 Transcript of interview with John Tiltman, NSA 06-78 DOCID: 4236153.

65 EA would later endow the annual RPS Emily Anderson Prize, of £2,500, under the terms of her will. The prize is awarded to an outstanding solo violinist early in their career, and is presented each year at a concert at the Wigmore Hall given by the winning violinist.

66 Concerts were held from 1 until 2 p.m., and tea, sandwiches and other refreshments could be purchased from a specially established canteen.

67 Greenberg, J., *Alastair Denniston: Code-Breaking from Room 40 to Berkeley Street and the Birth of GCHQ* (Frontline Books, 2017), p. 208.

68 Memo from Stewart Menzies, Director General GC&CS, to all
    staff, dated 8 May 1945, BPT OEF_4005, Bletchley Park Trust.
69 Filby, P. W., *Bletchley Park and Berkeley Street*, p. 281.

16. Eastcote and Beethoven

1 'Jumbo' Travis remained overall head of GCHQ, and served as its
   director until 15 April 1952, when he was replaced by Eric Jones.
2 Eastcote was the only GC&CS outstation also used by the US
   Army, whose 6812th Signals Security Detachment had a dedicated
   BOMBE bay on site, which contained ten machines.
3 De Grey, N., Handwritten memo on the need to invest in
   diplomatic SIGINT, 26 November 1940, HW 3/33, TNA.
4 The electoral registers for 1945–1951 record Anderson at the
   24 Ellerdale Road address.
5 Report of Joint Intelligence Sub-Committee of the Chiefs of Staff,
   dated 1 June 1945, J. I. C. (45) 181 (0), TNA.
6 The election took place on 5 July 1945. Labour won a landslide .
   victory, winning 47.7 per cent of the popular vote, the first time the
   Labour Party had won an outright majority.
7 Author's interview with Dr Friedrich von Busch, 26 June 2019.
8 Morris, C., 'Navy Ultra's Poor Relations', Hinsley, F. H., and
   Stripp, A. (eds), *Codebreakers: The Inside Story of Bletchley Park* (Oxford
   University Press, 1993), p. 243.
9 Most items were stored in a mineshaft in Siegen, some 120
   kilometres away, and others were brought to Homburg Castle near
   Nümbrecht, 50 kilometres from Bonn (Rößner-Richarz, M., *The
   Beethoven-Haus in Bonn during the Nazi Period*, vol. 6 (Beethoven-Haus,
   Bonn), p. 25).
10 Ibid.
11 Maria Floersheim-Koch was the daughter of the Frankfurt court
    jeweller Louis Koch. She and her sister Martha inherited his
    extensive collections of art, antiques and autographs in 1936. Maria
    and her husband, the agricultural economist Rudolf Flörsheim,
    were persecuted during the Nazi era because they were Jewish, and
    in 1936 the couple emigrated to Florence with their two children.
    Following Rudolf Flörsheim's imprisonment during Hitler's state
    visit to Italy in 1938, on his release the couple fled to Switzerland,
    where they settled in Wildegg, near Aarau.

12 Letter from EA to Hans Conrad Bodmer, 10 April 1948, Bequest of Bodmer Zürich, Beethoven-Haus Archive.

13 Erich Hertzmann was born in Germany in 1902. He studied musicology in Frankfurt and Berlin, receiving his PhD in 1931. In 1938 he emigrated to the US and taught at Columbia University until his death. Hertzmann also lectured at Princeton University from 1946 to 1949. He wrote extensively on Renaissance music, Mozart, and Beethoven. He died in California in 1963.

14 Beethoven-Haus, Bonn, Exhibition Catalogue, 'Auf den Spuren Beethovens: Hans Conrad Bodmer und seine Sammlung'/ 'In the Footsteps of Beethoven: Hans Conrad Bodmer and his Collection', 2006.

15 Obituary of Dr Hans Conrad Bodmer, written by EA, *The Times*, 6 June 1956.

16 Ibid.

17 Ibid.

18 Letter from EA to Hans Conrad Bodmer, 29 June 1948, Bequest of Bodmer Zurich, Beethoven-Haus Archive. All of EA's letters to Bodmer were written in German, and I am indebted to Dr Maria Rößner-Richarz, archivist at the Beethoven Haus Archive, Bonn, for these translations.

19 Letter from EA to Hans Conrad Bodmer, 3 July 1949, Bequest of Bodmer Zurich, Beethoven-Haus Archive.

20 Memo dated 4 August 1940, HW 14/6, TNA.

21 Letter from Alastair Denniston to T. J. Wilson, Foreign Office, 24 July 1940, FO 366/1110, TNA.

22 Telegram from T. J. Wilson, Foreign Office, to Miles Lampson, Ambassador to Egypt and High Commissioner for the Sudan, Foreign Office Cairo, 24 July 1940, FO 366/1110, TNA.

23 Anderson, E., Introduction to *The Letters of Beethoven*, volume I, p. x.

24 Known as the 'conversation books', Beethoven started using these notebooks in 1818, by which time his hearing had badly deteriorated. They enabled him not just to conduct conversations, but also served as shopping lists, notes regarding errands he needed to run, and for drafting memoranda pertaining to the lawsuits over the guardianship of his nephew. One hundred and thirty-nine of these notebooks have survived.

25 Russell, John, *A Tour in Germany And Some of the Southern Provinces of the Austrian Empire, in 1820, 1821, 1822*, vol. 1 (Constable & Co., 1928; first published 1827).

26 That the war created victims on both sides of the conflict is evidenced by the fact that Boucke's wife and his only child, a four-year-old son, were both killed on 23 November 1943 in the course of a heavy night-time bombing raid on Berlin by the RAF. Boucke himself died in 1989.

27 Alexander Hyatt King was appointed as Cataloguer in the British Museum in 1934, before, in December 1944, being appointed Superintendent of the Music Room at the Museum. He remained in that position until 1973, when he was named Music Librarian of the Reference Division at the British Library. He also served concurrently as the British Museum's Deputy Keeper of the Department of Printed Books, from 1959 until his retirement in 1976.

28 Douglas Barrett had read Classics at Oxford, and served in the Royal Artillery from 1939 to 1946.

29 *The Times*, 15 December 1959

30 Ibid.

31 Ibid, 20 November 1992.

32 Letter from Douglas Barrett to Theodor Wildeman, 20 April 1947, cited in Rößner-Richarz, M., *The Beethoven-Haus in Bonn during the Nazi Period*, p. 27.

33 Story recounted by John Amis, classical music critic and friend of Dame Myra Hess, 'National Gallery commemorates Second World War with special day of events and new online resource', press release, July 2010 (available at: https://www.nationalgallery.org.uk/about-us/press-and-media/press-releases/national-gallery-commemorates-second-world-war-with-special-day-of-events-and-new-online-resource, accessed 17/07/2022).

34 Cuthbert Morton Girdlestone was a British musicologist and literary scholar.

35 Letter from C. M. Girdlestone to EA, 25 July 1934.

36 Sonneck, O. G., Introduction, *Beethoven Letters in America* (The Beethoven Association, 1927).

37 The precise date of EA's retirement is unknown, as her personnel file no longer exists, but GCHQ records it as having

occurred in November 1950, EA having completed thirty years of service.

38 Jonathan Bliss, concert pianist, quoted in *The Wall Street Journal*, 13 January 2014.

17. Retirement and Beethoven

1 By 1941, the BBC was broadcasting news bulletins around the world in thirty-four languages.

2 Author's interview with Mrs Elizabeth Oliver, conducted 4 June 2020.

3 The two buildings were joined together as one during the time that 24 Ellerdale Road housed The King Alfred School.

4 Mrs Oliver's reference to a fire in No. 24 Ellerdale Road serves to clarify the reason why the address on EA's headed paper changed at some point in the early 1950s from 24 Ellerdale Road to 4 Ellerdale Court, presumably following the fire and the reconfiguration of the house.

5 When in Bonn, EA stayed at an hotel at Schloßstraße 35.

6 Letter from EA to Rupert Erlebach, 27 April 1952, Add MS 71037, British Library.

7 Letter from EA to Hans Conrad Bodmer, 10 March 1952, Bequest of Bodmer Zurich, Beethoven-Haus Archive.

8 The advertisement for the auction noted that 24 Ellerdale Road was divided into 'four self-contained flats, each let at an annual rent of £605 inclusive p.a.'

9 These included St Vincent's Orthopaedic Hospital, Pinner, and the National Temperance Hospital, London.

10 *Notes*, Second Series, vol. 9, no. 4 (September 1952), pp. 544–56.

11 *The Times*, 15 November 1961.

12 Anderson, E., *The Letters of Beethoven*, Volume I, p. xvi.

13 Ibid, p. xxii.

14 Letter from EA to Hans Conrad Bodmer, summer of 1954, Emily Anderson Papers, the Beethoven Haus Archiv, VHB 20.006.

15 Mason, C., 'Review of Anderson, E. *The Letters of Beethoven*', *The Musical Times*, vol. 103, no. 1438 (December 1962), p. 819.

16 The Russians had moved a good deal of valuable material from the library in Berlin, including the original manuscript of Beethoven's Fifth Symphony.

17 For more on the material removed from the Prussian State Library by the Russians, see Whitehead, P. J. P., 'The Lost Berlin Manuscripts', *Notes*, September 1976, vol. 33, no. 1 (Sept 1976), pp. 7–15.

18 VOH 20. 008, 3 October 1955, Beethoven-Haus Archive, Bonn.

19 Dr Wilhelm Virneisel was Director of the Music Department of the Public Scientific Library in East Berlin (formerly the Prussian State Library) from 1951 to 1956.

20 VOH 20. 008, 10 October 1953

21 Anderson, E., 'The Text of Beethoven's Letters', *Music & Letters*, vol. 34, No. 3 (July 1953), pp. 212–23.

22 Letter from Ludwig Misch, *Music & Letters*, vol. 34, no. 4 (October 1953), p. 363.

23 Ludwig Misch (1887–1967) was a German-Jewish musicologist and a leading authority on Beethoven. Having survived forced labour and a Russian prisoner-of-war camp during the Second World War, Misch emigrated to the United States in 1947, where he published several notable books about Beethoven and eventually donated his papers to the Leo Baeck Institute in New York.

24 *Music & Letters*, vol. 35, no. 2 (April 1954), p. 184.

25 Forbes was an American conductor and musicologist and a recognised Beethoven scholar.

26 Forbes, Elliot (ed.), *Thayer's Life of Beethoven*, vols I–II (Princeton University Press, 1967), p. xv.

27 EA's contact at Sotheby's was John Pashby, an acknowledged expert on music collections. She credits him for his help in acquiring copies of original Beethoven autographs in her article in *Notes*, 'The Letters of Beethoven: The Necessity for a Textually Accurate Edition'.

28 Letter from EA to Hans Conrad Bodmer, 17 July 1954.

29 The bag also contained letters to Grove from George Eliot, William Gladstone and William Morris (*The Times*, 7 December 1956).

30 *The Times*, 7 December 1956.

31 Letter from EA to Rupert Erlebach, 8 January 1955, British Library.

32 Proceedings of the Royal Musical Association, 81st Sess., 1954–1955, Taylor & Francis, Ltd. on behalf of the Royal Musical Association, (available at: https://www.jstor.org/stable/i231199, accessed 29/7/22).

33 *Manchester Guardian*, 5 July 1955.

34 The event took place at the Arts Council of Great Britain headquarters in St James Square, SW1.

35 Letter from EA to Rupert Erlebach, Correspondence of the Royal Musical Association, British Library, Add MS 71010-71064: 1874–1971.

36 *The Times*, 28 June 1957.

37 August Laube was an antiquarian book and art dealer based in Zürich, Switzerland. Having trained under Heinrich Eisemann, the bookshop he established in 1922 became a well-known address for international collectors and scholars. He was instrumental in establishing the Beethoven collection of Bodmer and also sourced material for Stefan Zweig.

38 *Irish Times*, 23 May 1956.

39 *The Times*, 6 June 1956.

40 Ibid.

41 Heinrich Eisemann was a Jewish book dealer who fled Germany due to persecution before the outbreak of the Second World War. Martin Bodmer, younger brother of H. C. Bodmer, and Stefan Zweig, the Austrian novelist, both collectors of manuscripts, were among his customers.

42 Sotheby's bill, 27 March 1956, H. C. Bodmer Collection, Beethoven-Haus Archive.

43 *The Times*, 31 May 1956.

44 Cagwin was also a good friend of Dagmar von Busch-Weise and Friedrich von Busch. She was a guest at their home in Bonn and they, in turn, stayed with her in the United States when Friedrich took up an academic position there.

45 File No. m2b0016, Beethoven Center Manuscripts, The Ira F. Brilliant Center for Beethoven Studies, San Jose State University.

46 *Westmeath Independent*, 2 November 1957.

47 I am grateful to Dr Dagmar von Busch-Weise for sharing this personal letter with me, and for translating its contents from the original German.

48 This was Chi Chi, who was installed in London Zoo on September 5, 1958, having been moved from Copenhagen Zoo. Chi Chi died in 1972.

49 Letter from EA to Alexander Hyatt King, 15 November 1958.

50 Letter from EA to Dr Dagmar von Busch-Weise, 4 December 1958.

51 My thanks to Dr Sabine Greger-Amanshauser of the Mozart-Archiv for confirming this detail. There is no indication in the Mozarteum records that Anderson accepted the award in person.

52 Anderson, E., 'A Note on Mozart's Bassa Selim', *Music and Letters*, vol. xxxv, issue 2 (April 1954), p. 120.

53 *Die Entführung aus dem Serail* (in English *The Abduction from the Seraglio*), also known as *Il Seraglio*, is an opera Singspiel in three acts by Mozart, first performed in Vienna on 16 July 1782.

54 Sir Stephen Lewis Courtauld was a member of the wealthy English Courtauld textile family. He served in the Machine Gun Corps and was awarded the Military Cross in the First World War. Following the war, he did not enter the family business, his wealthy background instead enabling him to travel extensively and to pursue cultural and philanthropic interests.

55 Anderson, E., 'A Note on Mozart's Bassa Selim', *Music and Letters*, vol. xxxv, issue 2 (April 1954), p. 120.

56 George Baker was a British opera singer and also a well-respected music administrator, serving as the BBC's Overseas Music Director from 1944 to 1947 and as committee member, treasurer and chairman of the Royal Philharmonic Society for over thirty years. He also served as a committee member of the Musicians' Benevolent Fund.

57 Letter from EA to George Baker, dated 17 May 1959, RPS MS 377, ff 186–187.

58 Letter from the Hon. Treasurer of the RPS to EA, dated 3 June 1959, RPS MS 377, f189.

59 Baker's letters stated: 'I know that you wanted our acceptance of your project, before you leave for Vienna on 16th June.' Letter from George Baker to EA, dated 3 June 1959, RPS MS 377, ff 186–187.

60 Nigel Fortune was one of Britain's leading musicologists of the post-Second World War generation. He served as Secretary of the Royal Musical Assocation from 1957–1971.

61 Paul Badura-Skoda was an Austrian concert pianist and musicologist.

62 Letter from EA to Nigel Fortune, 10 October 1959.

63 EA certainly did drink wine with her friends Dagmar and Friedrich when she visited them, but in moderation.

64 Richmond, J., 'Classics and Intelligence', *Classics Ireland*, vol. 9 (2002), p. 51.

65 Letter from EA to Nigel Fortune, 4 November 1959.

66 Letter from EA to Nigel Fortune, 9 January 1960.

67 Letter from EA to Nigel Fortune, April 1960.

68 Greenberg, J., *Alastair Denniston: Code-Breaking from Room 40 to Berkeley Street and the Birth of GCHQ* (Frontline Books, 2017), p. 216.

69 This is a reference to the BBC's *Newsnight*, the UK's leading TV news and current affairs programme (Typescript copy of a talk by Mavis Batey on British intelligence, for a living history tour of Oxfordshire. GBR/0014/BTEY 3/4).

70 The identity of the Irish cousins has not been established, but the term 'Irish Riviera' would refer to the counties of Waterford and Wexford, known as 'the sunny south-east' because of their generally favourable climate relative to the rest of the country.

71 Letter from EA to Cecil Oldman, 13 May 1951, Add MS 58075, British Library.

72 *Guardian*, 19 October 1961.

73 Forbes, E., 'Review of *The Letters of Beethoven*', *The New York Times*, 17 December 1961.

74 *The Times*, 10 October 1961.

75 Forbes, E. 'Review of *The Letters of Beethoven*'.

76 Described as 'the noblest novel of the twentieth century', *Jean-Christophe* is a novel in ten volumes by Romain Rolland, who was awarded the Nobel Prize for Literature in 1915. Rolland described the novel as 'the story of a life, from birth to death. My hero is a great German musician who is forced by circumstances to leave when he is 16–18 years old, living outside of Germany in Paris, Switzerland, etc. The setting is today's Europe [. . .] To spell it out, the hero is Beethoven in the modern world.'(*The Times*, 10 October 1961).

77 Forbes, E., 'Review of *The Letters of Beethoven*'.

78 Dean, Winton, 'Review of *The Letters of Beethoven*', *The Musical Times*, vol. 103, no. 1429 (March 1962), pp. 156–59.

79 *The Times*, 15 November 1961.

80 *The Times*, 29 October 1962.

81 *Guardian*, 19 October 1961

82 This refers to a letter written by Beethoven to his brothers Carl and Johannat Heiligenstadt in October 1802. The letter reflects Beethoven's despair over his increasing deafness, his contemplation of suicide, and his desire to overcome his physical and emotional difficulties in order to complete his artistic destiny, and was discovered in March 1827 after Beethoven's death.

83 *Guardian*, 19 October 1961.
84 Letter from Beethoven to Court Secretary Nikolaus Zmeskall von Donanovecz, sent 1798 (the date or month is not specified), Anderson, Emily, *The Letters of Beethoven*, (Macmillan & Co. Ltd., 1961), Vol. I, p. 32.
85 Letter from EA to Dr Dagmar von Busch-Weise, 21 October 1961.

18. Hiding in Plain Sight

1 *Second Supplement to the London Gazette*, 13 July 1943.
2 The interview was broadcast on 2 December 1961 on BBC radio's Third Programme.
3 Denis Stevens, CBE, was also an acclaimed musician and musicologist. At the time he interviewed EA, he was Editor of *Grove's Dictionary of Music and Musicians* (1959–63), had been appointed Professor at the Royal Academy of Music (1960) and subsequently became Professor of Musicology at Colombia University (1964).
4 The BBC Third Programme was a national radio station produced and broadcast from 1946 until 1967, when it was replaced by Radio 3. One of the leading cultural and intellectual forces in Britain, it played a crucial role in disseminating music and the arts.
5 *Radio Times*, 2 December 1961.
6 One of those was EA's long-time friend and collaborator Dr Dagmar von Busch-Weise, of the Beethoven-Haus Archive. Dr von Busch-Weise believes the other was Professor Josef Schmidt-Görg, musicologist, composer, music editor, and director of the Beethoven Archive from 1945–72.
7 An Oxford languages graduate, from 1942 to 1946 Denis Stevens had served in RAF Intelligence in India and Burma, decoding Japanese transmissions.

19. Acclaim, Illness and Death

1 Frank Howes was one of England's foremost music critics, who, from 1943 to 1960, was the music critic of *The Times*. He also served as president of the Royal Musical Association (1947–58), and as chairman of the Musicians' Benevolent Fund (1936–55).

2 Letter from EA to Dr Dagmar von Busch-Weise, 21 October 1961.

3 Milner-Barry's sister, Alda Milner-Barry, who had deputised for Anderson at University College, Galway, when she had originally been recruited to MI1(b), had died in 1940.

4 Hertzmann confirmed as much in a letter to Cecil Oldman, 13 November 1961, British Library.

5 Papers of Sir Philip Stuart Milner-Barry, Publications by Bletchley Park Staff, MNBY 7, CCAC.

6 *The Times*, 14 December 1961.

7 *Hebel's Bible Stories* was published by Barrie & Rockliff, London, in 1962.

8 Letter from EA to Geoffrey Robinson, publisher, illustrator and painter for Barrie & Rockliff Publishers, 14 March 1962. I am indebted to Dr Luigi Bellofatto for bringing this letter to my attention, and allowing me to cite from it.

9 Rehm, W., *Goethe und Johann Peter Hebel*. Speech delivered on Saturday, 21 May 1949, at the Goethe memorial service at the Albert-Ludwigs University of Freiburg im Breisgau.

10 Publisher's preface to the second edition of *The Letters of Mozart and his Family* by A. Hyatt King and M. Carolan (eds).

11 Cuthbert Girdlestone was Professor of French at King's College, Newcastle, and had written a much-lauded study of the Mozart Piano Concertos in 1939, published originally in French. He retired in 1960.

12 Letter from C. M. Girdleston to EA, 12 August (the year is not included). Other references in the letter, however, would indicate that the letter was written in 1961.

13 Letter from EA to Nigel Fortune, Royal Musical Association, 25 September 1961, Royal Musical Association Papers, vol. XXVIII, Add MS 71037.

14 Letter from EA to Nigel Fortune, Royal Musical Association, 2 October 1961, Royal Musical Association Papers, vol. XXVIII, Add MS 71037, The British Library.

15 Private letter from EA to Nigel Fortune, 2 October 1961, Royal Musical Association Papers, vol. XXVIII, Add MS 71037, The British Library.

16 A guinea was worth £1-1s, and there were ten shillings in a pound, so 30 guineas was £31-10s.

17 Letter from EA to Nigel Fortune, 4 December 1961, Royal Musical Association Papers, vol. XXVIII, Add MS 71037, The British Library.

18 Letter from EA to Nigel Fortune, 9 December 1961, Royal Musical Association Papers, vol. XXVIII, Add MS 71037, The British Library.

19 Letter from EA to Nigel Fortune, 12 March 1962, Royal Musical Association Papers, vol. XXVIII, Add MS 71037, The British Library.

20 Anderson, E., 'Beethoven's Operatic Plans', in *Proceedings of the Royal Musical Association*, 88th Sess. (1961–1962), pp. 61–71.

21 Ibid., p. 62.

22 Ibid., p. 61.

23 Oldman had originally written 'she spoke quietly but', and then decided to cross out 'quietly but'.

24 Dr Wilhelm A. Bauer was a noted musicologist and Mozart expert.

25 Letter to EA from Professor Otto Erich Deutsch, 22 July 1961, Papers of Alexander Hyatt King, Add MS 62678, British Library.

26 The document was dated 12 March 1962, Vorschlagsliste Nr. 2290.

27 Not to be confused with the former German Chancellor of the same name, Gerhard Schröder (1910–1989) served as Foreign Minister of the Federal Republic of Germany from 1961–66.

28 *Der Spiegel*, 20 January 1954.

29 Author's interview with Dr Dagmar von Busch-Weise, 12 January 2018.

30 In 1950, Villa Hammerschmidt became the official seat of the Federal President, and remained so until 1994, when Schloss Bellevue in Berlin became the official seat of the President of the united Germany.

31 The Bayreuther Festspiele, in English the Bayreuth Festival, is a music festival held annually in Bayreuth, Germany, at which performances of operas by the nineteenth-century German composer Richard Wagner are presented.

32 I am greatly indebted to Dr Luigi Bellofatto for copies of this, and other documents, from his private collection of music collection-related materials.

33 The friend may have been Monica Carolan, who lived a less than ten-minute walk from Anderson's flat, at 43 Rosslyn Hill,

Hampstead. Anderson was at that time collaborating with Carolan on the revised edition of the Mozart letters.

34 Until 1961, Carolan had shared a house with Madge Massey Cooper at 1 Windmill Hill, a short walk from Anderson's flat in Ellerdale Road.

35 General Register Office for England and Wales, certified copy of Death Certificate of Emily Anderson, 31 October 1962. The certificate states that the cause of death was 'confirmed after post mortem without inquest'.

36 Patricia Maud Crowden (*née* Anderson) and her husband, Frederick J. Crowden, lived at 41 Fairlawn Avenue, Chiswick. It is unclear which branch of the Anderson family Patricia was related to, but she would appear to have been born in Kilkeel, Co. Down, Northern Ireland, in 1914.

37 The wreath was to the value of 50 marks, and the receipt was dated 29 October 1962, for delivery on 1 November 1962 (Beethoven Haus Archive).

38 The florist was Marigold of Hampstead.

39 Letter from Professor Dr Joseph Schmidt-Görg to Mrs P. Crowden, 28 November 1962, Beethoven-Haus Archive.

40 Letter from Mrs P. Crowden to Professor Dr Joseph Schmidt-Görg, 23 January 1963, VBH 20.013, Beethoven Haus Archiv.

41 Cecil Oldman to Erich Hertzmann, 30 November 1962, British Library.

42 Cable from Erich Hertzmann's wife, Evelyn Chamberlain, to Cecil Oldman, 4 March 1963, British Library.

43 The term 'Atheromatous' refers to the fact that there was a build-up of cholesterol or 'plaque' in the vessel. I am grateful to Dr Eleanor Turner for this information.

44 Dr Trumpf later held the position of Secretary-General of the Council of the European Union from 1994 to 1999. From the beginning of 1999 until the end of his term of office, he also served as High Representative for the Common Foreign and Security Policy (CFSP).

45 I am deeply grateful to Stephen Andrews, grandson of Arthur Andrews, aka Alexander Anderson, for this and other information and photographs related to his grandfather and wider family.

46 Reverend Hall officiated at the funeral, and the service at Golders Green cemetery was conducted by Reverend Barney (*The Times*, 2 November 1962).

47 *The Times*, 29 October 1962.

48 Ibid.

49 Ibid.

50 Coutts & Co. is one of the world's most exclusive and oldest private banks, which counted Queen Elizabeth, the Queen Mother, among its clients.

51 William Norman Binns was the son of Anderson's uncle, William J. Binns, the brother of Anderson's mother, Emily Binns. Mrs Dorothy Binns was the widow of William Norman Binns, an engineer, who died in 1947. Mrs Dorothy Binns died in 1972.

52 Madge Massey Lings married Walter Lee Cooper of Manchester, a Jute and Linen merchant, in 1908. The couple had one son, but by 1919 the marriage appears to have broken down. Walter Lee Cooper died in 1925.

53 Massey Cooper also appears to have been an art lover, and donated a number of important pieces to public galleries, principally works by the artist Susan Isabel Dacre.

54 Mrs Patricia Maud Crowden lived at 41 Fairlawn Avenue, Chiswick, and it was she with whom the Beethoven-Haus corresponded following the death of Anderson. Patricia Maud Crowden was born in Kilkeel, Co. Down, Northern Ireland, in 1914, so she was clearly the daughter of one of Emily Anderson's father's first cousins, although the exact branch of the family has not been established. Mrs Crowden died in August 1991.

55 Pollak appears to have been an academic rather than a medical doctor. No further information has emerged to explain her relationship to Anderson, although for a time she lived close to Anderson at Canfield Gardens, Hampstead.

56 List of 'Female Enemy Aliens Exempt from Internment – Refugee, 1939–1945', HO 396/69/69A, TNA.

57 She is listed on the 1939 Register as a 'Companion Secretary (Librarian)' to Dr Moses Gaster.

58 Barbara Sidwell (*née* Hill), born in 1920, was a concert pianist who was appointed Professor of Piano at the Royal College of Music in 1964, eventually retiring from the post in 1990. In 1944, she married Martindale Sidwell, the organist, composer and teacher, and the couple moved to Hampstead in 1947. Martindale Sidwell was Music Director at Hampstead Parish Church, and is likely to have been responsible for arranging the music played at EA's

funeral. The Sidwells were clearly good friends of EA's, and it is significant that her *Hebel's Bible Stories* was dedicated to the Sidwell's sons, Peter and Timothy. EA's piano is now in the care of Timothy Sidwell.

59 England and Wales National Probate Calendar, 1963, p. 154. The equivalent value in 2022 is *c.* £280,000.

60 The 1963 electoral register lists EA as still being the occupier, but the 1964 register lists Michael and Katherina Baxandall as occupying Flat 4, 24 Ellerdale Road.

61 Baxandall was regarded as 'probably the most important art historian of his generation', and at the time he lived in Anderson's former flat, he was cataloguing the collection of German sculpture at the Victoria and Albert Museum. Obituary of Michael Baxandall, *Telegraph*, 17 August 2008.

20. Conclusion and Legacy

1 *The Times*, 29 October 1962.

2 Regulations for Applicants to GC&CS, FO366/815, X 8536, and CSC/30, TNA.

3 Ferris, John, *Behind the Enigma*, p. 459.

4 Ibid, p. 89.

5 'NSA Historical Figures: Elizebeth S. Friedman', NSA (available at: https://www.nsa. gov/About-Us/Current-Leadership/Article-View/Article/1623028/elizebeth-s-friedman/, accessed 20/04/2021).

6 'Remembering the First Ladt of naval cryptology', Station HYPO (available at: https://stationhypo.com/2019/07/24/remembering-mrs-agnes-driscoll-first-lady-of-naval-cryptology/, accessed 20/4/2021).

7 Layton, E. T., *And I Was There: Breaking the Secrets – Pearl Harbor and Midway*, (Konecky & Konecky, 2001), p. 33.

8 Johnson, Kevin W., *The Neglected Giant: Agnes Meyer Driscoll,* Volume 10 of Center for Cryptologic History special series, National Security Agency, Center for Cryptologic History, 2015.

9 Ewing, Sir A., 'Some Special War Work', p. 39 in unpublished Reginald Hall autobiography, Draft D, chapter 25, p. 22 (quoting Balfour memorandum of February 20, 1917), Papers of Admiral Sir Reginald Hall, CCAC.

10 Rowlett's input was crucial to breaking into the Japanese diplomatic cipher machine codenamed PURPLE. See 'NSA Historical Figures: Frank B. Rowlett', NSA (available at: https://www.nsa.gov/History/Cryptologic-History/Historical-Figures/Historical-Figures-View/Article/1623037/frank-b-rowlett/, accessed 29/08/2022).

11 Letter from Erich Hertzmann to Cecil Oldman, 30 November 1962, British Library.

12 Letter from EA to Rupert Erlebach, 8 January 1955, British Library.

13 *The Times*, 18 February 1967.

14 The annual concert is organised by *Music for Galway*.

15 Dr Lydon died at the British Military Hospital, Benghazi, Libya, where he had opened a clinic some months previously (*Irish Independent*, 6 July 1966).

16 I am grateful to Heather Wilson of the London Cremation Company at Golders Green crematorium for this information.

Image Credits

Page 1

Young Emily Anderson, with mother, sister and governess
© Courtesy of Special Collections, the Hardiman Library,
University of Galway

Young Emily Anderson, Queen's College, Galway © Courtesy of
Special Collections, the Hardiman Library, University of Galway

Page 2

Professor Alexander Anderson © Courtesy of Special Collections,
the Hardiman Library, University of Galway

Arthur Andrews and wife Lilian © Courtesy of the private collection
of Stephen Andrews

Page 3

Female staff of MI(1)b © 'MI(1)b, August 1919', MS 2788/2/17,
University of Aberdeen Museums and Special Collections,
licensed under CC BY 4.0

Commander Alastair Denniston © Courtesy of the private
collection of the Denniston family

Patricia Bartely © Illustrated London News Ltd./Mary Evans

Page 4

Bletchley Park © Stuart Robertson/Alamy

Emily Anderson in Cairo © Courtesy of the private collection of
Peter Carr

Image Credits

Page 5

British Embassy, Cairo / AP/Shutterstock

Dorothy Brooks at Mina © Courtesy of the private collection of
Peter Carr

GC&CS office, Berkley Street / US National Archives and Records
Administration

Page 6

German Diplomatic Section staff / Courtesy of Joel Greenberg on
behalf of Peter Sydney-Smith

Dr Dagmar Weise © Courtesy of the private collection of Dr
Dagmar von Busch Weise

Gerald Gover soirée / Anthony Wallace/ANL/Shutterstock

Page 7

Hans Conrad Bodmer © Courtesy of the private collection of
Dr Dagmar von Busch-Weise

Emily Anderson's piano © Author's own image

Page 8

Emily Anderson © Courtesy of the private collection
of Dr Dagmar von Busch-Weise

Select Bibliography

Anderson, E., *The Letters of Beethoven*, vols I–III (Macmillan & Co Ltd, 1961)

Anderson, E., *The Letters of Mozart and his Family*, vols I–III (Macmillan & Co Ltd, 1938)

Ashton-Gwatkin, Frank Trelawny Arthur, *The British Foreign Service: A Discussion of the Development and Function of the British Foreign Service* (Syracuse University Press, 1950)

Axelrod, Alan, *The Real History of World War II: A New Look at the Past* (Sterling Publishing, 2008)

Batey, Mavis, *Dilly: The Man Who Broke Enigmas* (Dialogue, 2009)

Beesley, Patrick, *Room 40: British Naval Intelligence 1914–1918* (Hamish Hamilton, 1982)

Bielenberg, Andy, *The Shannon Scheme and the Electrification of the Irish Free State* (Lilliput Press, 2002)

Brownrigg, Rear Admiral Sir Douglas, *Indiscretions of the Naval Censor* (George H. Doran & Co., 1920)

Cairncross, John, *The Enigma Spy: An Autobiography: The Story of the Man who Changed World War Two* (Century, 1997).

Carter, Dr Dan C., *A Short History of the Ministry of Education of Barbados* (Barbados, 2013)

Churchill, Winston S., *The Second World War*, vols I–VI
 (Cassell, 1948–1953)

Cunningham, John, '*A Town Tormented by the Sea': Galway
 1790–1914* (Geography Publication, 2004)

Denniston, Robin, *Thirty Secret Years: A. G. Denniston's Secret
 Work in Signals Intelligence 1914–1944* (Polperro Heritage
 Press, 2007)

Fara, Patricia, *A Lab of One's Own: Science and Suffrage in the
 First World War* (Oxford University Press, 2018)

Ferris, John, *Behind the Enigma: The Authorised History of
 GCHQ, Britain's Secret Cyber-Intelligence Agency*
 (Bloomsbury Publishing, 2020)

Foley, Tadhg (ed.), *From Queen's College to National University:
 Essays on the Academic History of QCG/UCG/NUIG,
 Galway* (Four Courts Press, 1999)

Forbes, Elliot (ed.), *Thayer's Life of Beethoven*, vols I–II
 (Princeton University Press, 1967)

Fraser, Lionel, *All to the Good* (Heineman, 1963)

Greenberg, J., *Alastair Denniston: Code-Breaking from Room 40 to
 Berkeley Street and the Birth of GCHQ* (Frontline Books,
 2017)

Hawking, S. W., and Israel, W. (eds), *300 Years of Gravitation*
 (Cambridge University Press, 1987)

Hinsley, F. H., and Stripp, A. (eds), *Codebreakers: The Inside
 Story of Bletchley Park* (Oxford University Press, 1993)

Hinsley, F. H., *British Intelligence in the Second World War*
 (Stationery Office Books, 1979)

Kelly, Michael, *Reminiscences of Michael Kelly of the King's
 Theatre, and Theatre Royal Drury Lane, Including a Period of
 Nearly Half a Century; with Original Anecdotes of Many
 Distinguished Persons, Political, Literary, and Musical*, vols
 I–II (Henry Colburn, 1826)

Layton, E. T., *And I Was There: Breaking the Secrets – Pearl Harbor and Midway*, (Konecky & Konecky, 2001)

Libby, F., *Horses Don't Fly* (Arcade Publishing, 2000)

McKay, Sinclair, *The Secret Lives of Codebreakers: The Men and Women Who Cracked the Enigma Code at Bletchley Park* (Aurum Press Ltd, 2010)

Miller Jr, James E., *T. S. Eliot: The Making of an American Poet, 1888–1922* (Pennsylvania State University Press, 2005)

Philby, K., *My Silent War: The Autobiography of a Spy* (Modern Library, reprint edition, 2002; first published 1968)

Raleigh, Sir. W. A., *The War in the Air: Being the Story of the Part Played in the Great War by the Royal Air Force* (Oxford University Press, 1922)

Robertson, K. G. (ed.), *British and American Approaches to Intelligence* (Palgrave Macmillan, 1987)

Rößner-Richarz, M., *The Beethoven-Haus in Bonn during the Nazi Period*, vol. 6 (Beethoven-Haus, 2017)

Russell-Jones, Mair and Gethin, *My Secret Life in Hut Six: One Woman's Experiences at Bletchley Park* (Lion Hudson, 2014)

Samson, Jim, (ed.), *The Cambridge History of Nineteenth-Century Music* (Cambridge University Press, 2001)

Schofield, Victoria, *Wavell: Soldier and Statesman* (Pen & Sword Military, 2010)

Smith, Michael, and Erskine, Ralph (ed.), *The Bletchley Park Code Breakers: How Ultra Shortened the War and Led to the Birth of the Computer* (Biteback, 2011; first published 2001)

Smith, Michael, *Station X: The Codebreakers of Bletchley Park* (Boxtree, 1998)

Smith, Michael, *The Secrets of Station X: How the Bletchley Park Helped Win the War* (Biteback, 2011)

Stone, Jean, *Mavis Batey: Bletchley Codebreaker – Garden Historian – Conservationist – Writer* (Matador Publishing, 2020)

Thirsk, James, *Bletchley Park: An Inmate's Story* (Hadlow, 2008)

Toye, F., *For What We Have Received* (A. A. Knopf, 1948)

Ward, Margaret, *Hanna Sheehy Skeffington: A Life* (Attic Press, 1997)

Welchman, G., *The Hut Six Story: Breaking the Enigma Codes* (Allen Lane, 1982)

Winterbotham, F. W., *Secret and Personal* (HarperCollins, 1969)

Winterbotham, F. W., *The Ultra Secret* (Harper & Row, 1974)

Wylie, J., and McKinley, M., *Codebreakers: The True Story of the Secret Intelligence Team that Changed the Course of the First World War* (Ebury, 2015)

Acknowledgements

In the six years it has taken me to research this biography, I was fortunate in receiving help and support from so many individuals and institutions. First and foremost, I want to acknowledge the role played by Professor Daniel Carey and Martha Shaughnessy of the Moore Institute for Research in the Humanities and Social Sciences at the University of Galway, who believed in this project from the outset, and provided me with the Visiting Fellowship, and a home, which made my initial research possible. My colleague Professor Dáibhí Ó Cróinín, meanwhile, shared his knowledge of intelligence history, and his library of books on the subject, with me – his guidance and enthusiasm were invaluable. Dr. Deirdre Ní Chonghaile – musician, music scholar and friend – was my guide into the world of Mozart and Beethoven, and I could not have asked for a better companion. And one of the first people to reach out in support of this biography was GCHQ historian (now retired) Tony Comer, whose confirmation of Anderson's status as Britain's foremost female codebreaker was a pivotal moment in the research process. His generosity in answering the innumerable questions of this intelligence history novice meant the world to me. Similarly, Professor John Ferris and James 'Jock' Bruce were unstinting in sharing both material and their extensive knowledge of intelligence history with me, and, for that, and their friendship, I owe them a debt I can never repay.

The respective staff of the National Archives at Kew, the British Library, Special Collections at the University of Galway – in particular Kieran Hoare – and the University of Aberdeen always went above and beyond to provide me with access to the material I needed; while, during the Covid lockdowns, Robinson McClellan and María Isabel Molestina of the Morgan Library and Museum, New York, generously scanned and forwarded documents related to Anderson's music research. I thank you all sincerely. The Beethoven Haus Archiv staff were also wonderful to work with, and my thanks in particular to Dr. Maria Rößner-Richarz, who took a personal interest in Anderson's story, and gave unstintingly of her time and expertise. I was particularly fortunate in being awarded an Archives By-Fellowship at Churchill College Archives Centre, Cambridge, and my time there, mining their remarkable collections from the First and Second World Wars, was a joy. Thank you all. With special thanks to the Director, Allen Packwood, who suggested many avenues of research I might not have considered, but which proved invaluable. The organisers of the Cambridge Intelligence Seminar – Professor Christopher Andrew, Dr Dan Larsen and Dr John Ranelagh – welcomed me into the world of intelligence history, and were unstinting in their help and support: thank you, gentlemen. And I wrote the Beethoven chapter during a Residency at the Tyrone Guthrie Centre at Annaghmakerrig, in the company of a group of wonderfully creative people – you know who you are! Ronnie O'Gorman and the *Galway Advertiser* were champions of this book from the outset, and their support was instrumental in getting it over the line – thank you.

Dr Dagmar von Busch-Weise and Dr Friedrich von Busch welcomed me into their home in Bonn on many occasions. As Emily's friends, they brought her to life for me in a way that would have been otherwise impossible, and I am blessed that her friends have now become mine. Andrew Brown introduced me to his remarkable mother, Patricia Brown (*née* Bartley), when she was 101 years old. The time I spent interviewing the last of the great Bletchley codebreakers was a privilege for which I will be forever grateful. Thank you, Andrew, for making my visits to your mother possible, and, in the process, becoming a valued friend. Another such friend is Peter Carr, who generously shared insights into the life of his mother, Dorothy Brooks Carr, and her remarkable career in SIGINT, thereby providing a window into Emily's time at Bletchley and in Cairo. He and his family have shared much valuable information with me about Dorothy, for which I am deeply in their debt. Stephen Andrews was also an invaluable source of information regarding his own branch of the Anderson family, and I thank him sincerely. Mrs Elizabeth Oliver, meanwhile, provided precious insights into her one-time neighbour, and Timothy and Elena Sidwell allowed me access to Emily's treasured piano: I thank them all as well. Karen Lewis, a research volunteer at Bletchley Park, and a talented historian, was incredibly generous in sharing her research material and insights on women codebreakers with me, and I gratefully acknowledge that, without her input, the chapter on CBME Cairo could not have been written.

Thanks also to my agent, Donald Winchester, who believed in this book from the start, and steered its progress towards finding the right home. That home was Headline Publishing, who have been a joy to deal with. Thanks to Iain MacGregor, who first brought the book to Headline, and to his successor, Bianca Bexton, who saw it over the line, with the able assistance of Holly Purdham, Anna Hervé and Tara O'Sullivan. Emily and I are in your debt.

Finally, I want to thank my family: those who generously hosted me during my lengthy research trips to the UK – Orna, Adair, Anne Marie and John – and those at home in Galway: my son Eoin, daughter Aoife, and husband Mícheál, who have lived with Emily as long as I have, and were willing to share me with her. Mo bhuíochas ó chroí libh go léir.

Index

    leadership style 85–6, 87
    learns to play piano 9–10
    leaves Barbados 36
    leaves Cairo 199, 201–2, 203
    legacy 325, 326
    life in London 95–7, 102–3
    loathing of publicity 3
    love of playing piano 103
    management responsibility 159
    in Marburg 20
    marriage question 317–19
    mental resilience 320–1
    MI1(b) appointment 44, 45
    move to Bletchley Park 139–40
    move to London 2
    Mozart Medal 271, 324
    music as safety valve 225–7,
        234, 321
    music scholarship 3, 4
    musicologist career 109
    OBE 4, 194, 211, 217–18, 229,
        259, 283, 299, 324
    obituaries 308–10
    Order of Merit, First Class 4,
        235, 299–303, 324
    parallel lives 4
    perception as a bully 159–60
    photographs 57
    pleasure in musicology work
        321–2
    post-war SIGINT work 232–3
    power as a Senior Assistant 138
    prelude to Second World War
        134–6
    promotion to Senior Assistant 87
    reactions to death 304–8
    recognition 217–18, 289
    recruits Bartley 153–4, 359n33

    relationship with Brooks 176–7,
        177–8, 179, 180, 201–2,
        318–19
    relationship with Denniston
        215, 221–2
    relationship with family 262–3
    relationship with father 118
    relationship with Ireland 237
    relationship with Josephine
        Morrissey 249–51, 261
    reputation 326
    reputation as a Beethoven
        scholar 264
    reputation as a music scholar 237
    resignation cover story 74–6
    resignation from UGC 45–7,
        73–7
    resumes academic career 67
    retirement 70, 231, 245–6,
        377–8n37
    return from Germany, 1914 21
    return to UK, 1943 204, 206
    reveals code-breaking career
        284–9
    RMA lecture 292–7
    RMA lecture invitation 274–6
    royalties 240
    sacrifice 269
    salaries 239–40, 342n21,
        363n14
    and secrecy 58, 76–7, 108, 289,
        307–8, 315–16
    self-control 322
    sense of duty 322–3
    sexuality question 318–19
    skills recognized 53
    sources of pride 324–5
    status 3–4, 82–3, 107,
        138, 214